Always an Immigrant

Always an Immigrant

A CULTURAL MEMOIR

Mohammad Yadegari
with Priscilla Yadegari

White River Press
Amherst, Massachusetts

First published 2020 by White River Press
PO Box 3561, Amherst, MA 01004
www.whiteriverpress.com

ISBN: 978-1-887043-67-0

Book design and cover by Lufkin Graphic Designs
Norwich, VT • www.LufkinGraphics.com

Excerpts from chapters 3, 13, 15 , 24, and 30 were first published in slightly different form as flash memoirs in **Write***Angles* **Journal**, https://writeanglesconference.com/wa-journal

Section illustrations by Roya Priscilla Lewis

Library of Congress Cataloging-in-Publication Data

Names: Yādgārī, Muḥammad, 1941 or 1942- author. | Yadegari, Priscilla,
    1945- editor.
Title: Always an immigrant : a cultural memoir / Mohammad Yadegari with
    Priscilla Yadegari.
Description: Amherst, Massachusetts : White River Press, 2020.
Identifiers: LCCN 2019057969 | ISBN 9781887043670 (paperback)
Subjects: LCSH: Yādgārī, Muḥammad, 1941 or 1942- | Iranians--United
    States--Biography. | Iranian Americans--Biography.
Classification: LCC E184.I5 Y337 2020 | DDC 973.92092 [B]--dc23
LC record available at https://lccn.loc.gov/2019057969

'Tis all a Chequer-board of Nights and Days
Where Destiny with Men for Pieces plays:
Hither and thither moves, and mates, and slays,
And one by one in the Closet lays.

— Omar Khayyam
Trans. by Edward J. Fitzgerald

Dedication

To my college students who urged me to write my "stories."

Contents

PART I

PART II

PART III

Acknowledgements

I OWE MUCH TO MANY. To my wife, Priscilla, I owe everything. This manuscript would not have become a book were it not for her effort. I initially began and ended with dozens of vignettes having no chronological order or topical relationship. I wrote one story after another, narrating my experiences in different countries. Priscilla moved them around, filling the skeleton with flesh and fashioning attire for the body. It began to make sense. She gave life to each one separately and as a whole. Together, we wrote and rewrote the manuscript. Slowly, we became convinced that it was the story we intended to present. We were both satisfied.

To Joan Axelrod-Contrada, managing editor of Write Angles Journal, I owe a great deal of thanks for editing the finished version. I had written more than needed. Joan used her skill to eliminate the extraneous material, resulting in a more concise narrative. All along she had one reassuring word after another and encouraged me to have the book published.

I have more than a dozen other people to thank for taking the time to read my manuscript. To the early readers, I apologize for daring to give them such unpolished drafts, but I am also grateful for their patience and words of encouragement for they were instrumental in urging me to continue. In alphabetical order, they are: Evelyn Akers, Amy Lewis, Mary Ann Lewis, Dominic Pannone, Warren Roberts, and Sarem Yadegari.

Also many thanks to those who read and commented on later versions: John Bini, Erika B. Harger, Jonathan Harger, Russell Miller, Hazel Landa, and Roya Priscilla Lewis.

My sister in law, Linda Millard, read the manuscript after the third draft and again in its near final form, both times with detailed letters of helpful remarks.

To my daughters, Shireen Fasciglione and Nasrene Yadegari-Lewis, and my son in law, Dominick Fasciglione, I owe special thanks for reading the manuscript several times and offering opinions, suggestions, and encouragement.

Introduction

THE DAY WAS DECEMBER 13, 2014, Arbain, one of the holiest days for Muslims. News reports indicated that millions from over sixty countries had converged on the city of Karbala, Iraq, to visit the shrine of Imam Hussein (the son of Ali and the grandson of Prophet Muhammad), one of the greatest martyrs in the history of Islam, particularly for followers of the Shi'ite faith. As I watched the news program, which showed throngs of people wailing in the streets, I remembered that I was once part of that scene, so vivid now in my memory.

Events of the past had crowded my memory imperceptibly, and those living moments had faded as they entered and traversed and were stored in crevices, shoved into compartments of my brain. Huddled together, memory after memory, moment after moment, were the happy and painful experiences of my life heaped pile upon pile. They were stored in hidden places nearly impossible to retrieve. Yet I felt I must draw them out. I felt compelled to write my memoir.

I am an American now. I live an American life. My two daughters, Shireen and Nasrene, are Americans with vague fond memories of Iranian family members who have visited over the years. They have met some of their cousins and relatives who live in California and Toronto; they have eaten some Persian food and sweets. They love baklava and halva and they cook some of the most common foods. Unfortunately, they do not speak the language, nor do they know the history of the Iranian people.

Additionally, I have four grandchildren whose descendants will never know who I was, where I lived, what I observed, or what I really thought.

By nature I am a storyteller. I like to talk about experiences and ideas I have had, and I like to listen to others relate their own experiences and thoughts. When I taught Middle East history in college, I often described historical events or cultural habits that caused my students to sit back smugly and think that the ways of foreigners were inferior and superstitious. I would then relate another story of life in these United States, which brought them face-to-face with the reality that similar incongruities exist right here in this country. They became fascinated. It was those students who first encouraged me to write down my stories.

As I started to write, my manuscript began to take form as the tale of my life's journey. However, there is an underlying message contained in many, if not all, of the stories narrated in this book.

Many people in America have only a scant idea of ordinary life in the Middle East. I dare say, they often consider the people religious zealots who keep women hidden behind veils. Most Americans know primarily what the mass media feeds them. This book will debunk some of those perceptions. My personal observations and the tales of my struggles show that life in the Middle East is as complex and real as it is in the United States.

The book consists of three parts. The first part takes place in Iraq, where I grew up as a child through the age of eighteen. The stories are presented from a child's point of view in a very simple style. The second part is about my life in Tehran in an environment of great personal freedom, when my life centered on having a good time doing what every teenage boy growing up into manhood would like to do. And the third part is the age of reason, where life becomes more complex and unpredictable in a society much different from that of the Middle East.

As a youth, being a "foreigner" in Iraq, Iraqi Arabs had directed insults at me at times. In the United States similar racist attitudes were covertly expressed because of religious intolerance. Having arrived in the U.S. during the Civil Rights Era that was ushered in by Martin Luther King Jr., the Kennedys, and Lyndon Johnson, who were able to promote passage of the Civil Rights Act of 1964, I found myself empowered in my struggles for my rights with no fear of recrimination, and completely protected by the law.

I have omitted the Trump Era, a late phenomenon in my life. However, his appearance on the scene has given me reason to ponder what kind of future others will have to deal with due to a resurgence of white supremacy.

I first began to think about the impact of Trump when, on my way to my grandson's soccer game, I saw a child of seven or eight shrink back in fear upon seeing me. In all my years and years of living in this country, I had not seen such a reaction from anyone. Instinctively, I felt sorry for the child. What kind of a parent would teach a boy to be wary and then learn to hate? For fear comes first, but then grows to hatred.

Another time, I was having lunch with an Iranian friend in a Chinese buffet, exchanging a few sentences in the Persian language. A couple sitting at the table next to us asked in what language we were conversing. Upon hearing that we were originally from Iran, he heartily "welcomed" us. Thanking him, I asked, "How old are you?"

"Forty," he replied.

With a smile, I explained, "I have been in this country for fifty-one years. I also welcome you." I realized that the gentleman genuinely, in his own way, said that, regardless of what Trump trumpets, immigrants should be respected and welcomed to the United States. I knew then that there is still hope for America.

Mohammad 1953

PART I

KARBALA, IRAQ

The Minarets of the Shrine of Husayn (Karbala)

CHAPTER 1

A Fork in the Road

I WAS BORN IN KARBALA, IRAQ, a pilgrimage city for many Muslims, especially Shi'ites. My Iranian parents owned a public bath in Karbala that catered to many of those pilgrims.

One day in 1948, my parents and I were going to take a train to a nearby city. The temperature in Iraq sometimes reaches as high as 110 degrees Fahrenheit in summer, and the heat was oppressive that day. We waited a long time in the train station, and time passes even more slowly for a young lad. Finally, we heard the train's whistle and the roar of the engine in the distance; I jumped with excitement at my mother's side, anticipating the ride on the magnificent train.

The train ride turned out to be a disappointment. From the moment we squeezed our way through the people who sat and stood shoulder-to-shoulder in the crowded passenger car, my parents seemed distressed. A kind gentleman rose up from his seat and offered it to my mother. My father and I grabbed hold of the handrail so as not to be jerked left and right.

I sensed my mother's anxiety and apprehension as her arms reached out to grab me. I heard her grumbling to herself, imploring God to bring down the rulers of Iraq. This was not unusual for her. My mother was a very verbal person, and she often softly mumbled her complaints as she called on God for assistance.

I looked around and noticed many gloomy faces. Most of the people were wearing worn and ill-fitting clothes. Their heads were bowed, and their eyes were glazed and inattentive to their surroundings. The train reeked of misery and despair. I had heard children's stories of genies and ghouls, and I thought we might be on their train. Something was wrong, but I could not tell what. My mother prayed quietly and periodically interjected a condemnation of the Iraqi government and a plea for the welfare of the people on the train. As the train stopped at the next station, she gripped my wrist and pushed me forward, forcing us to disembark. The passengers politely, yet indifferently, made room for us to leave.

Outside, my mother sat on a bench, tears running down her cheeks. She wiped them with her hand. "May God help them!" she pleaded. "Those Iraqi bastards put them on this train with what little they could carry. What have they done?"

My father stood nearby, puffing on his Kent cigarette. "Our turn will come," I heard him mutter between puffs.

Years later, I read about Iraq's premier Nuri al-Sa'id having made threats regarding the ouster of the Jews. There were also rumors circulating in Iraq regarding plans to oust Jews by trucking them to Jordan and leaving them near Israel's borders. I remembered that disturbing train ride, and I realized that those people probably had been Jews being deported from Iraq. The Iraqis had apparently confiscated their homes, lands, and money in the name of the Palestinians and, in the struggle between Arabs and Israelis, had been ousting them from their country. They had been successful businessmen and women who had known no other place but Iraq. Their families had lived for centuries in Mesopotamia, as Iraq was known centuries ago. Some of them may have been descendants of the captives of Babylon. They were as Iraqi as anyone else. What I witnessed on the train may have been a personal choice of flight out of fright; however, the large number of people more likely indicated their forced ouster rather than a voluntary departure.

In any case, it was a known fact that the Jews of Iraq were in danger, and such persecution did not sit well with many of the God-fearing and upright people living in that country. They knew well that greedy business competitors who coveted the jobs, properties, and money of the Jewish citizens were using them as scapegoats. My father did not want to end up in the same position.

We were Iranians living in Iraq. As non-citizens, we carried our Iranian birth certificates and passports as identification when traveling. The children in our families went to special Iranian schools, and many of us did not even speak Arabic. It was said that the Iranian residents of Iraq constituted almost 20 percent of the population of the country at that time, an exaggeration, perhaps, but commonly accepted as fact.

The Iranians who lived and worked in Karbala were an industrious, hardworking group. Being such a large segment of the Iraqi population, they had a great effect on its economy. Thus, at the time, Iranian residents of Iraq perceived no danger to their immigrant status there. Why would the government deport them when Iraq's economy was sluggish and Iranians were a significant source of investment and income?

But the scene on that train convinced my father of the fragility of our position in Iraq. He gathered our large family together one night and made us promise to keep his plans secret. He predicted that someday, maybe twenty years from then, he did not know when, the Iraqi government would expel all the Iranian citizens, confiscating their properties and belongings. As an initial step, he planned to go back to Iran for a visit to explore the possibilities for buying land and setting up businesses there. He would later send the older children individually to Iran under the guise of finishing their educations in our original homeland. He promised that he'd send us monthly allowances sufficient to support us. In the meantime, he'd sell the properties that he owned in Iraq. He was not pleased that he had to do this, but he beseeched God to give us guidance and aid us in our own individual endeavors. It took some time, but he finally accomplished his plan by the late 1960s.

My father's ominous prediction, made in 1948, came true many years later when Saddam Hussein finally forced the departure of Iranians from Iraq in the spring of 1980. Many of our relatives and friends who had remained in Iraq lost everything when they were forced to flee. Our family fortune was saved from total loss because of my father's foresight, and my destiny was diverted to a new path.

CHAPTER 2

Karbala, Iraq

KARBALA: *"karb"* and *"bala"* (agony and calamity). That's how my mother described it, although the word's actual origin had nothing to do with the meanings of its two parts. In her mind, Karbala, a city some sixty miles southwest of Baghdad, was a land destined to ooze unhappiness, great pain, and suffering. She blamed every moment of sadness on the city of Karbala, that land of tragedy and affliction, the land that had swallowed the most courageous man history has ever known, the grandson of Prophet Muhammad, the son of Fatimah and Ali. That land was not going to be gentle to ordinary people.

Pessimistic by nature, my mother lamented that tragedy always followed even fleeting moments of happiness. She really believed it. At least, she uttered it a sufficient number of times for me to think so. At such times she would console herself with a special tea made by steeping a desiccated lemon in a pot of hot water. Lemon tea was thought to lower blood pressure and calm the nerves.

While Iraq was a patchwork of many ethnicities, languages, and religious groups, it was considered largely an Arab country. Its primary language was Arabic, and the religion was Islam with two main sects, Sunnism and Shi'ism. Karbala was one of the wealthiest cities in Iraq for various reasons. It was an important agricultural area, where dates were one of its most abundant crops. Second, as one of the cultural centers of Shi'ite Islam, it attracted many visitors who came to study under the learned scholars there. By far the most important reason for its wealth was that it was a center for pilgrimage. While the pilgrimage to Mecca is well known, there are other sites of pilgrimage. Karbala is the burial place of Imam Husayn, the son of Ali, who is one of the most revered martyrs of Shi'ite Islam. For the Shi'ites, Husayn's shrine was, and still is, one of the holiest destinations for pilgrimage, surpassed in importance only by the Sacred Mosque in Mecca, the Prophet's mosque in Medina, and the Aqsa Mosque in Jerusalem.

Since Iran is geographically contiguous to Iraq, Husayn's shrine drew an unusual concentration of Iranians to Karbala. While my father moved to Karbala around 1917 to be with his cousin's family after his own father died young, many Shi'ites chose to live in that city to be close to the spirit of Husayn and finally to be buried near him for eternity. There was a constant flow of pilgrims throughout the year. On the holy days of Ashura[1] and Arbain, the heights of the pilgrimage season, hundreds of thousands flocked to the city. Many pilgrims came to Karbala from Kuwait, Bahrain, and other Persian Gulf States, and from faraway places such as Egypt and India. We occasionally saw some Muslims from countries such as Albania, Yugoslavia, and Bulgaria, but Iranians were the largest group of pilgrims.

Pilgrims were the lifeblood of the Iraq's economy. Before oil became a major factor in Iraq's wealth in the 1940s and 1950s, the country's exports were limited to agricultural products such as dates and citrus fruits. Thus the impact of pilgrims, especially those from Iran, was enormous on Iraq's finances, particularly in the holy cities. Year-round, pilgrims traveled to the holy centers supporting the economic growth of those cities. Karbala was the most important focal point of pilgrimage. It was no wonder that Iranian businessmen also flocked there in droves, as business opportunities abounded.

Due to the constant influx of visitors, many Iranian residents opened businesses to cater to their needs. Over generations, those businessmen, whose native language was Persian, became bilingual, speaking both Arabic and Persian. In the early 1900s, Iranians were the largest community in Karbala. Over time, this proportion decreased due to naturalization and

---

1 Ashura is the tenth day of the month of Muharram in the Islamic calendar. Husayn was martyred on that day in the year 680. Arbain is the fortieth day after his death.

periods of forced ouster of Iranians, especially during the rule of Saddam Hussein (fifth president of Iraq, 1979-2003).

Karbala offered a great deal of opportunity to those who chose to open businesses. With hundreds of thousands of pilgrims traveling to Karbala each year, businessmen had plenty of customers looking for places to stay, food to eat, places to bathe, and places to shop for gifts for hosts and for those back home.

Many apartments, rooms, and houses were available for rent in Karbala. However, at peak times, when the number of pilgrims exceeded hundreds of thousands, some slept in mosques or in other religious sites, while others stayed with relatives, friends, and acquaintances. It was not unusual for visitors to arrive in Karbala knowing only the name of a local businessman who was a casual acquaintance. They would arrive without notice at the businessman's door, expecting hospitality. Usually they would receive it, since hospitality to travelers, especially pilgrims, was an integral part of the culture. My family had our share of visitors. Most of them turned out to be honest and decent people who thanked us with gifts and entertained us with stories of their travels.

Food was abundantly available in shops, restaurants, and from small vendors. There were bakeries that sold hot flatbreads. Vegetables and fruits were plentiful. Grilled meats called kebabs were sold at a variety of restaurants that were open for breakfast, lunch, and dinner.

For breakfast, street vendors sold traditional ground lamb kebabs as well as kebabs of liver, gizzard, and kidney. There were also specialty shops that supplied take-out food. While people usually ate a simple breakfast of flatbread, cheese, and tea, occasionally they would want something special and more substantial. *Kalleh paacheh* (literally "head and feet") was a soup of stewed lamb's head and feet, similar to pig's head and feet that one sometimes sees in supermarkets in the United States. It was a popular breakfast food and diners often vied for the most prized portions such as the brain or tongue. The cooks devoted a great deal of time cutting, washing, and cleaning the head and feet of a ritually slaughtered lamb. They then simmered the lamb parts with spices in large pots over low heat for hours until the meat was extremely tender and ready to fall away from the bone into the broth, making a delicious soup. *Kalleh paacheh* was served with hot flat bread. Another choice for breakfast was *haleem*, which was similar to hot cereal, but it contained meat. Wheat, barley, sugar, meat, and spices such as cardamom and cinnamon were simmered overnight so the meat became very tender. Before serving, it was mashed with a wooden mallet so the meat and grains became as if they'd been pureed in a food processor. The resulting *haleem* was often served with melted butter.

Occasionally my father would order *kalleh paacheh* or *haleem* the night before, and the next morning I would be sent to pick up the stew from the store. I enjoyed those excursions because as I approached the shop, I was enveloped in invisible layers of enticing aromas. As I passed stores that were preparing liver kebab and *kofte* kebab, the pleasant smell of sizzling meat made me inhale with pleasure. Then the spicy smell of *kalleh paacheh* would attract my attention and my mouth would water. I didn't have to be hungry to feel those sensations. I greeted the proprietor cheerfully as he ladled some of the hot stew from his large pot into a small covered pan for me to take home. Another member of the family was picking up the hot flat bread from a different store, and I hurried so we would be back home at the same time. The whole family of eight people, as well as several guests, sat down to eat the delicious stew and hot bread while laughing and joking about who would get the eyes and who would get the brain or the tongue. As for the pan that the shop provided, it was washed and dried before being returned.

For gifts and other personal shopping, people went to the bazaar, which was a domed structure with arcade-like offshoots that housed many small and large shops. It was similar to an enclosed shopping mall. However, it was characteristic of the bazaars to assign specific areas for sellers dealing with certain types of wares. For example, all the sellers of handcrafted copper trays and urns would be in one area, all the jewelry sellers in another area, and all fabric sellers in yet another section. Additionally, there were some stores here and there that were not organized into sections. Haberdasheries, shoe stores, tailor shops (which imported the finest cloth from Damascus, Syria, and Manchester, England), and butcher shops (where the customers chose live fowl and had it butchered in front of them) were found in nooks here and there or just outside of the bazaar.

For personal cleanliness in Karbala, a traveler or a local resident would go to a hammam (public bath). Though houses had indoor toilets and sinks, bathrooms with showers or bathtubs were not common at that time in Iraq. Thus, with the multitudes of pilgrims, hammams were successful businesses.

My father, Abbasali Yadegari, was originally from Yazd, at that time a small town in central Iran known as a center of Zoroastrian culture. His family members were recent converts to Shi'ite Islam. Abbasali had no siblings, and he lost his father at an early age. He subsequently quit school in the fourth grade to help earn a living for himself and his mother. His older cousin on his father's side, Mohammad Ibrahim Hajebrahimi, owned a public bath in Karbala. When Mohammad Ibrahim offered his younger cousin employment in his public bath, Abbasali and his mother moved to Karbala.

My mother, Khadijah Hajebrahimi, was born in Karbala to an Iranian family and was more fluent in the Arabic language than my father. My father still spoke Arabic with a heavy Persian accent, so it was easy to detect that he was Iranian. That was a source of consternation for him, but he tried not to show it. His polite and solicitous manner made him a very likable person regardless of his accent.

Though bilingual, Iranians in Karbala spoke Persian in the streets, the bazaar, the stores, and in their homes. We spoke Arabic only when necessary. Iranian businessmen had an advantage over most of the Arabs of the city because most pilgrims who visited the city were Iranians and preferred to deal with the Persian-speaking inhabitants. A great number of the visitors did not speak any Arabic.

The public bath, known in the West as the Turkish bath, was similar to the baths of the Greeks and the Romans. For centuries, public baths were ubiquitous throughout the Muslim world. There were separate baths for men and women. Typically, they consisted of two main areas: a changing area and a bathing area. Some public baths also had private shower rooms.

The changing area consisted of several large cubicles where customers would undress and wrap themselves in long towels. Then they proceeded to the bathing area where there usually were three small pools: one cold, one lukewarm, and one very warm. After soaking in the pools (still wrapped in the towel), a customer would get out of the pool to wash with soap and an exfoliating product using a mitten-like scrub cloth called *keeseh*. Occasionally, the customer might hire an attendant to do a more efficient exfoliation. After showering, the wet towel would be replaced with at least two warm, dry towels when the customer left the bathing area. Some bathers might request a massage, of course for an additional fee. In some public baths, there were several masseurs who were expert in giving different kinds of massages. The gentle Swiss massage was the most popular although some preferred the more strenuous Russian massage.

Most public baths had tea and small pastries available for those who wished to purchase them while relaxing after their baths. (In earlier centuries, many public baths featured elaborate teahouses with floor cushions to sit upon; in modern public baths, a visitor might occasionally find a cafe where tables and chairs have replaced the earlier floor cushions.)

My father's first job in the public bath as a young boy was to bring clean towels and to serve glasses of water to customers. He was hard working, honest, polite, and congenial. By the time he was in his teens, he was well versed in all aspects of running a public bath and was well liked by his extended family.

Around 1928, a large old public bath became available for rent at a low price because it was in disrepair. With some savings of his own, help from his mother, and very likely the backing of his cousin, my father arranged to rent it. The building was large enough to accommodate several hundred customers at full capacity. However, it needed a lot of work remodeling and redecorating. After much renovation, my father opened the bath for business. Soon after, Mohammad Ibrahim arranged a marriage between Abbasali and one of his daughters, Khadijah[2].

The harder my father worked and the more charm and humor he exhibited, the more popular his place of business became with both the local population and the itinerant pilgrims. He made many friends with people from all walks of life among the locals and with many wealthy and prominent visitors who periodically journeyed to Karbala.

My father was deeply religious. I never recall seeing him miss his daily prayers, fail to pay his religious dues, or neglect to fast. At the earliest possible time, he took his obligatory pilgrimage to Mecca. After that pilgrimage, he was always referred to as Haji Abbasali. (*Haji* simply means one who has performed the pilgrimage to Mecca.) Knowing my father, I

---

2 The marriage of cousins was common. In addition, almost all marriages were arranged.

am sure that his journey was not to earn the title but to fulfill his religious duty. However, the title always comes with the trip.

If I were to describe my father's personality traits, the first and foremost would be generosity. Perhaps because of his own good fortune in life, he was generous to the extreme. He often donated money to charity, and he was generous to his workers. He helped them with their wedding expenses, purchased houses for some of them when they got married and needed a place to call home, paid for their doctor and hospital bills, invited them to our house often, and treated them with respect. If a loyal worker who had shown an upright attitude and true honesty wished to part ways and open his own business, my father did not hinder his endeavor. He lent him support in words and cash. Several small business owners and shopkeepers owed their independence to him.

One day a Kuwaiti friend who was visiting Karbala offered to sell him a piece of desert land in that British protectorate. He offered it specifically to him saying, "Dear Haji Abbasali, the British are digging for oil and finding it everywhere. If you hit oil on that land, you'll make a lot of money." My father thanked him profoundly but refused the offer. He abhorred the idea of being "filthy rich." As he so often put it, "It would change me. Money is the filthiest thing in the world. It is good to have it but not a huge amount of it. It causes one to deviate from the path of righteousness."

Hearing my father decline the offer, one of his workers stepped forward and politely asked him if he minded if his "humble servant" purchased the land. When my father asked if the fellow had the money, he replied that he had only three thousand dinars. The worker explained that he was hoping to borrow the other two thousand from him. At that point, my father let out a full belly laugh. So did the owner of the land who was really offering to sell the land to my father as a sign of friendship and generosity. After a good laugh and many joking repartees, my father looked at the young man, offered a prayer for him, and said, "By God, if you want it, you will have it. Repay me the two thousand dinars whenever you earn it. May God be with you."

The young man came back to Karbala several years later wearing exquisite clothing with a silk cloak draped over his shoulders. He greeted my father, kissed his cheeks and hands, and hugged him warmly. He handed him the money he had borrowed and told him that he had, indeed, made a great deal of money in Kuwait. My father took the money but refused any additional favors or cash. He was genuinely happy to see his previous employee succeed. I never knew whether the fellow made his money in oil or in some other endeavor. However, it was commonly known that anyone who could tolerate the searing heat of Kuwait (they did not have air conditioners then) to live and work there could easily make a fortune.

My father was generous and kind, but he also had a quick temper and loud voice. If anyone crossed the line and acted improperly, hell would be unleashed on that day. The worst kind of language would spout from his mouth humiliating liars, pilferers, or other miscreants.

He also had some faults. The most glaring was that he was a flagrant philanderer. While the number of monogamous men greatly exceeded the number of polygamous men, it was religiously acceptable to have up to four wives as long as each was equally provided for. Permission of the existing wife was a necessary condition. However, this requirement was not always followed. In addition, the Shi'ites allowed the practice of temporary marriage (*sighah*), a short-term legal liaison for the purpose of sex. If a child was conceived, the process provided legal status, support, and hereditary rights to any offspring. The woman was enjoined to wait until she was sure a child had not been conceived before she entered into another temporary marriage. However, it was common knowledge that some women who entered into temporary marriages did not always wait the allotted period (two full cycles of menstruation), and men often turned a blind eye to this. The practice of multiple wives and temporary marriage is still permitted today in some countries.

Whatever one may think of this practice, it was effective in reducing the numbers of illegitimate children. Children of temporary marriages were fully recognized as legitimate offspring bearing the father's name and legally entitled to inheritance. No one ever considered such a child a "bastard," and the father was responsible for his support and upbringing.

Temporary marriage did not originate with Islam. It was a pre-Islamic custom, also practiced during the early Islamic period in Arabia. Furthermore, it is likely that this practice was prevalent in Babylonia. Taking of concubines (*pilegesh*) among the Jews in ancient times was similar to temporary marriage among the Shi'ites. The taking of concubines

Abbasali, Khadijah and some of their grandchildren

was approved in the *halakhah*, and the concubines had rights similar to those of a married woman. It appears that various forms of "temporary marriage" existed in various societies, Arab and non-Arab alike.

For whatever reason, my father had to have a dalliance here and there. The practice of temporary marriage allowed him to retain his religious persona and also indulge himself. Sometimes, he went overboard. Once, he married another woman as a second wife (not temporary) and kept it a secret for some years. She bore him two children.

My mother hated my father's dalliances and threatened to divorce him. That finally made him discontinue his womanizing ways. But when it came to the two children of the second wife, she accepted them and treated them as if they were her own. My mother actually raised the boy, who preferred to live with our family rather than with his mother. His sister chose to stay with her mother. My mother taught us that both children were genuinely our siblings.

My mother had a keen eye for business. Though not officially an actual part owner of the public baths, she was in total control of the women's bath. She was not salaried, yet she took as much cash as she needed to pay the workers and to order all kinds of supplies. The everyday management of the household, the hiring and firing of maids, the purchase of furniture, paying for food, clothes, children's allowances, and all other necessary and incidental expenses were under her purview.

As business was good in the women's bath, my mother had access to money that needed to be invested. It was not considered proper or ladylike for a woman to purchase property, although some women did. She, and many other women, invested in gold. She had an array of solid gold bracelets, anklets, and necklaces. These were not just for appearance. They were her "insurance," a nest egg that could be converted to cash in time of need. However, she gave me money and encouraged me to buy and sell land when small suburbs began to spring up outside of Karbala. Since Karbala was growing rapidly, many people were buying properties, speculating on their increase in value.

My mother was also generous like my father. This became obvious to anyone who noticed how well she treated employees of the women's bath or her own successive maids.

One of our maids, Naneh Sakineh, stayed with us for over fifteen years. We liked her a lot and she was fond of us all. However, she had frequent altercations with one of my discourteous brothers. When he would ask for something, he'd shout and be rude to her. Often, he would arrogantly demand a glass of water, something that he could have easily gotten himself. In return, he received vigorous admonishment but no water. Using the occasion to show up my brother, I would politely request a cup of tea. Naneh Sakineh would immediately serve me some tea, all the while offering blessings and prayers for my good health and well-being. "Here you are, Mohammad, may God grant you long life and good health." Since my brother never changed his manners, these exchanges were a constant source of amusement and laughter for the rest of the family.

Naneh Sakineh had a son my age. His name was also Mohammad, and he was my classmate and friend. When he finished elementary school, he decided to become a carpentry apprentice to one of our relatives who made and sold furniture. I tried to convince him to continue his education, but he assured me that his lifetime goal was to become a carpenter and that he was happy to have the opportunity to achieve his wish. As it turned out, he was quick in learning the craft and soon opened his own small business in a building where he built sofas and chairs in the back room and sold them in a store in the front.

On one occasion, he expressed gratitude for my mother's generosity in arranging and supporting his business, not knowing that I was unaware of her help in his venture. When Mohammad got married, his mother purchased a home where the three of them lived. The family rumor was that my mother had also contributed to his wedding and the purchase of their home.

One of the misfortunes of my mother's life was the fact that, born in 1911, she'd never had the opportunity to go to school and was not able to read and write. Without a doubt, that was why she encouraged me to pursue education and become an avid reader at an early age. At the time, I was not aware that modern education had not been introduced in Iraq until the 1920s, and that almost all elementary and secondary schools were for boys. From my observations, Iraq's genuine pursuit of education for the populace did not really gain momentum until the early 1950s. At that time, thanks to the rivalry between Iraq's prime minister, Nuri al-Sa'id, and Jamal Abdul Nasser of Egypt, Iraq embarked on a vigorous program of building schools for both boys and girls.

When my mother was young, most people in Karbala were illiterate. Because of the chauvinistic attitude of the male-dominated society, the number of literate women in Iraq was only a handful (most of whom probably were taught by their parents).

As in the case of my father, I can say much about my mother. But most importantly, no one in my life ever affected my love of learning and intellectual pursuit more than my mother.

CHAPTER 3

The Day My Sister Drowned

MOST HOUSES IN THE MIDDLE EAST are built around a central courtyard and have a *howz* (decorative pool), usually in the center. From the Taj Mahal of India to tiny village homes, the *howz* is a universal feature of Muslim architecture. The *howz* might be simple in an ordinary home but is usually ornate in the homes of the wealthy. Most are rectangular, though some have other geometric shapes. A faucet provides running water for ritual ablution before prayers. There are also similar shallow pools in mosques and schools.

I don't remember exactly how old I was when my little sister drowned in a *howz*. I couldn't have been older than four. My sister was around one year old, still crawling, and the delight of all who knew her. It has been so many years that I seem to even have forgotten her name. Maybe my memory refuses to remember it. Raziah sounds familiar.

My mother had taken her along when she walked to a seamstress's house in our neighborhood to arrange for a dress to be made and to pick out cloth for the dress. My sister had crawled out of the room without being noticed. My mother swore that she had kept a watchful eye on her all the time, but, like any accident, it happened quickly. Maybe it was because of that tragedy that my mother always reminded us to be careful. "Accidents happen within seconds, and, if they do, nothing can reverse them." (I don't think I have to tell you that people can get busy talking and chatting about serious as well as trivial matters and forget to be watchful.)

The *howz* at the seamstress's house was rectangular, approximately eighteen inches deep, built in the middle of the yard. While I did not go on that day, I had been there with my mother several times. According to her, on that particular day, it was full of leaves that had fallen from nearby trees. The seamstress had not cleaned them out. Though relatively shallow, the *howz* was deep enough to drown a crawling baby, my young sister. The water shimmering in the sun or newly fallen leaves floating on the water may have attracted her. After all, crawling babies are not afraid of anything. They don't know what danger is. One second my sister was alive and exuberant, and the next she was floating, unresponsive, on the surface of the water. That is how my mother found her.

When she was brought home, my sister was laid out on the floor. Her small dress was torn away so her body was bare. She looked soft, her skin fair, her stomach smooth, but she did not move. My mother was constantly patting and kissing her on the lips, on the cheek, on her abdomen. I stood there, a little boy in a circle of weeping women. I did not cry because my feelings were numb. I did not know how to react. All I knew was that she was dead. She was dead and gone, and she did not move.

She did not look at me, the one who had been her constant companion and playmate. On the night before, this little sister of mine had been so happy when I put her on a big metal serving tray and spun her around and around as I pushed the tray around the room. She had laughed loudly, her squeals of delight making everyone turn and look and smile. My mother had stopped me. Some people say that spinning a child on a tray brings bad luck. Call it superstition, call it a mother's intuition, call it whatever you wish. I distinctly remember my mother stopping me and saying with a nervous smile and a worried look that it was not good to put a baby on a tray and push her around. Something bad could happen to her.

And there I was with my wide eyes looking down at my sister's abdomen because I couldn't understand why mother kept kissing her there. It was white and soft and different from mine. A woman next to me slapped me lightly on my forehead. "Stop ogling her bare body," she shouted. "You ought to be ashamed of yourself!" I could not understand why. I was bewildered at the whole affair. I had never seen my mother so sad, wishing she'd been the one who had drowned instead of her daughter. And then I heard a wail that seemed to swell up from the depth of her soul. "Leave Mohammad alone! My dear son, you want to look? Look, look, look. She is beautiful." She bent down again, kissing my sister's cold abdomen. Less than four years old, too young to understand, I witnessed the pain that a mother feels at the loss of her own flesh and blood.

It was over seventy years ago, and no one knew about CPR. And by all accounts, I can surmise that my poor sister had no chance of survival at that point anyway. My mother pleaded with God but He did not answer. A short silence was followed by a weak sigh of desperation and resignation. Only later, when I had children of my own and could comprehend the finality of life and death, did I begin to imagine what really had gone through my mother's mind during that fateful moment.

My mother never wore the dress she had ordered that day. And, though it is said that time heals all wounds, she never forgot that awful moment. I doubt if she fell asleep that night. I am also sure that, although she did not voice an objection to the will of the Master of the Universe, she still blamed the city of Karbala whose earth was always thirsty for new flesh, that city of agony and calamity: *"karb"* and *"bala"*!

CHAPTER 4

Babajoon

MY GRANDFATHER ON MY MOTHER'S SIDE, Mohammad Ibrahim Hajebrahimi, lived a long life. Some said 115 years and others, 108. Records of birth were not the best in those days. We called him Babajoon (Dearest Father). His image in my mind is that of the man I last saw in 1963. Though old in comparison to me, he was still vibrant and physically strong.

His mustache always reminded me of Shah Abbas the Great (1587-1629). He often twisted the ends and curled them upward on both sides. His eyes were penetrating. If he wished, he could send a piercing glance to fill his victim with trepidation. However, he always bestowed a smile upon his twenty-one grandchildren. We received his perpetual love and admiration. He made us laugh by twitching his mustache one side at a time, making it dance in the air. He hugged us and kissed us on the cheeks. He perched the little ones on his lap. He made small talk but mainly smiled while praising us all.

His first question whenever he picked me up and placed me on the bench next to him was, "Have you been good to your mother?" I would reply, "Yes Babajoon," even if I had not been good, though, somehow, I felt he could tell by looking into my eyes if I had been honest or not. "Then you deserve a Coke." He'd laugh loudly and would call out, "Bring my grandson a Coca-Cola." There was an icebox in the corner of his public bath. Babajoon would insist on opening the bottle of Coca-Cola himself.

He would dry it with a towel gently, gingerly, and patiently, before handing it to me. My hand would get chilled, but I would switch the bottle to my other hand and try to tolerate the cold bottle. He'd take it from me, wrap it up with his clean white handkerchief, and hand it back to me. "Does that feel a little better?" Yes, it did but only for a moment. "Have you been a good boy?" I would nod affirmatively.

"Repeat after me, *pendare neek, guftare neek, kerdare neek*" (good thoughts, good words, good deeds). I would repeat the words carefully, making sure I did not disappoint him. This was his motto in life: having good thoughts, speaking good words about other people, and treating everyone with kindness. As I grew up, I began to notice that this motto and his other pieces of advice were centered on the positive. He rarely used such words as, "Don't ever," "Never," or "Thou shall not." His own actions and words exemplified his entire philosophy of life. I don't recall ever hearing him admonish anyone or gossip behind anyone's back. If he did not have anything good to say about a person, he did not say anything. I attributed his cheerful demeanor to the fact that he was a happy man and very proud of his children and grandchildren.

His wife, my grandmother, had died from rheumatic fever when she was in her forties, leaving him with two sons and three daughters. We never saw our maternal grandmother, but we heard our mother talk about her. Everyone said that Babajoon loved her. Even so, he married another woman a few years later. She was also a wonderful woman, young and beautiful, but my mother never got along well with her stepmother. "Look at the way she fixes her hair and uses makeup!" Apparently, my mother was a bit jealous of her, but we never thought much about the rivalry. "And see how she is always pregnant. Every year she gives him a new baby. With time spent cooking and cleaning and having her hair done, how will she find time to raise all these kids? And she can't even cook. She knows only one dish."

We loved that dish, *khoresh maahi* (baked, stuffed fish). Periodically, she'd invite our family of ten (including our parents) for dinner, and she would always serve the fish. But the way she prepared it was elaborate. A large whole fish was split in half, each side lying flat piled high with a stuffing of pistachios, chopped almonds, small pieces of walnut, and just the right amount of raisins mixed with diced tomatoes and then baked to perfection. Hidden under each child's plate there was a dirham (equal to one shilling). We all knew what to expect and waited for the moment Babajoon directed us to pick up our plates to see what was underneath. Our eyes and excited expressions and giggles were more than words of thanks. He loved to see us smile and be happy. He started the meal with his usual ritual. "Repeat after me," he would say. *"Pendare neek, guftare neek, kerdare neek."* We'd shout it happily. Then we'd eat.

It wasn't until later in life that I learned the significance of those words. I was eighteen and in Iran when I met my great aunt on my father's side. She was also old in age but as young at heart as her nephew, Babajoon, in Karbala, Iraq. She was extremely thin, her cheeks hollow over her jaws. I knew she wore dentures because I saw her clean them. This great aunt constantly talked. I asked her how old she was and she replied that she was 135 years old. "That's impossible," I said. "You must be exaggerating."

"I never exaggerate, young man. I saw the nephew of Nasir al-Din Shah [1848-1896] in the bazaar of Isfahan when I was only eight years old." She repeated, "I was eight years old." Apparently she had had a crush on the nephew of the Shah. She talked of him as her "prince." I asked her why she talked so much. She said that was one reason she was still alive. The other, apparently, was eating a lot of yogurt. She lived with her daughter in Shemiran, north of Tehran, in an affluent neighborhood. She refused to be treated as old and incapable of taking care of herself. I asked her, "Whom do you talk to when you're alone in the house and no one is around?"

"The wall, son, the wall. I just knock on the wall and yell at it, 'Hey wall, I am talking to you.' " We loved her for her sense of humor, her vigor, and her independence. But we knew she couldn't be 135 years old, not even 125, though maybe over 100. Otherwise, the dates just didn't add up. Whatever the case, she would advise us, just like Babajoon, *"Pendare neek, guftare neek, kerdare neek."* By then, I knew what religious doctrine this motto represented. I asked her why she and Babajoon kept repeating this motto. "We used to be Zoroastrians. Didn't anyone tell you that?" she explained with a smile bordering on a smirk. "Of course, we're Muslims now, but we're all originally from Na'in [near Yazd]. Islam teaches the same kinds of things but we still like the old ways that we have followed for many centuries."

CHAPTER 5

Ya Husayn

I WAS ONLY SEVEN YEARS OLD, walking with my elder brother and his friends along the river that meandered in an arc on the outskirts of Karbala. We were on a dry, dirt road that bordered orchards of date palms and citrus trees when we saw three Arabs, each wearing a *kafiyyah* on his head and a long *dishdashah* that dragged on the ground sweeping the dust. They were ambling haughtily behind us. Long walls identified the property lines, separating one orchard from another. The shade from the trees cooled us as we walked.

In the 1940s, Karbala was like an oasis located between the main Euphrates River and a wide canal that branched off from it called Shatt al-Husayniayyah (the Husayniayyah River). Irrigation canals for the purpose of supporting agriculture had existed in Iraq as far back as the Persian Sassanid Empire (224-651 CE), which had controlled much of the Fertile Crescent at that time.

In truth, my main interest in tagging along with my brother and his friends was to have ice cream afterward. Most of the time, my hope for ice cream was dashed because, even though they often talked about going to the ice cream parlor, they seldom had enough money. But that did not prevent me from daydreaming about a trip to the ice cream parlor and hoping that we'd actually go. I loved ice cream, especially in that particular store. The place was large enough for a couple of dozen people to sit at tables with comfortable chairs. The ice cream was flavored with rose water and saffron and its mere scent made my mouth water.

In any case, on that day I was tired of standing next to the circle of my brother's friends who strolled along aimlessly but periodically stopped to continue chatting. I decided to sit on the ground, a short distance from their vociferous exchange of ideas, and I began writing simple words in the sand with a stick.

I had just learned to write *"Ya Husayn"* meaning "O Husayn!"[3] Who in Karbala didn't know how to read or write *"Ya Husayn"*? I felt proud of my masterpiece. As a child, I expected to be praised for my achievement. I did not notice the three inquisitive men passing by me. As they passed, they slowed their pace, lingered, and looked at my work of art. They glanced at one another with frowns on their faces and then gave us all dirty looks that tore my heart apart. My brother and his companions rushed to see what I had been up to. Fear gripped them and anger made their cheeks flush. What had I done? I asked myself. One of my brother's friends grabbed my arm and dragged me away while another scuffed out the writing with his shoes. Another one shouted at me in Arabic that I should never again commit such a blasphemy. "You should never write '*Ya Husayn*' again," he yelled into my face. "Don't you know that Husayn was only a man? We never pray to a man, we pray to Allah and only Allah."

What was he talking about? I asked myself. And why did he speak Arabic and not Persian? While my brother and his friends knew Arabic, they usually spoke our mother tongue, Persian.

As the men disdainfully walked away, my brother's friend quieted down and, when he was sure that the three strangers were out of range of both sight and hearing, he heaved a sigh of relief. Everyone else began to relax. Then their nervous laughter filled the air. One of them smiled and pretended to wipe the sweat from his forehead. Once again speaking Persian they explained to me, "Those men are Sunnis. We have to make sure they don't know we are Shi'ite. They hate Shi'ites, and we've been told

---

3   This expression identifies the speaker as Shi'ite. Although many Sunnis have their own Sufi saints, they consider Shi'ites' devotion to certain religious figures as anathema.

to practice *taqiyya*[4] [dissimulation] when Sunnis are around. You never know when they might pull out a dagger and cut your throat."

"What is *taqiyya*?" I asked. The whole affair was bothering me, and *taqiyya* had no meaning for me.

"You'll learn when you grow up!" was the only answer I was given. Of course, I was instructed never to write *Ya Husayn* or *Ya Ali* or "*Ya* anybody" again in front of people I did not know.

---

4 Dissimulation is the practice of disguising one's views on subjects such as religion, politics, or sexual orientation from other groups with antagonistic attitudes. It has been practiced for centuries by various groups of people such as Shi'ites, Jews, or homosexuals who are subjects of discriminatory acts.

CHAPTER 6

Chador

*I*WAS ABOUT SEVEN YEARS OLD when my nineteen-year old brother got married. His eighteen-year-old wife was very beautiful. Young and vibrant, her eyes hazel green and her hair lustrous brown with streaks of gold, she wore a touch of makeup on her face. The young couple lived with our family, which was common for newlyweds.

One evening during dinner, as usual, she was wearing a *chador* (Persian for women's veil). Sitting across from her, I felt sorry for her as I saw how difficult it was for her to use her right hand to eat with a spoon and her left hand to hold her *chador* to cover her hair. We were fourteen people sitting around a *sofreh*, a tablecloth spread out over a Persian rug on the floor. Food and place settings were arranged on the *sofreh*, and we sat on the floor and ate "picnic style." As we ate, we talked and laughed freely. Unaccustomed to seeing so many of her new in-laws and relatives, she looked very uncomfortable. At home during the day when men were not present, she did not wear her *chador* in front of me, a seven-year-old boy. But she wore it now because my other brother, Hadi, was seventeen. He was above the official age of maturity, fifteen, and therefore was called *namahram* (any man not permitted to see a woman without her *chador*).

New to the family and shy, my sister-in-law did not ask for water or salt or pepper or more bread. When someone offered her anything, she'd say, "No, thank you." I was convinced something had to be done. An idea popped into my head. I had found a solution that would end this dilemma.

If my brother the *namahram* had a chance to see her only once, then there would no longer be a mystery. Then she could take off her *chador* and be able to eat comfortably. To me, it was not a big deal anyway. I had seen her many times without her *chador*. With that thought in mind, I rose from my seat moving deftly and quietly and stood behind her. No one paid any attention. They were busy eating, talking, and laughing.

I called Hadi's name. He instinctively looked up and without hesitation I pulled the *chador* off my sister-in-law's head. She sat there looking exquisitely beautiful but extremely embarrassed. Her cheeks were red.

"Do you see, Hadi?" I shouted triumphantly. "Now she doesn't have to wear a *chador* anymore." I thought I had performed a heroic act. I had found a solution that was so logical!

The adults' eyebrows raised in surprise and disapproval. But some began to chuckle, and my mother admonished me gently, saying, "Mohammad *joon* (dear Mohammad), Hadi is *namahram* to her."

My confident smile began to fade. Why didn't they understand my simple solution to this complex issue? My sister-in-law said nothing at all. She simply picked up her *chador* and slowly relocated it on her head. I walked back to my place, circling the people sitting around the *sofreh*. I said nothing; they said nothing. Their heads were lowered; my head was down. But I could see a couple of amused, askance looks. We started to eat again.

CHAPTER 7

The Cure

THE IRANIAN AND IRAQI GOVERNMENTS had reciprocal agreements to build a number of schools in each other's countries to teach the children of their respective citizens their own curriculum in their own language. However, the curriculum of the host country was mandatory as well. Thus, those who studied in an Iranian school in Karbala or Baghdad underwent rigorous training in the Iraqi system of education conducted in Arabic, as well as the Iranian system of education conducted in Persian. I graduated from elementary school with two diplomas: one diploma certified that I had fulfilled the requirements of the Iraqi curriculum; the other certified that I had fulfilled the requirements of the Iranian system of education. Because of that, our school days were much longer than the school days of those who attended just the Iraqi school system. Since this rigorous double duty was difficult for some Iranian children, many Iranian families sent their children only to the Iraqi-operated schools. This speeded up the Arabization of the resident Iranians and slowly many Iranians opted to become Iraqi citizens (which was welcomed and encouraged by Iraqi officials).

The advantage of going to the Iranian school for me was that we had small classes with excellent teachers. Teachers' salaries there were much higher than salaries of their counterparts in both countries. The Iranian Ministry of Education spent a good amount of money to provide us with the best available education.

When I was in the elementary school and junior high, I read many books. Actually, by the time I left Iraq for Iran in 1959, I had read 999 books, some fiction but mostly nonfiction. I counted them. It was surprising to see that I had read so many books. I went around and bragged about it. I had read one less than a thousand books and had arranged them in my own personal library. I don't want to give the impression that I really had a library. I had makeshift shelves in my room where I kept my books. Every time I finished reading a book, I put it next to the previous one. Most of the people we knew were interested in reading. Actually, our Arabic and Persian literature teachers often exchanged books with us, and we discussed them afterwards. The culture of Karbala encouraged it.

Translations of books by foreign writers were readily available. Works of Victor Hugo, Tolstoy, and Dostoevsky could be found in bookstores. Books written by philosophers such as Fredrick Nietzsche and Schopenhauer were my favorites. I used to memorize interesting quotes and slip them into my conversation. Well-to-do businessmen who were patrons of scholarship would often hold book discussion sessions in their homes, in teahouses, or in madrasahs during the day as well as weekends and evenings. I often attended these discussions because the hosts were friends of our family.

Even though I became a proficient and avid reader, I had been very slow to learn in the early grades. I was sent to kindergarten when I was six years old, but I often played hooky because I was afraid of the teacher. His teeth were menacingly scary. He smiled and leaned forward to reassure me, but that sent shivers up my spine. As soon as I found an opening, I ran home and hid so that no one knew I was there. I lost one year of my life because I was made to repeat kindergarten.

When I was in the second grade, I could not read more than a few words. I remember distinctly the day I was moved from the second grade back to the first grade. There were six other students in my category. None of us could read and write, yet we were in the second grade. Some teachers had complained about it, and one day a representative from the Supervisory Board of Iranian Schools in Iraq, located in Baghdad, came with his entourage to inspect our school. They sent us to the board, and, one by one, we were asked to write the name of our school. None of us could. The entourage decided we had to repeat first grade. All seven of us were escorted immediately to the first grade.

My mother had many encouraging words for me that night. "You're very smart, Mohammad *joon*. All you have to do is learn to read. You're so smart that you pretend to read without knowing the words. When someone reads a book to you, you take it back and read it page by page and everyone thinks you can read. But I know what you're doing. You look at the pictures, and, since you've memorized the story, you recite it. But you really don't recognize the words."

That was true. I had fooled everyone. Not purposely. It had been so easy for me to remember the words, and the pictures helped me turn the pages at the proper moment. But I didn't know how to read. One of my older brothers was asked to tutor me. He did his best, but, even though he knew how to read, he didn't know how to teach me. However, he was able to teach me the alphabet and how to connect the letters to make a word.

I lost another year because I was moved from the second grade back to the first grade. By the time I was back in the second grade again, I must have been ten years old. Additionally, I lisped through second grade. Up until that time no one had made fun of me, and my lisp did not bother me.

In the second grade, a new teacher was hired to teach us mathematics. He was amused when he first heard me talk. I will never forget when he came to our second-grade classroom for the first time. He made us stand up one by one to introduce ourselves. When he got to me, he detected my special "genius." You see, I always thought I was very smart. Never mind that I couldn't write my name and that I had played hooky from kindergarten for most of the year, or that I was so bad in second grade that they sent me back to first grade, I still thought I was somebody special. I didn't even realize that I lisped. When the new teacher called on me to tell him my name, I saw him smiling curiously. He continued asking questions. I felt great because the other students were not given the special attention he was so generously bestowing upon me. Peripherally, I saw my classmates gesturing, trying to communicate with him. He couldn't understand them at first but when he finally grasped the fact that I lisped, an amused smile brightened his face. "Come here, Mr. Yadegari," he said. I was on cloud nine. Our new teacher liked me. He was going to pat my head and ruffle my hair tenderly because he had found a cute and lively boy who was truly special. I went out in front of the class and stood by his side smiling and happy. So was he, or so I thought. He asked me to count the number of metal support beams in the ceiling of the classroom. I told him there were "theven." He asked me to count them one by one. "As you count, say, 'one support beam, two support beams, three support beams, so on and so forth.'" I eagerly counted them, "One thupport beam, two thupport beamth, three thupport beamth," to the end. There were "theven thupport beamth." When I looked at my classmates and saw all of them giggling, I suddenly realized that I lisped and had just been made the butt of a joke. That was a rude awakening. How could a boy who was so smart and so special be the subject of such humiliation? The teacher's interest was to get a good laugh at my expense. My friends didn't look me in the eye, but they were still laughing and smiling and chuckling. They had gone along with the charade. I wished the earth would open its mouth and swallow me up. I quietly went back and sat dejectedly in my chair.

Arriving home after school, I told my mother the story. She became indignant and embarked on the tedious task of finding a cure for my lisping. She consulted everyone she could find and tried one remedy after another. None worked. Then one auspicious day, she returned to the house exclaiming that she had found a solution. She had purchased thirty little sparrows from Ma'sumah, a "wonderful and wise" woman. The birds were in a cage, singing nonstop.

"This is going to cure you. I am going to make you a wonderful soup, sparrow soup. Ma'sumah emphasized that there had to be thirty of them, no more, no less. It will work. Wait and see." I waited with anticipation.

She faced Mecca, saying *Bismillah*[5]. Then she cut off the sparrows' heads, blanched them in boiling water, and plucked their feathers. Finally, she cleaned their entrails. They looked tiny and almost meatless. She added water and some salt and pepper to the birds in a new pan and boiled them until tender. She poured the broth into a bowl, and instructed me, "Don't leave a drop when you drink it. When you finish, your lisp will disappear, I promise you."

---

5 *Bismillah al-Rahman al-Rahim* (In the Name of God, the Most Gracious, the Dispenser of Grace). This blessing is always said when butchering an animal to be cooked and consumed as food.

My skeptical older sister was watching in anticipation. It seemed to her that it was only an exercise in futility. Our mother was too naïve, my sister thought. I drank the broth expectantly. It was warm and soothing, with just the right touch of salt and pepper. I finished it and put the bowl down. "Well, say something!" my mother insisted. "What do you want me to say?" Even though I felt no different, I saw tears rolling down my mother's cheeks. My sister looked with wide eyes. How could this silly soup of thirty sparrows cure years of lisping? Everyone examined me by asking me to repeat words that a lisper has difficulty pronouncing. I had passed the test!

I had conquered my lisping but still was sitting in the second grade for the second time, and all I knew was the alphabet and how to slowly, very slowly, read a few words. Again, my mother, who could not read or write, came to the rescue. In her own way, she pleaded with me to read to her. "Mohammad *joon*. I can see, but I can't read. You read to me. Promise me this. You're going to read this book to me every day. Follow me around while I cook and clean. Read it to me." I had no choice. First of all, she was the one who had miraculously cured my lisp. Also, she was my mother, and I felt sorry for her not having had the opportunity to go to school.

I looked at the book. It was not a normal looking book. It was a lithograph of text that was handwritten, and the handwriting was terrible. Every word seemed to be joined to the next. There was a space in the middle of each line. I told her it didn't look like a normal book. She told me it was poetry. It was an epic about Mukhtar's revolt against the Umayyads (661-750 CE) in 686 when he avenged Husayn's martyrdom that had occurred in 680. It extolled the courage of Mukhtar who had killed and even boiled (according to the enthusiastic poet) those who'd had the audacity to kill the grandson of the Prophet.

"You can do it, Mohammad. Do it for me. I cannot read, you read it to me." So, it all began. Every time I could not read a word, she told me what it was. "I thought you couldn't read," I challenged her once. My mother really could not read or write but, apparently, she had heard it enough times that she had almost memorized the entire epic poem. Greatly encouraged, I started to read. By the end of the summer, I was surprised to find out that I could read any book given to me. I had "graduated" to *Haydar-nameh* and *Hamzeh-nameh*. Both were epics praising the virtues and the courage of Haydar (another name for Ali, the first Shi'ite Imam) and Hamzeh (Muhammad's uncle) respectively.

When my mother was confident that I could read, she promised that she would pay for any book I wished to buy. This was apart from my daily allowance. I had to make a solemn promise to her, though. I swore that I would not believe everything I read. Only the Quran and the Bible were to be believed implicitly and the Bible ranked second because the Jews and Christians, though God-fearing, had "corrupted" their holy books. Why else would God send Muhammad to reteach humankind?[6] By the time I was in sixth grade, she heard me read what is now considered to be pornographic by some. Not knowing that she was in the room, I read it out loud. *"Do lab bar lab nihad-o naaf bar naaf, alif ra kard raast bar khane-ye kaaf."* (He laid his lips upon her lips, putting his navel on her navel, entering the house of V. with his straightened P.). Looking at me askance, she was pensively perturbed. Then, she saw me hide Karl Marx's *Communist Manifesto* whenever my father entered the house. After Mosaddeq of Iran and Nasser of Egypt became major political figures, everyone was into politics, including me.

My mother told me that she didn't want to know what I was reading anymore. "Just show me the book you have purchased, and I will pay you its cost. But remember your solemn promise, do not believe everything you read. The written word is that of a person and people can be wrong in their views. Never forget that!" I nodded in agreement.

---

6 Muslims believe that the original message brought by previous prophets (Moses, Jesus, and others) had been corrupted over time. Therefore, God revealed the Quran to Prophet Muhammad to clarify His wishes.

CHAPTER 8

Ya Mahdi

I WAS ABOUT TEN YEARS OLD. My mother was in labor. At that time, women did not go to a hospital to deliver a baby. Midwives did everything. Our homes did not have chairs and sofas to sit on. We sat on floors covered with Persian carpets and slept on padded mats on the floor. For birthing in those days, a makeshift apparatus was constructed. Sturdy concrete blocks were stacked up to form a chair-like structure.

Imagine being in a campsite in a state park. Then look at the concrete fireplace. Just like that. Now imagine this construct packed with covers and huge pillows. The pregnant woman would put her feet one on each side and lean against the back that was covered with piles of soft and fluffy covers, her legs apart, and she would keep pushing.

There were two or three midwives and more than a half-dozen women helping the midwives. Buckets of water had been boiled, and buckets more were being boiled. Clean towels were piled ready to be used. My mother, I was told, was crouching on this apparatus and pushing, pushing with all the strength she possessed. She was screaming with pain. At one point, we children were standing by the door, peeking in. One of the women saw us and instead of scolding us she asked us to go out on top of the roof and call out, *"Ya Mahdi."*[7] Our cries would attract the Hidden Imam's attention, and he would help ease the pain of delivery. We ran up to the rooftop and started entreating the Imam. Some of us were shouting at the top of our lungs eagerly awaiting the intercession of the Expected One.

I began to wonder why we were calling on Mahdi and not God. I stopped shouting and was angry with the Mahdi. Here I was fervently calling his name, yet he did not show up and ease my mother's pain. I began praying and calling on God to come to the aid of my mother. I yelled, *"Ya Khoda (O God)."* Pausing for a moment, I continued yelling, *"Khodaya,* help my mother, ease her pain, and show mercy. *Ya Khoda, Ya Khoda, Ya Khoda."*[8]

One of the children in the group reminded me that we were instructed to call on the Mahdi. It was Mahdi (the "patron saint") who was supposed to help pregnant women in labor. I went along with the rest and continued calling on the Mahdi. But I kept thinking that, if the Mahdi was alive and in occultation, he should hear me and come quickly and help my mother deliver her baby. Where in the world was he? And again, if God created us all, why did I have to call Mahdi's name and not God's name? God, I was told, was omnipotent and omnipresent. He was everywhere. The Mahdi, though an Imam, was only a man. Maybe he had been busy with a much less fortunate person. Still, I wasn't happy with him. My mother was more important than any other person. She had been in labor for many hours, and this wonderful person—the best mother and the best person in the world—was in trouble. The Mahdi did not seem to care.

---

7 Muslims, Sunnis, as well as Shi'ites, believe that when injustice and oppression have become the order of the day and all hope is gone, the Mahdi, the Expected One, will come to bring peace and tranquility to this planet. The belief in the coming of the Mahdi among Muslims has its roots in poorly validated sayings attributed to the Prophet. That is, the authenticity of these sayings is questionable. One such saying mentions Prophet Muhammad stating, "The Mahdi resembles me: forehead broad, nose aquiline." However, there is no mention of a "Mahdi" in the Quran.

The concept of the Messiah is common to many religions. The Zoroastrians call him *Saoshyant* (the Deliverer or the World Savior), the Jews name him the Messiah, the Christians believe in the Second Coming of Jesus. Many world religions and their denominations have sketched their savior based on their own situational conditions. Messianic belief seems to be a very ancient concept reflecting humans' dissatisfaction with their present conditions and their yearning for a savior to bring a better life.

8 While Allah is the Arabic word for God, the Persian word for God is Khoda. In fact, German Gott, English God, and Persian Khoda are linguistically related, all belonging to the Indo-European language group.

As I grew older, I began to appreciate how traditions can affect our mindsets. Most people need tangible results. They need constant reassurance, care, and compassion, and, since God is believed to be a transcendent Being and, thus, inaccessible to those who need Him, people look for the next best available entity: a saint, an imam, a shaman, or a Sufi peer (guide). In the Catholic tradition, there are apparently thousands of such saints: St. Gregory, St. Jude, St. Monica, St. Girard, and St. Nicholas among them. Though deceased, they are more "available" than the One whose domain is in the heavens.

At that age, however, I didn't know about saints and good luck charms, nor did I know about spirits in rocks or what karma meant. The bitter truth is that I would have called on all of them. For me, at that moment, the safety and health of my mother was important. Nothing else mattered. Unfortunately, it took several more hours before my mother delivered the baby. Apparently my sister had a big head.

CHAPTER 9

What Do You Want to Be When You Grow Up?

TEACHING IS AN ART, and teachers are among the greatest artists in the world. The secret to successful teaching is the ability to impart knowledge to students in such a way that they can understand it. Period. Students don't have to love a teacher, but they must respect him or her. We were taught to respect all our teachers.

We particularly respected our English teacher in the fifth grade. Mr. Naseri was tall and hefty, an impressive figure in the classroom. He spoke in English the first day even though we did not understand what he was saying. His son was our classmate and had been instructed well in advance on how to behave. For example, when his father entered the classroom on the first day and commanded in English, "Stand," his son stood, and we followed his example. After the order to "Sit" was given, we immediately followed his son's example and sat. Of course, since he gestured very obviously, moving his arms upward and downward, his intentions soon became very clear to us.

During the first two weeks of class with new students, Mr. Naseri was strict and gruff. His piercing gaze froze students in their seats. He concentrated on an intensive study of the English alphabet and required students to memorize a list of some two hundred words by repeating the words and their spellings over and over. To this day, I remember many of those words and how to pronounce them the way I did then.

In the Iranian school of Karbala, our classes were usually very small, only about eight to ten students per class. We were all close friends as well as constant competitors. We all tried to excel and surpass one another, but the size of our class and the closeness of the students' grades was such that jealousy did not enter our hearts.

I didn't think our English teacher regarded any of us as individuals during the first two weeks. He seemed unfriendly. It was later that we discovered that his demeanor was all an act. His philosophy was to be tough in the beginning to establish his position: he was the teacher, and we should never forget it.

Then, one day during the third week, we were allowed to see the real personality behind the mask. He spoke in Persian and let English take a rest. He became friendly, kind, and polite. He greeted us and treated us with respect. He earned our respect in return.

On that day, while pacing around the room reflectively, he turned around and announced that he wished to take a break from teaching English for the day. "Let's do something else," he suggested. We asked him to tell us some stories. "Later, later, not today," was his reply. Later he did, indeed, keep his word. Our English teacher was a master storyteller. His body language and his expressive eyes added depth to the stories he shared. I remember him telling us about George Washington and the cherry tree, and that George could never lie. His retelling of the stories of Washington Irving's "The Legend of Sleepy Hollow" and Mark Twain's *The Adventures of Huckleberry Finn* fascinated us. Other stories about ghosts and monsters kept us on the edges of our seats.

On the day that he shed his strict demeanor, he began the class by asking each of us what goal we had set for ourselves in life. "What would you like to be when you grow up?" he asked.

As each boy (yes, it was a boys' school) related his wish for the future, the teacher made comments, asked questions, and gave advice. When I think back, I realize that he was giving us guidance to be clear about our goals and to pursue them earnestly. His demeanor was fatherly and friendly.

When my turn came, I was timid because I was afraid he might laugh at me. I whispered my answer softly, saying that I wanted to "change the world." He looked down at the floor suppressing a smile. He was thinking. Then, looking up into my eyes, he asked, "How?"

I didn't like his challenge. What did he mean "How?" He should know what it meant to change the world. But I dared not tell him. I repeated, "I want to change the world." My voice was a bit louder this time, deliberately emphasizing the words. He understood that I was annoyed as well as confused. He stubbornly persisted. "But HOW do you want to change the world?"

"I don't understand your question," I said respectfully, wishing I had not revealed my inner thoughts. I could have said I wanted to be a doctor, lawyer, teacher, anything. Why in the world did I tell him my secret dream? Instead, I just stood there, saying nothing. I saw him eyeing me with admiration but with a puzzling look.

"The janitor who is sweeping the floors of this school is changing the world in his own way. As a teacher, I am changing the world because I prepare you for the future. English may be a foreign language and seemingly useless, but you never know where and when you may need it. I am changing your lives by teaching you English. That could affect your future. By doing so I am changing the world. Now, think about it, Mr. Yadegari, and tell me what profession you plan to choose in order to serve the people and change the world." As a habit, surnames were used to address each other. (By the way, "surname" was one of the first two hundred words he made us memorize during the first two weeks.)

"I want to be a writer who changes the world."

A sigh of satisfaction, at last! "So," he said, "you want to be a writer."

I felt that he was going to elaborate on writing. When he did not, I thought he still didn't understand me. I interrupted him. "I want to be a writer who changes the world," I replied. I heard a few giggles.

Mr. Naseri's sharp glance silenced everyone in class. "Mr. Yadegari, how do you want to change the world with your writing?"

This was turning into an interrogation now. Why didn't he leave me alone and go to the next person? And why did I keep trying to show off?

"I want my writing to make people think about the conditions of life and affect them so they would change the way they think. There are a lot of religious hypocrites who are wolves in sheep's clothing. There are a lot of poor people shivering from cold right now without an Aladdin heater." (I pointed to the Aladdin kerosene space heater that warmed our classroom.) "Some people don't have enough food to eat," I continued, "and then there are a lot of very rich people. I want to change people's lives. I want to become a great writer and win the Nobel Prize. Hopefully, my writing will help my readers understand that the truth is not as they see it." I felt I was digging a deep hole in which to bury myself. My exasperation and perspiration overwhelmed me. I didn't know that some writers' works did exactly what I was suggesting.

He smiled. "Lofty goal, Mr. Yadegari. Lofty goal. Well said," he reassured me, though, by then, I was too spent from the pressure to appreciate his compliment.

After nearly forty years of teaching, I still see poor homeless people, hungry people, ignorant people, bigoted people, and rich greedy people, avaricious people whose only aim in life is to accumulate wealth. As my father used to say, no one becomes "filthy rich" without stepping on someone else's skull on the way up the ladder of financial success. Yes, indeed, I still want to change the world, but I don't know how.

The child in me still hopes.

CHAPTER 10

The Sword

WHEN YOU LIVE IN A CITY where almost every aspect of human life is intermingled with some religious dogma and one's destiny intertwines with the dictates of men who speak for God, it is inevitable that you feel that your actions and words are somehow controlled from the Beyond. But, for whatever reason, I always doubted that. It was unbelievable to me that God took a specific interest in me and other human beings. In this regard, my family considered me odd but they loved me, anyway. "There goes the philosopher again," was a common reference to my questions and arguments. I am really glad that their reaction to me was not negative because if, for example, they had said, "There goes the big mouth," my character and psychological development would have been different. Adults can be cruel to children. They could have admonished me with a slap and sharp words. For whatever reason, they smiled and tolerated me. When I think of all the people in my family, the one who had the most tolerance for my questions was my mother. She looked with pride at me whenever I challenged the learned elders who made a great deal of sense to those who believed them, but not to me.

My brother-in-law was very religious. One day he came home with a sword, a great shiny one. It had a sheath decorated with what appeared to be jewels, but they were actually imitation. These glass "jewels" twinkled and sparkled in the light. He was very proud of his treasure and handled it with much care. He slowly unsheathed the sharp steel blade, showing us how magnificent it was. And it was. I had never seen such a large, curved blade. It could chop off a head with one stroke. What was it for? Why had he bought it? Proudly, he hung the sword on two hooks that he had fastened on the wall above a mirror. He stood beneath it and rested his right elbow on the mantel beneath the mirror, striking the pose of a conqueror awaiting a picture-taking event. "I am ready," he proclaimed. He told us that he was ready for the coming of the Mahdi, and that he would fight by his side.

The Mahdi was expected to reappear to set all wrongs aright. First, he was to kill Dajjal who was an evil liar (someone similar to the Antichrist). Then, with the aid of Jesus, who would descend from the Heavens at the same time, the Expected One would end misery and poverty, establishing an equitable social order.

"Do you think he is coming soon?" I asked skeptically. "He's been absent for a thousand years. He may not come for another thousand years." My mother chuckled quietly. This was not an acceptable question for a believer. The reappearance of the Mahdi was considered an absolute truth. My brother-in-law considered himself to be well versed in Islamic teachings and a man of God. I don't think he liked my comments. My mother was smart enough to hide her smile. "Mohammad is only a kid," she offered quickly.

I could not comprehend the power of Almighty God. God had breathed His Spirit into a virgin, impregnating her. He had sent terrible rains that had filled the earth with a great flood. God, through Moses, had parted the sea and through Jesus had raised the dead and cured the lepers. This God was obviously capable of hiding a little boy for as long as He wished and could just as easily send him back to sack the unbelieving and corrupt rulers.

For the next several years, my brother-in-law remained full of zeal and anticipation of using his sword against the evildoers in the army of the Hidden Imam. As time went on, the eminent expectation of the Imam's appearance was slowly forgotten. The sword still hung there, though. I don't know if it was ever removed.

About fifty years later, some people undoubtedly thought that Saddam Hussein was Dajjal. And, finally, a resident of the White House,[9] under orders from his Supreme Being, took up the "sword," invaded the fertile land of Mesopotamia, and hanged "Dajjal" (Saddam Hussein).

---

9   George W. Bush (March 20, 2003).

CHAPTER 11

The Fortress

KARBALA ABOUNDED WITH ORCHARDS. There were orange and lemon groves in the midst of which numerous date palms stretched their fronds upward toward the sky in supplication. Walls approximately five feet high not only separated the individual orchards but also fenced in the groves, preventing pedestrians from plucking samples as they walked by on the roads that bordered the citrus trees.

Our family was growing, and our original home was becoming too small to accommodate all of us. There were eight of us children. My eldest brother and eldest sister were married and lived in our house with their spouses. My father decided to give the house to his eldest son and daughter and rent a house for the rest of the family. We stayed in the rented house a short time and then had to move again. An Arab Iraqi friend offered to sell his house to my father. It was located in the corner of a five-acre orchard on the road to the village of Hurr, just outside the city limit of Karbala. The man assured my father that the house was solidly built. He explained, "True, it appears to be in the middle of nowhere, being the only residential home in the midst of a sea of orange groves but don't worry, it is built like a fortress." The neighborhood was named Sa'diyyah but not many people lived in the area. Even though it was actually less than quarter of a mile walking distance from the hammam, the numerous orchards made it appear to be situated in a rural location. Our previous houses in the heart of Karbala had been built very close to neighboring dwellings.

Ahmad Ali proudly pointed out that his house would be the first line of defense if and when the Wahhabis, a militant Muslim sect that had originated in Saudi Arabia, dared to attack Karbala again. He showed us a long narrow window in the wall of a room that faced the road and claimed that with his rifle he could prevent the advance of Bedouin invaders who might arrive riding camels and horses. My mother had many times related the story of the massacre of 1802 as she had heard it from her mother, who had heard it from earlier generations. The memory of Saudi-Wahhabi attackers was still vivid in the minds of the residents of the city, and we were all familiar with it. As it turned out, Ahmad Ali's "prediction" about the Saudi-Wahhabi "invasion" of Iraq did not materialize until the beginning of the twenty-first century with ISIL (Islamic State of Iraq and the Levant), not from the south but from the north.

Muhammad Ibn Abd al-Wahhab (1703-1792) preached an ultraconservative version of Islam, the tenets of which were in conflict with historical Islam. The majority of Muslim scholars, Sunni and Shi'ite alike, regarded him as a man of superficial learning and shallow intellect. Muhammad ibn Saud (1710-1765), the head of the House of Saud, was attracted by the ideas promoted by al-Wahhab and also realized that Wahhab's version of Islam would provide the ideological basis for the Saud family to expand its territory. Ibn Abd al-Wahhab and Muhammad ibn Saud established a politico-religious alliance in the mid-eighteenth century. With urging from the House of Wahhab, the Saudis expanded territorial control from one oasis to another and from one tribe to the next.

Rejection of the veneration of any idea or personality other than God became a central theme of Wahhab's fragmented teachings. Any nonliteral interpretations of the Quran were repudiated. Non-Wahhabi Muslims were accused of practicing *shirk* (polytheism). For the Wahhabis, the real Muslims were only themselves, while everyone else, including mainstream Muslims, were unbelievers.

Many practices prevalent among traditional Muslims—Sunni and Shi'ite—were condemned. Drawing images and erecting statues, building domes over burial places, marking graves, venerating saints (dead or alive) by seeking their assistance in obtaining divine intervention, and visiting shrines of highly regarded personalities were forbidden. Those who destroyed the ancient statues of Buddha in Bamiyan, Afghanistan, in March 2001 and Palmyra, Syria, in 2015, were following Wahhabi doctrines.[10]

Wahhabis insisted that their teachings were the "real" Islam and they were determined to convert everyone to their version of the religion by force. They unleashed their rage upon the Shi'ites, the Sufis, and the Sunnis. In 1802, Saudi-Wahhabi forces attacked the city of Karbala, razing the Shrine of Husayn to the ground and killing thousands of people: old, young, men, and women. They stole the silver, gold, and jewels that had been donated to Imam Husayn's shrine by the faithful. The looting of Karbala remained fresh in the memories of later generations. That was the raid that Ahmad Ali and others remembered when they prepared themselves for future attacks.

Despite Ahmad Ali's allusion to possible danger, when we visited the property for the first time, we found the house and the orchard to be an island of tranquility. There, we encountered nature in its most glorious moments. When I spotted a graceful date palm growing in the yard close to one end of the house, I immediately ran upstairs onto the flat roof to see its fronds bending overhead. Raising my hand, I was able to pluck a date. Less than two inches long, its color was dark honey, and it was very sweet.

Later, when we expressed our delight to Ahmad Ali, he smiled with satisfaction. It was clear that he was proud of the house he had designed. "The tree is a medjool date palm. Do you think I would plant any other kind in my yard?" He continued telling us how he had calculated carefully to ensure that the tree grew close enough to the roof but not so close that it would harm the structure and the walkway on the rooftop. We used the rooftop for sleeping in the summers as well as sometimes in spring and

---

10 The Wahhabi position that demands destruction of statues is a literal interpretation and is not the position of mainstream Muslims.

fall. Also, for us children, it served us as a running track. Oh, the joy of running around the perimeter and plucking a ripe date as I passed!

I recall sitting at my desk in my room facing a large window that overlooked an orange tree. I was struck with awe by the sight of raindrops falling on a ripe orange, rolling down its thick rind, gliding slowly around its curvature, and then plummeting to the ground. Random rays of sun in the faraway distance tried to sneak through patches between the clouds, while raindrops dripped from the oranges. That image and the quiet solitude of that moment are forever etched in my brain.

We were the only non-farmers in that neighborhood, which appeared to us as a vast island of green. The owners of the surrounding orchards were all Arabs who were friendly and decent people except for the one across the road. His reputation as a thief preceded him. This was an oddity for Karbala in those days. The city was safe and crimes were almost nonexistent. If any, they consisted of petty larceny and occasional fights among young people.

It was, therefore, highly surprising to hear rumors that the owner of the large orchard directly across from our house expanded his crop by stealing from his neighbors. With four armed employees, he would sneak into neighboring orchards in the dark hours of the night picking as many oranges as possible. Yet, for reasons mysterious to us, he avoided our property. We attributed this to the fact that, though our orchard produced thousands of oranges annually, it was, in fact, comparatively small. Furthermore, my father usually gave the produce of the orchard to our friends and relatives as well as to his workers in the hammam. He also showered our ill-reputed neighbor with gifts and lavish flattery.

Unfortunately, our luck changed. One morning we looked out over the orchard to notice that the sea of ripe oranges was gone. The trees were bare. Everyone, including the police (who were quite possibly on the take), probably suspected our neighbor, but no one would make an accusation. In such circumstances, it is often wise to keep silent. Neither the neighbor nor my father ever discussed the incident, and both continued their friendly conversations and amicable relations.

My father devised a plan for the next season. A week or two before the oranges were ripe, he hired a few workers to pluck half of the oranges and bury them in one of the cellars in the house. He directed them to pour a one-inch layer of sand over the concrete floor and to lay the green oranges one by one on top. Then, they poured another layer of sand, burying the oranges. This process continued until all of the oranges were buried. His logic was simple and convincing. If the oranges rotted, at least we would have the satisfaction of not losing them to a thief. If the plan worked successfully, then we would have the gratification of having prevented the thief from stealing them, and we would have the oranges.

The green oranges, smaller than usual, ripened in the sand and turned out to be extremely sweet and juicy. This worked for several years. However, my father was not one to keep his successes to himself. One day, he invited a group of people, our neighbor among them, for dinner. I can only surmise that his vanity made him boast by showing the guests how cleverly he had hidden his oranges and bragging that thieves no longer tried to outsmart him. "Yes, indeed, I taught them a good lesson." Our neighbor may have taken that as a challenge.

Another dark night when the moon was dim and even the wild dogs and jackals had retired to their lairs, my mother was awakened by the sound of tools digging into the bricks around the back door. She woke my father who became alarmed. "He is going to rob us," my mother wailed. "Not only will we lose the rugs and the furniture and money and jewelry, he may go so far as to leave no witnesses."

As usual, we had a few guests staying overnight. My father woke them up and directed them to the roof where they began to shout loudly and shine flashlights in all directions. My father ran to the side closest to where our guilty neighbor was supposedly sleeping in his small hut. Calling his name at the top of his voice, he urged him to come to our aid. Though we all knew the neighbor and his cohorts were crouching near the back door silently waiting for us to go back to sleep, my father pretended to ask for his help.

In the dark, we saw the outlines of the men scurrying back into the hut. Claiming to be just awakened and feigning drowsiness, the neighbor came out to ask what he could do. "Call the police," replied my father, "we're being burglarized!"

As we waited for the arrival of the police, our family was reluctant to accuse the neighbor and his cohorts outright. Our neighbor expressed his outrage over the audacity of the criminals, and my father thanked him for coming to our aid. Politeness abounded. When the police investigators arrived, statements were taken, and our neighbor was the first to sign his name as a witness to the crime of attempted burglary. One of his comments, though, hinted at his surprise and disappointment during his venture. "Who in the world would build such a thick wall, four or five bricks deep?" My father's ready response was scathing. "Ahmad Ali did say that he built his house like a fortress. God bless his soul. If it were not for him we would have been slaughtered by those bastards."

Our neighbor was no longer interested in approaching our home or the orchard. It is possible that his "retreat" was due to a superstitious belief that "forces from beyond" were foiling his attempts. He sold his orchard and moved away. Yet his forays into other orchards continued until one night he was shot dead by an owner whom, as rumor had it, he had robbed years earlier. Whoever shot our former neighbor removed his corpse from the orchard and dumped it in the road by the river. No one shed a tear.

CHAPTER 12

Karbala, a Cultural City

ARBALA WAS A CULTURAL CITY. True, there were some dirt roads and lanes. It was not as clean as Paris, but it was a vibrant environment for those of us who were fortunate enough to experience it.

The streets of Karbala periodically presented sideshows of colorful and bizarre characters. The dervishes[11] were always entertaining. They claimed to be mystics devoted to their religious rites. While the original goal of their Sufi orders had been the quest for knowledge of, and union with, the Divine, the superstitious dervishes remaining in the 1940s and 1950s had become spectacles of superhuman feats. They would swallow swords, exhale fire from their mouths, read the future, and tell fortunes.

Ashura, the commemoration of Husayn's martyrdom on the tenth of Muharram, was, and still is, the highlight of the year in Karbala, but the nine days preceding Ashura were also a time of displays of remorse and anguish over the barbaric and inhumane killing of Husayn and his band of seventy-two followers centuries earlier. On those days, my cousin Jalal and I would walk to his father's dental office on the main street. His father usually gave us candy and pistachios from bowls placed on a table next to the samovar that always had hot tea ready for his customers. Then he would send us out to the street to watch the passing parades of mourners.

---

11 Those of the Sufi order of Muslims, which dates back to the twelfth century, who ritually whirled, danced, and otherwise entertained, often putting themselves into a trance.

We saw men, some shirtless and some wearing black, slowly walking in procession down the street, flagellating their backs with barbed chains and slapping their chests and foreheads, crying out "Ya Husayn," whipping themselves into a frenzy. Many had welts on their skin and some were bleeding. There was also a group of men holding an empty cradle aloft, tears streaming down their faces as they recalled the diabolical slaying of the infant son of Husayn.

In addition to the parade, numerous reenactments took place in private homes and in public halls. I had seen that scene many times: the besieged band of Husayn's men with their wives and children, crying out in vain, asking for a bit of water for Husayn's infant son; then the cruel Shemr with his thousands of men attacking and killing all of Husayn's men and taking their families as prisoners.

One year, Jalal and I went to a reenactment in the yard of a large private home. About a hundred spectators had gathered around to watch. Three soldiers, who represented many more, attacked Husayn, and the traditional fight ensued. When Husayn was finally defeated, the audience was distraught. Women were crying and men were choked up with emotion, slapping their foreheads with their palms from sadness. As Shemr bent down to decapitate Husayn with his saber, a stone was thrown from the angry audience hitting him in the rump. He jerked around to scan the spectators. Again, a stone flew hitting him on his cheek. Blood began to trickle down his face. Suddenly understanding his situation, he became angry. A tirade of oaths ran from his mouth. "I am not the real Shemr, you imbeciles. I am an actor!" The actor threw down his saber and walked out, leaving the audience bereft of their expected catharsis.

The tenth day of Muharram (Ashura) was the climax of the events. A replica of Husayn's tent was set up in the main square of the town, and a lavish reenactment took place. Actors volunteered to portray Shemr and his band of attackers. Since the square was near my father's hammam, our family all gathered there to watch the scene from the flat rooftop. Thousands of people were in the streets for the event. The commemoration began with a parade of mourners as in the previous nine days, but the participants wore shrouds to indicate their willingness to die for Husayn. They inflicted superficial gashes on their heads, and their blood ran down, staining their shrouds. In support of this commemoration, my father had hired medics to be on hand to treat their bleeding lacerations with styptic and bandage their wounds. He also gave them tea and sweets and free use of the hammam.

The crowd was assembled near Husayn's tent and waited with trepidation for the travesty they knew was coming. Suddenly, Shemr, wearing an elaborate red uniform, galloped on his horse toward the tent and set it on fire. As the tent went up in flames, the crowd was worked into a state of grief and indignation.

I looked forward to these spectacles every year, but I found the bleeding disturbing, and for many days after I was haunted in my dreams by the cruel face of Shemr as he approached Husayn's tent and ignited it with his torch.

In retrospect, I would compare these reenactments and flagellations to Christian passion plays that commemorate the passion of Christ. Commemorations of the crucifixion of Jesus on Easter have been performed in various parts of the world, particularly in the Philippines, Spain, South America, and even in some cities and towns of the United States and Canada. At some of these commemorations, especially in the Philippines and South America, Christian devotees have become so immersed in the reenactment that some have died on the cross.

The Muslim world, so culturally and scientifically advanced in the Middle Ages, had been in decline for several centuries, but the Shi'ite centers of Karbala and Najaf in Iraq—as well as Qom and Mashhad in Iran—remained intellectually alive long after the waning of the educational achievements of Muslims centuries earlier. While the rest of the Muslim world lived and, in many places, still lives in the dark, Karbala and other Shi'ite centers kept the tradition of learning and scholarship alive.

We didn't have cinemas, but there were seminars. We didn't have bars, but we frequented teahouses where coffee, tea, and sparkling water were served. We didn't have music halls, but political and philosophical discussions were common. For people who wished to gather in discussion groups, there were mosques, madrasahs, and the shrines of Husayn and his half brother, Abbas. Tutors were available for those who sought additional learning beyond routine school subjects.

Books were abundant in bookshops, libraries, and in the homes of the savants and pseudo-savants. It was common for friends and acquaintances to exchange books. Quite often, my teachers lent me their books, and I reciprocated their generosity by lending mine.

Iraq, at that time, had several publishing companies, and distributors imported translated and original books from Lebanon, Syria, and Egypt. Christian authors in Lebanon wrote extremely popular reading material for the voracious readers of the Arab world. There were all kinds of books: philosophy of Avicenna and of Friedrich Nietzsche, classic novels such as *Les Miserables* by Victor Hugo, alongside the Lebanese Christian George Jardaq's five-volume biographical masterpiece on the popular hero, Imam Ali.

Besides the vibrant religious and social institutions that encouraged thought-provoking study and discourse, Karbala had excellent secular schools that were styled after the British system of education. After World War I, the British and the French had divided the area of the Fertile Crescent between themselves. The modern states of Iraq, Syria, Lebanon, and Palestine (later Israel) were created arbitrarily. The British even carved out a new kingdom called Transjordan with a king who was brought in from Arabia and placed on a throne. The Iraq of the 1950s was a European brainchild, and the country was mandated to the British by the League of Nations.

The British were colonialists. However, their educational system served as a model for the development of Iraq's modern, secular system of education. The British colonialists who ruled Iraq under the authority of their mandate were usually clever enough to keep their distance from the local population. After a period of uprisings and rebellions in the country, they learned to keep a low profile, stationing most of their Royal Air Force and supporting personnel on a base in central Iraq. Thus, the Brits were rarely seen wandering in Iraqi cities and towns, especially not in the holy cities of Karbala or Najaf. They were not welcome and they knew it.

Therefore, it was surprising when, one day, we saw two men strolling lazily down the street as if they owned the world. Their light skin and blonde hair were hard to miss. They were clean-cut with crisply ironed pants and newly shined shoes. It was obvious that they were British.

We were a small group of four or five sixth graders standing outside a teahouse, listening to a lively discussion among some adults regarding their understanding of Nietzsche's statement, "God is dead." Loud voices of the men preoccupied with their debate filled the teahouse and spilled out to the street. We were outside, talking and listening with fascination at the depth of the intense philosophical discussion. As the two Brits passed the teahouse, they clearly heard the loud discussion and noticed the enthusiastic gesticulation of the men inside. They began to smirk. I must admit that the cacophony of the lively discussion, the language of the participants, and the exaggerated facial expressions must have seemed ridiculous to those staid and unemotional British men. But when we saw their supercilious and arrogant smirks, we were angry. Who were these "tourist" colonizers to pass judgment on people whose conversation they could not even understand? "Why don't these idiots learn Persian and Arabic so at least they can understand what they overhear?" one of the boys commented indignantly.

Though we were children, we knew exactly what the two British men were smirking about. They only heard noise: loud conversation and discordant discussion. They thought that the ignorant, uncouth natives were arguing about trivial matters. They were completely oblivious to the subject of discussion. They did not know that it was a gathering of book club members who had just finished reading Nietzsche's *Thus Spake Zarathustra*. They did not know that those who gesticulated and loudly expounded on the matter at hand were well-read and well-informed citizens of a world that was undergoing a sea of change.

Neither could they have known that their days in Iraq were numbered.

CHAPTER 13

Horse and Buggy

WHILE KARBALA WAS A MAJOR DESTINATION for Shi'ite pilgrims, Hurr, a village approximately five miles from Karbala, was another, albeit less important, destination of pilgrimage. It marked the site where Hurr, one of the commanders of the Syrian army who had defected to Husayn's side, was killed in the Battle of Karbala in 680 CE. Pilgrims to Karbala often made side trips to Hurr, usually by horse-drawn carriages hired for the trip. The place where the carriages lined up to wait for customers was a block away from my father's public bath, and I passed it nearly every day.

I loved the horse and buggy carriages that transported the pilgrims. It was fun to ride in the carriages and watch the horses, letting the breeze caress my face and rumple my hair as my curly black locks flew in the wind. Watching those horses gallop in unison fascinated me. Most drivers of the carriages did not whip the horses, that apparently knew the route and how fast they were expected to go. Occasionally, to impress the passengers, some of the drivers twirled their whips enthusiastically and brushed them softly on the horses' rumps. The horses would then pick up speed. They knew that at the end of the ride they would be pampered with hay and water and the loving touch of their owners. But those horses had no respect for the passengers. They farted a lot. The pungent stench wafted through the air. Adult passengers tried to maintain their decorum but not I. I could not stop laughing. One by one, other passengers would also laugh. Now and then, a woman would complain that the owner's whip scared the poor animals and their flatulence was a sign of their fear. Others pointed out that animals did not observe etiquette, nor did they have inhibitions. Someone would joke that the horses did it purposely. "Animals are not dumb. They know how to get even. They are taking their revenge for being worked so hard."

During slow seasons when the pilgrims from the Gulf region and from Iran only trickled in and there were few customers, I would see the carriage owners tenderly but firmly brushing the horses' bodies from front to back. They would squat on the ground lifting the horse's hooves one by one, cleaning them and massaging their legs. They would feed them lumps of sugar and constantly whisper in their ears, praising them.

They tended to their horses and worked on the interiors of their carriages, sewing or replacing torn seats. They bought cushions or whatever was needed to make their vehicles comfortable for the passengers. People would tip the drivers more if they kept their carriages clean and tidy.

The carriage owners made a living, enough to feed their families, enough to buy hay, sugar cubes, and horseshoes for their animals. Then, one day out of nowhere, modern life intruded. Some taxis appeared and took up positions waiting for customers who were seeking transportation to Hurr. Almost a dozen carriages had parked in a row, in the usual place. It was modernity versus tradition, and fast versus slow. The newly arrived taxi owners had encroached upon the territory of the carriage drivers. I did not know that it was a matter of life or death of an entire industry and lifestyle. It became a war for survival.

As I was passing by, I overheard a loud discussion that led to pushing and shoving. Then swear words were spewed. The argument became louder and louder. They were yelling and shouting at each other. The buggy drivers tried, calmly and deliberately, to convince the taxi drivers that their profession was "sacred" because for years they and their ancestors had been "servants of Husayn," doing what their religion and God had destined them to do. The Karbala-Hurr highway (a dirt road that got wet and muddy when it rained) belonged to them, not the fancy taxis. It was almost irreligious and an insult to both Imam Husayn and Hurr. How could anyone think of desecrating the time-honored tradition? The taxi drivers were without shame because they had insulted tradition, they had insulted Husayn and, by extension, the religion of Islam. The taxi drivers shrugged and argued that they had spent a lot of money buying the cars, training, and learning how to drive just to make some money for their families, but it was obvious in their faces that they were haughtily proud of their new mode of making more money. A taxicab zooming back and forth between Karbala and Hurr could make the trip much faster and much more efficiently than the twenty minutes it took by carriage. The drivers smirked and joked about the old carriages and how slow they were, how dirty they looked. They advised the owners to go and buy cars. They reminded them of the increase in the number of pilgrims visiting the shrines of Husayn and his brother Abbas. To go round-trip by carriage and stay a few hours in Hurr would take almost a half-day and sometimes a full day, including the time the pilgrims would have to wait in long lines under the torrid sun. The taxi drivers said God would punish the horse and buggy drivers in hell for that imposition on the pilgrims.

Suddenly I heard the crack of a whip as it knifed the air over the heads of the group and hit a taxi driver in the face. It slashed his right cheek as if it were a sharp blade cutting butter. Blood poured from his face. That was all that was needed. Blood had been shed and vengeance was required. In the melee that followed, hands, legs, and bodies were at work beating and stomping and fighting. A crowd gathered, watching the scene. The carriage owners and the taxi drivers were all local people. The crowd knew that it all had to do with money, livelihood, change, and progress. When it came to another man feeding his family, the crowd understood that they had no right to interfere. Children's lives on both sides were at stake. I asked a person next to me why no one spoke up to support the carriage owners. Deep down, I preferred the horse and buggy. He cautioned that it was not our business to interfere.

Within minutes, the fight came to a halt. It was so surprising, so poignant, that I still remember the short period of the noise and punches and curses, followed by an exhausted and total silence. The carriage owners were crestfallen. Almost all of them were sitting with their backs leaning against the wall and gently sobbing. They knew and the crowd knew and the taxi drivers knew that the old way was being pushed aside.

The defeated men would no longer be able to provide for their children, wives, mothers, and sisters. By then, even I knew. I was too young to comprehend the immensity of dejection that these men were feeling inside. All I knew was that they sobbed for a loss that was too hard for me to imagine.

CHAPTER 14
Political Awakening

AS A CHILD, I was fascinated by the discussions of Iranian pilgrims at my father's public bath. At times, nearly a dozen people lingered in the open areas just inside the entrance, socializing with each other and conversing about politics. They talked mainly about Iran, not Iraq, and the subject was usually the politics of oil. To keep abreast of the events in Iran, we subscribed to some Iranian magazines that were distributed in Karbala. For the first time in modern history, Iran was asserting its rights vis-à-vis Britain, a colonial power that had infringed upon Iranian rights by outright theft of its most precious natural resource, oil. Visitors from Iran enlightened us about the British and Russian rush to exploit the country politically and economically.

The history of oil exploration in Iran goes as far back as 1872 when Nasir al-Din Shah (1848-1896) gave an exclusive concession to a British subject, Baron Julius de Reuter, for the exploration of all natural resources, and for the construction of railroads, telegraph lines, and irrigation throughout the entire country.

In 1941, during the occupation of the country by the Allied forces, the British deposed Reza Shah (1925-1941), who had proved to be uncooperative in the area of oil agreements, and installed his son, Mohammad Reza, as the Shah of Iran. Young and inexperienced, in addition to being keenly aware of his father's fate, the new Shah was very pliant to British demands. The governing system at the time was an elected Majlis (Iranian Parliament), which approved or disapproved the Shah's choice of a prime minister.

At the public bath, Iranian pilgrims often talked about Ahmad Qavam (five-term prime minister of Iran), who was nicknamed the "Old Fox" because of a deal he had negotiated with Joseph Stalin. Soviet forces had been stationed in Iran during World War II and remained after the war's end. In 1946, Ahmad Qavam convinced Stalin to withdraw his forces from Iran, promising him an oil concession in the north of the country. Yet, after the Soviet withdrawal, the Majlis failed to approve the concession. People suspected that Qavam had known all along that it would not be approved, but that he used the promised agreement as bait anyway. The people admired his guile in dealing with the Soviets but resented his subservient approach toward the British.

In 1949, amid a growing tide of nationalistic sentiment, the Iranian National Front, comprised of an amalgam of many parties, unions, and organizations, was formed. It unanimously chose Dr. Mohammad Mosaddeq to head the coalition. Mosaddeq believed that Iran needed to negotiate a much better deal with the Anglo-Iranian Oil Company.

During negotiations in 1948-49, Iranians tried to obtain a fifty-fifty profit sharing. The British did not agree but submitted a counteroffer called the Supplemental Agreement that was unacceptable to the nationalists. But under British pressure, the Shah supported it and sent it for approval to the Majlis. However, the term of the Majlis was soon to expire, and the representatives, cognizant of the nationalistic sentiment of the people, dragged their feet in dealing with the proposal until finally their term expired on July 28, 1949. When elections for the new term were held, the Shah rigged the elections. Thousands of people followed Mosaddeq in protest, demanding that the Shah hold new, fair elections. The Shah gave in, and the new elections added a great number of ardent nationalists to the Majlis. Thereafter, the Majlis became more insistent on getting Iran's fair share of the oil revenues. In December 1950, the Supplemental Agreement was withdrawn from consideration.

The new Majlis elected Dr. Mohammad Mosaddeq as Prime Minister on April 28, 1951, and passed a law nationalizing the oil industry on the same day. Days later, on May 1, Mosaddeq implemented the law, which was a symbol of resistance to British interference in Iran. By his actions,

Mosaddeq became popular not only with Iranians but throughout the entire Middle East. When Mosaddeq traveled to Egypt during his return from Washington in 1951, the Egyptians hailed him as a great hero. Wherever he went he was received with cheers of approval and applause. Mosaddeq had become an emblematic statesman of the Third World.

I was ten years old when the Iranian Majlis elected Dr. Mosaddeq by an overwhelming majority to become Iran's prime minister. Almost all Iranians, whether they were in Iran or were expatriates like us, were enamored with that strong-willed personality who remained steadfast in his devotion to the principles of democracy and in his efforts to promote the national interest. Among his early acts were the introduction of an unemployment benefit, a requirement that factory owners provide health care for workers, and the establishment of a fund to support public services such as providing housing for the poor and improving sanitary conditions. Landlords were required to finance this fund by paying 20 percent of their rent collections.

During the 1950s, in our discussions at the public bath, we learned a great deal about the history of British efforts to find petroleum in Iran, about the politics of oil, and about the history of the Anglo-Iranian Oil Company. Most distressing were the stories of the squalid conditions of Iranian workers under British management at the Abadan oil refinery. We heard about the workers' strikes demanding better health care, greater compensation for their labor, and improvement of their housing conditions. The British intimidated them in one form or another, hiring thugs to violently squash the workers' determination.

When Mosaddeq nationalized the oil industry, he had the full blessing of the great majority of Iranians. In retaliation, the British, supported by their Western Allies, imposed economic sanctions on Iran, forbidding exportation of oil from Iran, claiming that it was the property of the Anglo-Iranian Oil Company. To emphasize that they were serious about this boycott, the Royal Navy commandeered the Italian tanker, *Rose Mary*, which had filled up with oil in Iran and was headed back to Italy. This alarmed the rest of the world and effectively kept them from approaching Iranian oil ports thereafter.

Economic problems and internal dissension convinced Mosaddeq that, in order to combat chaos and violence, he would be most effective if he were to take charge of the armed forces by assuming the post of Minister of Defense. The Shah was in charge of the army at the time. When Mosaddeq formally requested a change, noting that it would be constitutionally proper, the Shah refused. Mosaddeq submitted his resignation.

The Shah, who had been looking for such an opportunity, accepted it immediately and replaced him the next day with the Old Fox, who had a long history of smooth relationships with the British. One day, as I arrived home, I heard Tehran Radio blasting at high volume and found my sixteen-year-old brother pacing the living room, clearly dismayed and angry.

I was glued to the radio while my brother issued constant comments. We heard that thousands had poured into the streets of the cities of Iran, protesting Mosaddeq's replacement. The demonstrators wore white shrouds to signify their readiness to die as they shouted in unison, *"Ya marg ya mosaddeq"* (Give me Mosaddeq or give me death). Soon, the streets were awash with the colors of white and red as the *Kafan Pooshaan* (Shroud Wearers) began to bleed from wounds inflicted by the Shah's army. Many were killed.

"How could the Shah dismiss Mosaddeq? How dare he?" my brother shouted in disgust. And I would ask one question after another.

In the aftermath of those worrisome days, I immersed myself in studying the politics of intrigue, past misdeeds, and the continuous political and economic pressures exerted on Iran by the British and the Russians. It was then that I realized that Iran and many other countries in the world had been either colonized or manipulated politically and economically. At that time, I, along with my brother and many Iranians, naively looked to the United States, and the democratic ideals it espoused, as a beacon of liberty and an honest broker.

The demonstrations were effective in forcing the Shah to bring Mosaddeq back as prime minister after only five days. During those five days, I had become infatuated by the world of politics and world affairs, and I owed this self-awakening to Mosaddeq.

At that time I knew very little about how the imperialist forces around the world operated and how cunning they were. Churchill convinced President Eisenhower that Iran was a threat to the strategic interests of both Britain and the United States. As the economy was crippled and the National Front was weakened, political opinions began to split. Some held firm in supporting Mosaddeq's strict nationalism, while others, swayed by the Shah, called for moderation and compromise with the foreign concessionaries.

Mosaddeq was so dedicated to the principles of democracy and political freedom that he allowed unhampered discussion of the matter. He allowed the papers to criticize him openly and to publish unflattering cartoons of him as a dog or a pig. He reminded people that Iran was a democracy with the right of free speech. He even allowed the Communist Party (the *Tudeh*) to function freely, despite the fact that the party had designs against him. This turned the religious element against him because they were staunchly anti-Communist.

On August 13, 1953, the Shah ordered Mosaddeq to resign. He refused. On August 16, when the people poured into the streets demonstrating overwhelming popular support for Mosaddeq, the Shah was forced to flee to Rome. Three days of jubilation and victory celebrations followed in Iran.

Throughout the months of debate among the populace that preceded the Shah's departure, America's Central Intelligence Agency (CIA) had been active fomenting dissension against Mosaddeq. It had hired journalists to write inflammatory articles and cartoonists to portray Mosaddeq in a poor light; it hired thugs to demonstrate in the streets, creating a sense that the government was not in control. Currying favor with key Iranian military leaders, the CIA promised to support and fund a military takeover. Finally, on the evening of August 18, 1953, the agency arranged a military coup and toppled Mosaddeq's nationalist government, returning the Shah to his throne on August 19, 1953. Yet, in the aftermath, Mosaddeq remained immensely popular, and American opposition to him helped tarnish the reputation of the U.S. government in the eyes of the Iranian people.

Mosaddeq awakened every Iranian. Men, women, and children were intoxicated with Iranian nationalism. In those emotional days, blood would flow to my brain as if it was clear and cleansing water, opening a new world, previously unknown, in my psyche.

Thenceforth, I was no longer a simple sheep.

CHAPTER 15

Trips to Iran

AS IRANIANS LIVING IN IRAQ, every summer when school was out, and occasionally in between, some of us would take a long trip to Iran to visit relatives and friends. We often went for several months at a time, but we did not all go at once. My parents would go; my brother and sister with their respective spouses and children would go. Sometimes, I accompanied my parents. Often, travelers from several families would make the trip together for both safety and sociability.

A trip was a big deal. The travelers were sent off by family, neighbors, and friends, who would hold a copy of the Quran aloft for them to pass beneath. Prayers that entreated a successful venture and safe return were said. Then, in the lane just outside the door, a sheep would be sacrificed, and the travelers would step across it. Later, pieces of meat from this sacrifice would be distributed among the poor. I don't know when that custom started. I can surmise that, since, in the past, roads were unpatrolled and unsafe, with bandits roaming the countryside and robbing travelers, people turned to prayers, sacrifices, and vows to ward off harm. Slowly, as time went by, these customs died away. When I accompanied my parents in the summer of 1953, no one made a fuss. They had stopped such rituals a few years earlier.

We went to several cities to visit various relatives, but we stayed mostly in the city of Mashhad in northeast Iran. Apparently, most of the people my parents knew were there. Besides, it is the resting place of Imam Reza, the eighth Shi'ite Imam (d. 818). He is the only Imam who is buried in Iran. There are many other shrines in various other cities of the country, but these are shrines of Imamzadehs (descendants of Imams). The shrine of Imam Reza's sister, Ma'sumah, in Qum is well known. The cities of Mashhad and Qum are both centers of learning and scholarship. Actually, the huge Imam Reza Library in Mashhad is very famous for housing many old manuscripts. I never got to see it, though. When I suggested to my cousin that we go to that library, he laughed. He was definitely not interested in old manuscripts.

Iranians are extremely hospitable people. When visitors arrive in town, the relatives argue with each other, seeking to be the first to invite them to their houses. After much insistence by all parties, finally there is an agreement as to who will be the hosts and on what days. Sometimes, visitors end up eating lunch in one house and supper in another. A lot of times, the visitors have no choice in the matter. Furthermore (I am beginning to chuckle), the hosts try to outdo one another in presenting the best *sofreh* ever. The food is abundant and delicious and the arrangement and decoration of the *sofreh* is elaborate. The hosts graciously entreat you to eat, and it is understood that it is your duty to eat. You had better eat, even if you are not hungry.

There is also a great deal of ceremonial politeness (*ta'aruf*) involved. When a guest arrives at a house, the host and guest exchange many formal niceties, asking each other again and again "How are you?" They ask about each other and about children, relatives, and friends by name. The hosts feign subservience to the guests. "*Khosh amadeed, azizam*. Welcome, my dearest. Welcome to my humble house. I am your servant and at your disposal. I kiss your feet and the ground upon which you walk." As a teenager, I was amused at such exaggerations and would chuckle quietly. Of course, the guests have an elaborate routine of their own in reciprocating. Respect and *ta'aruf* abound. Actually entering a house is a chore in itself. "After you, my dear master."

"Absolutely not, you go first, great scholar and best friend."

"No, no, no. I am here to serve you and fulfill all your wishes. You are the greatest, most honored guest." The host and guests pat each other's backs, applying a slight pressure each trying to get the other to move in, and yet each must resist.

Of course, politeness is very common among many societies in the world, but it must be noted that the Iranian *ta'aruf* is an extreme form of such nicety. Let me digress for a short moment. A lesser form of the ceremonial politeness I have described is also common in other countries of the Middle East. I remember when Israeli Prime Minister Ehud Barak and Palestinian Chairman Yasser Arafat were invited by U.S. President Bill Clinton to Camp David for peace talks in 1999. The two Middle Easterners indulged in some back and forth *"ta'aruf."* American reporters and pundits mistakenly took their respective back and forth niceties as an indication of the likelihood for a positive outcome.

In another instance, a professor of anthropology from Tehran University came to the United States in 1976. He was invited to an Exxon party thrown periodically for scholars. As American parties go, caterers circulated around the guests, carrying trays of warm appetizers, offering them to the attendees. The professor politely and ceremoniously refused the appetizers, and the waiters moved on. While it is customary for Iranian guests to say "No, thank you," twice, it is also expected that the host insist at least three times. To make a long story short, the poor professor spent all afternoon hungry. We had a good laugh when he told us of that *ta'aruf* episode.

Iranians usually eat supper late, especially on such occasions when they have guests, and it may take several hours. Lunch itself is almost a two-hour affair. A dinner or lunch invitation during our trip to Mashhad commonly occurred as follows: A long *sofreh* (tablecloth) was laid out on the floor over a large Persian rug. Around the *sofreh,* mattress-like mats were placed as seating, and bowls of fruit were arranged on top. Watermelon cut from the rind and then cut into small cubes, Persian honeydew melon cut similarly, along with apples, cherries, all kinds of berries, and oranges were offered on the *sofreh*. After we had eaten our fill of fruit, the *sofreh* was cleared and removed by the family members. Another *sofreh* was laid out. Four to six different dishes were then brought out: *bademjan* (eggplant with stewed meat), *qormeh sabzi* (lamb and parsley stew), *fesenjoon* (chicken or duck cooked in pomegranate-walnut sauce), and *bamiyah* (okra with tomato and stewed meat). Chicken and lamb were the main meat items in the dishes. These were accompanied by several kinds of rice dishes: *sabzi polow* (rice with greens), *baqella polow* (rice with lima beans), and a crispy orange rice called *tahdig*.

"Eat, Mohammad *joon*, eat," our host would urge. So I ate. The *sofreh* was cleared again. A third *sofreh*, the dessert *sofreh*, was laid out. This was often very elaborate, offering baklava, halva, and various pastries. After all, it is said that Iranians had invented sweets. I could not comfortably eat more than one piece of baklava but usually was "forced" with kindness to eat more. Cup after cup of tea was served during and after the dessert *sofreh*.

One evening, we were at the house of a family friend waiting for dinner. It was before dusk and we were sitting in the yard talking. The sun was low in the sky. As I glanced up, I saw something yellowish and round fixed momentarily in the sky. Seconds go fast but they can linger when you recognize something odd. I shouted loud enough to get the attention of my family and our hosts. They looked up, too. We all saw the strange saucer-like object. Silence was followed by oohs and ahs and repeated questions about what it was. The object seemed fixed in the air and many people saw it. It remained close to half a minute as it rotated slowly and smoothly about half a dozen times. Every turn was vividly visible. Then it took off quickly and disappeared. We asked one another what it could have been. No plane had that shape or hovering motion.

A woman said that they (not it, but *they*) were the fourteen Ma'suums[12] who were visiting Imam Reza. I was thinking that, since Imam Reza was one of the Ma'suums buried in Mashhad, then those visiting him would have to have been thirteen in number, not fourteen. Couldn't religious people even count? But that was not a time to argue with the woman. I just looked at her and shook my head slightly.

The next day I learned that almost everyone in Mashhad had seen the object too. I was at a public bath lying on a towel getting a loofa bath. Other customers described the object almost verbatim to the way I had seen it. Many pondered what it was. A young man of approximately thirty years passed nearby explaining with great confidence that it was some new Soviet invention. "They're experimenting with some kind of technically

---

12 Infallible beings. Mohammad, his daughter Fatimah, and the twelve Imams are considered by the Twelver Shi'ites to be the fourteen infallible (*ma'suum*) beings.

advanced flying machine that is extremely fast and very silent." I did not believe him. "Probably a communist," I mused to myself. The timing was shortly after the fall of Dr. Mosaddeq, and many Iranians were dreaming of a miracle. Some looked to the Soviet Union to aid Iranians in their quest to reinstate Mosaddeq. But I know one thing for sure; no one can tell me it was a figment of my imagination. I saw what is called a UFO (Unidentified Flying Object).

Years later in America, I shared the experience with my father-in-law, who believed in UFOs. He had a book that listed all such sightings. Sure enough, in 1953, people from Mashhad, Iran, had reported seeing a UFO.

Tell me then, why do some people laugh when former U.S. President Jimmy Carter and Congressman Dennis Kucinich claim to have seen UFOs, yet they don't laugh at the concept of Moses "Parting the Red Sea"?

CHAPTER 16

The Madrasah

HERE HAS ALWAYS BEEN AN INTEREST in learning for learning's sake in the Muslim world. This attitude has its basis in the Quran, which urges humankind to study the mysteries of the universe in order to discern the majesty of God. Prophet Muhammad made it the duty of every Muslim man and woman to seek knowledge. This responsibility created a spirit of inquiry and learning that gave rise to various types of educational institutions from primary to university prototypes during the rule of the Abbasids (750-1258). Many historians consider the Abbasid dynasty to be the golden age of the Muslim world economically, politically, educationally, and scientifically. Unfortunately, this level of advancement did not endure.

One of the most important reasons for the abandonment of educational pursuits was the conflict between Muslim theology and Greek-inspired philosophy. This controversy led to the slow but steady ebb in the pursuit of philosophy and the sciences. Much of the Muslim world slipped into a degree of ignorance. However, the old spirit of learning and inquiry was kept alive in the Shi'ite world, especially in Iran where the Usuli branch of the Ja'fari Shi'ite School of Law has been dominant. One of the types of schools developed during the Abbasid dynasty was the madrasah, literally the place of learning.

Today, thanks to television and online news outlets, when the word madrasah is mentioned, poor, decrepit, makeshift tent schools with semiliterate teachers who force children to memorize the Quran without being able to read it or understand it parade through the mind. However, before the Muslim world's decline in education, madrasahs had become the equivalent of modern colleges. At the peak of their success, beginning in the ninth and tenth centuries, some of these "universities" were quite large, with tens of thousands of students pursuing all the branches of science and learning. In Karbala in the 1950s, the madrasahs were remnants of this type of school on a smaller scale.

When I was in junior high school, I was very interested in philosophy and religion, and I asked my older brother, Mehdi, to arrange for me to attend a madrasah. Soon after, Mehdi met me after school, and we walked to the madrasah. It was a two-story building that was about twenty minutes from our house and was essentially a boarding school for students who were studying to be clergy. Most of the school's full-time students were sponsored by an established ayatollah and were given room and board and a monthly stipend. Mehdi told me that he had found an upper level student to tutor me.

The first floor of the madrasah had lecture halls, a kitchen, and a dining area. Mehdi and I climbed the stairs to the second floor, where resident students had individual rooms. Mehdi knocked on a door; a young man opened it. He was about thirty years old, neatly dressed, and smiling politely. Mehdi introduced me to Mirza Hasan and left the two of us in that modestly furnished 12' × 12' room, to talk. When I asked about the charge for my tutoring, Mirza Hasan insisted that there would be no charge, as knowledge was not a commodity to sell. We planned to meet three times a week after school.

We sat on cushions on the floor of his room, and Mirza Hasan spent an hour discussing what he planned to do and how we should proceed with my learning process. Even though I had studied Arabic and Persian grammar in the secular school, he suggested a more in-depth study that delved into Arabic grammar and etymology. I found the material on Arabic grammar difficult, but I persevered since a good grasp of that subject was essential for understanding Arabic literature. I particularly enjoyed learning about the origin and the development of various Arabic words. I recall him telling me that in the Arabic language there were seventy different words describing a camel at various stages of the animal's life.

Logic and philosophy were next. I did not like Aristotle's logic, but the philosophical treatises of Ibn Sina (d. 1036), al-Farabi (d. 950), and Kant (d. 1804) were thought provoking. Sahrawardi's *Ishraqi*[13] philosophy (Illuminationism) presented complex ideas that were completely new to me. I found the artfully crafted symbolic language of Sufi poets such as Rumi (d. 1273) and Attar (d. 1220) to be fascinating and beautiful.

Mirza Hasan was a higher-level student who took various philosophy courses with different professors. As I progressed and he noticed my interest, he invited me to come with him to some of his classes. I recall attending a few sessions with him, listening to the discussions that took place among students and the teacher. In one such class, the discussion centered on the controversial concept of *Wahdat al-Wujud* (Unity of Being) attributed to Ibn 'Arabi (d. 1240). The professor presented it for discussion even though many Muslims had condemned the idea as pantheistic. Ibn 'Arabi had maintained that the entire universe was an interconnected unitary whole with sense perception. Many Muslims interpreted this concept as saying that everything is God. For me, Ibn 'Arabi's idea defied logic. However, at the time I was taken aback by the demeanor of one of the students, who continued to refute the theory as if trying to elicit a reaction from the teacher. The student was visibly irate that Ibn 'Arabi's name would even be mentioned in that class. Mirza Hasan was deep in thought and offered no apparent reaction. The professor continued, unfazed.

Years later, in America, I read about James Lovelock's Gaia Theory, which describes earth as a "living," self regulating system. At that time, I was teaching mysticism (Sufism) in the university and was much more in tune with such ideas.

In the madrasah, I learned to respect the power of ideas. I came to understand what the madrasah actually had been originally intended to teach. Its methods of teaching were vestiges of an older tradition that had begun by the Ghaznavids (977-1186), whose rule stretched from western Iran to the greater parts of Transoxiana to northern India, and whose capital, Ghazna, was in present-day Afghanistan.

---

13 Shihab al-Din al-Sahrawardi (1154-91), Persian philosopher and Sufi, founded the Illuminationist philosophy (*hikmat al-ishraq*).

In Karbala, discussion of these kinds of ideas was as common as discussion of football in the United States. The ideas of those scholars were still vibrant and often discussed in the homes of the savants and business places of Karbala, challenging us constantly. This was the Karbala of both the ancient and modern age, outwardly quiet, almost sluggish, yet, beneath the surface, vibrant with new vistas of ideas. There were many reactionary and hypocritical people in Karbala but there were also some free thinkers. All I had to do was to discover them.

CHAPTER 17

A Tall Tale

*I*N ONE FORM OR ANOTHER, Iraq was a colony of Britain from the early 1920s until July 1958. The British were unpopular in Iraq, and their hold in that country was initially tenuous. During the Great Iraqi Revolt of 1920,[14] some two thousand British soldiers were killed. However, after two years of bitter fighting, the British finally established a firm foothold in Iraq.

From 1936 to 1959, the British stationed their Royal Air Force (RAF) at Habbanyyah, some fifty miles west of Baghdad on the banks of the Euphrates River. But as a result of the revolt, the British learned to keep a low profile. Rarely did they venture into the cities and towns of Iraq. This policy of "out of sight, out of mind" was very successful for them.

Even so, people despised them. People do not like occupiers, no matter what the circumstance. When they appeared in Karbala, they were subjects of ridicule and insult, surreptitiously, of course. They would never be allowed to approach the shrines of Husayn and Abbas. Those places were sacred and home to scholarly pursuit and religious discourse. How could non-Muslims be allowed to visit them as sightseers, taking pictures, paying a few cents to children to pose, instructing them to stand in a

---

14 A mass revolt against the British began in Iraq in 1920. Though all segments of the Iraqi population (Sunni, Shi'ite, and Kurds) participated, the Shi'ites in the south were most effective. Shaykh Mahdi al-Khalisi, a chief Shi'ite Ayatollah, who issued a *fatwa* (a legal opinion on an Islamic law) against the British in Iraq, was one of the main leaders of this revolt.

particular place against a specific background in the sacrosanct shrine of Husayn?

Many fanciful stories were woven about the British. I heard a *mullah*[15] urging his listeners to be vigilant against encroachment of Christians in Muslim lands, "All you have to do is to look at the electric poles they are erecting. What do they look like?"

"What?" I asked, curiously looking at the electric pole.

"A cross, my son. It looks like a cross. The cross is a Christian sign. Why are these electric poles built in the shape of a cross? First come the signs and the symbols, then the missionaries and their religious zealotry."

I looked incredulously at the mullah who told me this story. "How else would one design an electric pole?" I countered. His logic had not impressed me. I went on to offer a positive contribution of the occupiers. "Many people are being educated. Look at the growth of well-educated people in Iraq." But to tell the truth, I didn't like their presence in the country either. After all, they were stealing Iranian oil, and Dr. Mosaddeq had alerted everyone in Iran and the entire Middle East about how European oil companies were robbing the Third World nations of their most precious natural resources and paying very small royalties.

Rumors and innuendos about the British abounded and were not limited to political intrigue. The English were dirty and did not wash properly. They would fill the sink with water, shave, brush their teeth, and wash their faces and hands in the same stale water. Their women were loose and would engage in extramarital sex. They were arrogant snobs who considered the Iraqis beneath them.

Some tales were tantalizing to the imagination of an adolescent boy like me. One such tale was told to me by the son of one of the workers at my father's public bath.

The water in the bath was heated by a system of heavy pipes that stretched beneath the floors. A husky fire stoker fed a tremendous furnace to heat up the pipes. The stoker was a burly man who seemed to have

---

15 A Shi'ite Muslim who has decided to dedicate his life to religious activities such as performing marriages, reading verses of the Quran at religious gatherings, performing funerals, and offering religious advice. There are no stringent requirements pertaining to the level of education of a mullah. Some are highly educated, while others are only minimally educated.

the strength to withstand the tremendous heat of this huge furnace. His job was to add coal just like the men who stoked the engines of trains in nineteenth-century America. This kind of job was not easy. He had to have a great deal of physical stamina to perform his task on a daily basis. In summer, Karbala's temperatures sometimes hit 40 degrees Celsius (104 Fahrenheit). Besides the heat generated from the furnace, there were noxious gases. Looking back, I feel sorry for the fire stoker.

This man had a fifteen-year old son, Ali, who helped him a few hours a week. I used to go up and sit near them, but away from the heat, talking to Ali. The father was too sweaty, dirty, and busy to carry on a conversation with a young boy like me. Sometimes Ali and I roamed the rooftop, peeking through the glass panes or open spaces built into the small domes to allow the entry of fresh air and sunlight into the building. We would look down to see the nude women taking their baths in the women's public bath. I had never seen breasts so firm and tantalizing before. I saw breasts that were large and small and some in between. I saw symmetrical breasts and some asymmetrical ones. Some women were old, and some were young. Some women were heavy with stretch marks on their abdomens, and some were slim and curvaceous. Those who had finished bathing relaxed on benches sipping tea. The women were very noisy, gossiping and laughing loudly.

One day, when we were peeking into the women's public bath, two big hands suddenly reached down and lifted each of us by our shirts. It was the fire stoker; he was angry. He uttered no words but his eyes tore my heart in two. I began to cry. His rough appearance made him look like a huge genie, a very dirty genie recently liberated from a lamp. He dropped me abruptly on the rooftop; I scraped my knees and hands. "If I ever see you here again . . ." There was no need for him to finish his sentence. I never approached those domes again. Afterward, I rarely saw his son, Ali, either.

About three years later, I bumped into Ali. At eighteen, he had chosen to become an Iraqi citizen and had been drafted into the army. He looked dashing in his army uniform. As a private, he was assigned to be a *khedmatkaar* (servant) in a young RAF officer's home. He ran errands for the officer and his wife, did chores around the house, and drove the missus around. This was common in those days. After training, some soldiers were selected to serve the higher-ups. They lived in the officers' homes rather than in the barracks. They ate good food, dressed well, and had some free time. Ali was lucky to have been assigned to the British couple.

The officer and his wife were very good to him, treating him well. We sat near the small garden across from the public bath, reminiscing about the past. I asked him about his service and how it was going; he told me that he had a good routine and lots of fun. He often took the couple and their friends to a lake to swim. I was surprised that women went swimming. "Oh yes. They go swimming to get a tan." Had they no shame to take off their clothes in front of him? "No. They even went topless." The description was intoxicating. I kept prodding. "How could they do that?" He laughed. "You won't believe how white their skin is," he told me. "It has no color. White, white, white, but they like to look bronze. That's the color they like." I tried to imagine. I told myself that we didn't need to lie in the sun. Our olive skins were already tanned.

"One day," Ali went on, "I took the wife and her guest, who was about her age, thirty or so, to their favorite spot by the water and as soon as we got there this new woman took off her clothes and jumped into the water totally naked, laughing and splashing. I was dumbfounded and kept looking at her. I was so preoccupied watching her swimming that I didn't even notice the missus taking off her clothes behind me. All I saw were her wonderful tiny buttocks jiggling as she ran toward the water to join her friend. I stood there with my eyes wide open, just looking. They kept splashing and talking in English and looking at me. I couldn't turn my eyes away."

My imagination ran wild. "Then what happened?"

"The guest came out of the water looking at me, smiling and laughing, and she started taking my clothes off. Then she began fondling my private parts. I could not resist and had sex with her right there on the sand." His tale was sounding less believable, especially when he asserted that the missus joined in, holding him from behind, kissing his back and scratching it like a cat.

Though hard to believe, I imagined being there instead of Ali. It didn't matter to me that Ali was older, bigger, and more muscular than me.

"I had sex with both of them a few times," was his final sentence of this tale. I was curious whether he had had the same experience afterwards.

"What happened next?" I persisted.

"Nothing," he said. He was still the *khedmatkaar*, and no one mentioned the incident again. Both women acted as if nothing had taken place, and he was prudent enough to keep silent. After all, he was their servant and was comfortable where he was. However, the perception about British women that was created in my mind persisted for many years afterward.

CHAPTER 18

Mystical Awakening

HERE WERE A LOT OF CROOKS and con men around, and we encountered our share of them. Among the many travelers we met was a mullah who came to take baths several times and always struck up a long conversation with my father. One year, about a month and a half before the pilgrimage to Mecca, he suddenly appeared at our house, knocked on the door, and invited himself in. With his usual largesse, my father asked him to stay for supper, then overnight, and then he stayed on. He showed great piety, taking a long time to pray, and asking not to be disturbed during his meditation. He had prayer beads and said hundreds of *zikr*[16] after prayer. How could my father not trust him? The rest of the family was slightly suspicious, but we did not dislike him. After all, he was a guest in our house and we were taught to respect guests. My mother, however, claimed that she saw him peek through the curtain that opened to the yard where women were unveiled. In any case, just a day or two before leaving on his pilgrimage to Mecca, while packing his suitcase, he handed several boxes of baklava to my father who was helping him pack. He even gave his holy Quran to him. Suddenly, he froze, his face pale, his eyes fixed on his suitcase.

"What's wrong?" my father asked worriedly.

---

16 "Remembrance of God." A word or phrase used by devoted Muslims, which is repeated many times silently or aloud as a means of ingratiating them to the Divine. At the same time, this repetitious chanting brings tranquility and peace of mind.

There was no answer. This respectable mullah was in a coma-like condition. My father repeatedly entreated him to answer and finally shook him to bring him back to reality. The man confessed that he had forgotten to bring his pilgrimage money with him from Tehran. "How much?" my father asked anxiously. "Ten thousand *toman*."[17] With tears running down his cheeks, he bemoaned the fact that he would not be able to fulfill his lifelong dream of making the hajj. Mind you, we did not witness this scene but were told in detail with much sympathy by my father. Well, guess what? My father gave him the ten thousand to perform his pilgrimage to Mecca on the condition that he would repay him soon after his hajj. The man thanked him and tried to kiss his hands, but my father would not allow him to do so. The man then took the money and returned to Tehran, Iran, instead of performing his religious duty. It is a long story, but we heard that upon his return to Tehran, he married a beautiful young woman. We were flabbergasted but not sorry for my father because this was not the only time he had been conned. We had gotten tired of his naiveté. He had more faith in strangers than he did in his family. And his dalliances were beyond forgiveness. "He deserved it," we said. We even wondered if my father's intense anger was just because he'd been conned or because he'd been conned by a man who used the money to marry such a beautiful woman (as she was described to us). We thought it was funny that my father would dish out ten thousand *toman* for somebody else's sexual adventures.

But my father fought back. He went to Tehran and pursued the mullah from place to place, shouting at the top of his lungs that the man was a crook, telling all his neighbors what he'd done. Week after week, my father took a taxi from Karaj (a suburb of Tehran) and went to the con man's house. When no one answered the door, he would call the mullah's name loudly and demand, "Give me my money, you no-good crook. Under the guise of going to Mecca and performing the hajj you stole my money and used it to be married? You're a bastard. God will burn you in hell." The whole neighborhood was aware of my father's complaints against the man.

---

17 *Toman* is an Iranian currency. It was equivalent to one eighth of an American dollar in 1960.

Mamdasan c. 1960

To our total surprise, my father got his money back; he used it to purchase a good piece of land in Karaj, where he built a modern public bath. In the passageway leading to the public bath, there were several stores and apartments that he rented out. Of course, the ten thousand *toman* was a very small initial investment toward the purchase of the land. It took much more to build his business, but where there is a will there is a way. Having so many wealthy friends who loved him and trusted him, he had no problem borrowing a great deal of money to build his new business in Iran. Which fit in well with his plan to sell everything in Iraq and move to Iran.

My father had seen the coming of Saddam Hussein long before Hussein was around. Having seen how the Jews in Iraq had been treated after the establishment of Israel, my father knew it was only a matter of time before the Iraqi government would force the Iranians out. He was one of the few who saw this coming. Most minorities often get so involved with their everyday lives that they don't realize their own neighbors and friends could easily turn against them. They don't see the coming of fascism. They wait and dilly-dally until it is too late. The Muslims of Bosnia-Herzegovina in 1992 did not anticipate the coming carnage. There are many such examples. My father had a realistic view of the future, and in this instance, he was lucky.

Later, another person attached himself to our family. Fortunately, he was not a crook. His full name was Muhammad Hasan Yazdani, but he called himself Mamdasan, connecting two of his names together. He showed up one day at the public bath and, after bathing, he sat drinking tea and chatting. Soon, he attracted my father's interest. He had a sense of humor and an honest demeanor. When he was asked what he did for a living, Mamdasan replied, "I run errands. Anything. I don't need much to live on. I can work for no pay. All I need to stay here in Karbala are food and a shirt to cover my back." That was his ticket to enter our lives.

Soon Mamdasan was considered a member of the family. He got to know all of us and many of our relatives. In no time, he also became well known to many others including some ayatollahs. Since he was a good cook, he was jokingly given the title of *Tabbaakh al-Ulama'* (Chef of the Religious Scholars). Because of his versatility and ability to do whatever was asked, he gained a good reputation among all who knew him. A rumor had it that once one of the local ayatollahs had invited a number of guests for dinner, and he'd called on Mamdasan for help. He asked him to cook *qormeh sabzi* (stew of lamb and parsley). Mamdasan did not have enough parsley, so he improvised by supplementing the parsley with thoroughly washed and finely chopped grass. Luckily, the dish was delicious and the diners did not notice anything amiss.

Mamdasan made time to chat with all of us. He never said no to anyone, and he spoke to each person on his or her own level. Kids loved him because he would act silly. Adults trusted him because he was respectful, honest, hardworking, and polite. With me, he was more than a friend. He was a mentor without letting me know it. He said many things that made me think and sent me searching through books for more answers. Was he educated? As far as I could see, he did not read or write, pretending to be uninterested in such matters. But when he divulged some flickers of insight that did not follow the accepted line of religious thought, I began to doubt his sincere belief. Even though I was negligent in performing the required daily prayers and avoided fasting whenever I could, I was still part of a society whose focus was total absorption in religion. He would say that there was no physical heaven or hell and that God was "too busy to manage the lives of ants or humans personally." Though I agreed with him, I could not believe that a respected adult such as Mamdasan would contradict the Quran. Jesus was the son of the Virgin Mary to Muslims. That was repeatedly written in the Quran. He was not God or His son, as Christians claimed, but the Spirit of God, as far as Muslims were concerned. Mamdasan contradicted it.

"Read about Mitra,"[18] he'd say.

"Who is Mitra?" I would ask.

"The original Jesus," he'd answer.

"But the Quran speaks only of Jesus," I would say.

"Yes, yes, it is the same person."

Mamdasan often bewildered me. After making a serious remark, he'd act silly, as if he had been kidding. He'd suddenly change the conversation, repeating the word *herebereh*.[19]

"What is *herebereh*?"

"You know, *herebereh*."

I would give up asking and just laugh. *Herebereh* had no meaning at all to me. Obviously, when he realized he'd gone too far, he'd use the word to divert the discussion to silly things. As time went by I began to realize that Mamdasan had a point. He was a mystic who lived among the blind, and he had to be careful.

Like many teenagers, I had doubts about religion and talked about those doubts to anyone who would listen and was ready to engage in a dialogue. How could there be heaven and hell? It was hard for me to believe that God, who was described as the Most Gracious, the Dispenser

---

18 Many mystery religions that existed before Christianity and became popular among the Romans have astonishing similarities to Christianity. Dionysus, Osiris, and Mithras are among the "divinities" around which these cults revolved. Mithraism has an Iranian origin but was popular in Europe until its rival, Christianity, became the State religion during the reign of Emperor Constantine (d. 337). Thus, Mamdasan, a Persian, may have been familiar with Mitra (Mithras), whose birth, life, and crucifixion were similar to that of Christ.

19 A bit of gibberish that has no meaning.

of Grace, would choose some who would go to heaven and some who would go to hell.

I decided to approach my elementary school principal for guidance. I wrote him a six-page, handwritten letter that was full of questions that dealt with metaphysics. All I got back were big words too hard to understand and quotations from the hadiths (sayings of Prophet Muhammad and the Shi'ite Imams). Apparently, the principal confided the contents of my letter and his own responses to our Persian Literature teacher. The teacher approached me afterward saying that he was more impressed by my questions than with the principal's answers. "Keep on questioning, Mr. Yadegari. You'll find the answers on your own." I felt important.

It was Mamdasan who directed me toward answers to some of my questions, saying, "The concept of heaven and hell is very interesting. There are several verses in the Quran with explicit references to the fact that many of the stories, including those about heaven and hell, are actually allegories." His comment contradicted the Muslim belief in the physical nature of the Hereafter. I knew, in my heart, that if I were to tell others what he had said, they would not approve.

So what is God? Mamdasan had an enigmatic answer for that as well. God is not in heaven. He is everywhere. Didn't He say I am closer to you than your jugular vein? Didn't He say, wherever you turn you see the face of God? Didn't He say, "Ask and you shall receive?" He is the light of the heavens and the earth. That light, Mamdasan maintained, was in my heart, guiding me whenever and wherever He chose to succor me. Thus, everything is united as one in multiple facets that seem unrelated, yet they are related. "Remember the first fundamental of faith: *Tauhid* (Unity)," he used to say. Then, suddenly everything was *herebereh* for him. "And you'll find the answer, my son. If there is anyone who'd find it, it's you. Now, what are you going to get me when you become rich and famous? *Herebererh, herebereh.*"

"Stop fooling around, Mamdasan," I would object. The conversation was serious, and he was throwing in *herebereh* to end the discussion.

"Keep reading. Read Hallaj.[20] You'll find the answer," said Mamdasan.

---

20 Mansur al-Hallaj (tortured and dismembered in 922) was a mystic whose beautiful poems attracted the attention of many and the disapproval of the traditionalists.

"Wasn't Hallaj the crazy fellow who said, 'I am the Truth,' and then he was chopped to pieces?"

"Absolutely. Hallaj found himself. He was telling the truth. But they killed him. People are sheep. Sheep don't think. They only follow shepherds whose task is to sell their version of gods as a commodity. It is all *herebereh*!"

At that time, over sixty years ago, I could not understand. Nor do I claim that I understand today. *Herebereh* is beginning to make sense to me, though. Deception, fraud, illusion, nonsense, gibberish! All I know is that I find life more mysterious than I ever imagined. Mamdasan makes a bit more sense to me now than then. If, as I suspect, he was a Sufi (mystic, gnostic), then for him, Mitra and Jesus and Osiris and many like them were one and the same. Mamdasan knew what happened to Mitra and Hallaj. Today, I understand why he had developed a tactical diversion from serious discussions to *herebereh*.

The man was sane and wished to remain alive.

CHAPTER 19

Junior High School

THE IRANIAN SCHOOL did not offer classes past sixth grade. Thus, upon completion of elementary school in 1955, I attended the Iraqi high school for boys that offered a diploma after successful completion of eleventh grade. Karbala at that time also had an Iraqi secondary school for girls. Though not as excellent as the Iranian school, I found the Iraqi school sufficiently challenging, especially in light of the fact that the Iranian students were held to high standards. Most of the teachers were well qualified. One of them was even on leave, having been given a grant to study for his doctoral degree in Washington, D.C. This was very impressive.

For whatever reason, the science teacher who was on sabbatical leave discontinued his doctoral pursuit and returned home after a couple of months. Speculations and rumors abounded, but he did not usually talk about it. Once, when he and three other Iranian students were discussing race relations in America, I asked him if that or similar social issues in the United States made him cut short his study. He told us that he really didn't like living in America. "Americans are not clean," he said. "Men use urinals close to each other, standing, while urinating." That made us grimace. He continued saying that the odor of the urine was dizzying. Also, the hotel was smelly. Worse yet, men used the public showers collectively while fully naked. That was unacceptable for the modest people of Karbala. However, rumor had it that the real reason was that he was extremely homesick and could not tolerate living alone in a foreign country.

In July 1956, Nasser nationalized the Suez Canal, creating a crisis that gripped the world for many months with ramifications for years to come. I was in the eighth grade when, on October 29, 1956, Britain, France, and Israel attacked Egypt but were faced with stiff resistance that lasted over a week. Under pressure, especially from President Eisenhower, the British and French forces retreated. The Israeli occupation of the Sinai ended later in 1957. Nasser's popularity increased throughout the Arab countries, and Iraq was caught up in a whirlwind of Arab nationalism.

Immediately during and after the 1956 war, waves of emotion surfaced on every Arab city street. Iraq was no exception. Unrest over the government of Prime Minister Nuri al-Sa'id, a British lackey, festered. One day after dismissal time, as I headed out of the main gate to leave school, a senior student shoved me aside and pushed to the front of the departing crowd. Several dozen of his classmates had gathered, anticipating his next move. He thrust his right arm upward with clenched fist. I was near enough to hear his breath rush in and out as if he were a bull getting ready to charge. He began to chant, "Down with the government of Nuri al-Sa'id." With another deep breath came a much louder cry, "Down with the government of Nuri al-Sa'id." Hundreds of other students joined in. Then the students poured into the street shouting slogans, slowly dispersing into the shadows.

The next day, as the first bell rang, students remained in the schoolyard, refusing to attend class. I was one of the few who did not join the strike. Complying with my family's instructions, I tried to stay out of Iraqi politics. I saw one of my closest Iranian friends circle the school with the student strikers. I walked over to him and attempted to persuade him to leave. "Come on," I said. "This is not our fight. Leave it to them." He was obviously scared but did not dare to call attention to himself by leaving. Failing to convince him, I walked away, leaving hundreds of students gathered there. I realized my mistake immediately when I heard derogatory remarks directed toward me. It was a humiliating experience. Some shouted the slur *'ajam*[21] as well. Double insult.

---

21 Ajam means non-Arab and is usually applied to Iranians. It is often used as a derogatory term.

On the third day, as I approached the school, I could see students already gathered outside the entrance ready to march in the streets. I was several blocks away. I decided that the day was going to be wasted, and I prudently turned to head home. A carriage that was carrying two of our teachers was heading toward the school. One of the teachers, Mr. Taha Hussein, called me, asking why I was walking in the wrong direction. I explained that, because of the unruly students, the day was going to be a waste of time. There was no reason to stay and stand around doing nothing. He invited me to join them in the carriage, insisting that classes would be held and reassuring me, "No one will dare to touch you while you are with us. Hop in and we'll take you to school." I was hesitant but did not want to refuse the teacher's invitation.

Mr. Hussein had a reputation for being tough with students, occasionally even slapping them. When the strikes began, he had openly reprimanded the students for skipping classes and taking part in the demonstrations and chided them, saying that if they wished to change the political system they should seek a better education first. As the carriage approached the crowd, the students directed their attention toward Mr. Hussein. They dragged him out of the carriage and beat him. The strikers, however, left me alone with the other teacher, who quickly advised me to go home and not worry about school that day. Then he sought help for his injured colleague.

Life had become intolerable for my Iranian friend and me. Our classmates shunned us. Most distressing was the day that our Arabic literature instructor unintentionally alluded to the evils of being an informer. The whole class turned to stare in unison at the two of us. The instructor recognized that his remarks had been ill advised, and he did his best to explain that his lesson had nothing to do with any specific person but was related to the story we had read a week earlier. Some believed him and remembered the lesson, yet my friend and I felt that we had been "targeted." To be honest, we did not fault the teacher. It was just an awkward moment in the overall scheme of events. We decided to talk to our parents.

As fate had it, the Iranian School in Karbala had just begun instruction in seventh grade with plans to continue providing education through the ninth grade. The principal of the school was consulted. Fortunately, he invited us to attend the seventh grade. Several other classmates who had chosen to skip school for one year rather than attend the Iraqi high school, also returned. The newly established seventh grade now consisted of about twelve students.

By transferring from eighth grade in the Iraqi school to seventh grade in the Iranian school, I delayed my graduation one more year.

CHAPTER 20

A Student Strike

RETURNING TO THE IRANIAN SCHOOL extended my school years but turned out to be extremely important in the development of my spirit and independence of mind. When I attended the Iraqi school, my parents had cautioned me to keep a low profile and to avoid any political discussions.

However, in the Iranian elementary school, I had been a confident and bold speaker. My older brother, Mehdi, had encouraged me to practice public speaking, and then he arranged for me to give a speech welcoming Dr. Hossein Fatemi (d. 1954), Mosaddeq's Foreign Minister. Dr. Fatemi came for a visit to Karbala and was cheered by thousands of Iranians and Iraqis at the consulate. As a fourth grader from the only Iranian school in that city, I delivered a welcome speech on behalf of our school. Bolstered by enthusiastic encouragement, I continued public speaking on every occasion that was feasible and appropriate, and such occasions abounded.

Our school was built around a central schoolyard. In the morning, each grade stood outside their respective classrooms, and our *naazem* (literally, one who keeps order, but is really a dean or director) took attendance. Then he asked anyone interested in speaking to the student body to come forth and deliver his speech. He never previewed the content of the talk beforehand. Mehdi continued helping me write speeches and urged me to deliver them. I spoke on subjects like the evils of jealousy, the need for a school paper, and the need to make all books in the library available to the students. In addition, I read a few poems by well-known poets. I had a good speaking style for a student and soon became very comfortable in this role.

In sixth grade, in one of my speeches, I chided the principal—a kind and erudite gentleman and a good friend of our family—for keeping a private library at the school and not allowing students to use it. Disgruntled by my words, he patiently unlocked the door to the library and showed me the exquisite and extremely valuable glass-door mahogany bookcases that housed several hundred tomes. "If I let every single elementary student come in without careful supervision, they might break the glass doors by throwing balls and running around. Not only would we lose the library, but we would also have injuries on our hands," he cautioned kindly. As I looked around the room, I was embarrassed because, indeed, he was telling the truth. Apparently, an Indian visitor to Karbala had donated the library to support scholarly pursuit. Our principal seemed forthcoming, though. He gave me a list of books and asked me to select one to borrow. Not having any idea which book would be good to read, I chose one with the title, "Muhammad" written in Persian.

His smile made me think my choice was appropriate. He offered an excuse that he didn't have the key to the locked bookcase with him, but he promised he would call me the next day to come to the office for the book. It was dismissal time when he called. As I walked in, I was surprised to see all of the school's teachers sitting primly in their chairs, regarding me with interest. I approached the principal's huge desk, asking for the book. He handed it to me. I was turning to leave when I heard him ask, "Don't you want to look at it? Open it." I did as he advised. Totally surprised, I burst out, "This book is in English!"

"You chose it, Mohammad," was his gleeful remark. For whatever reason, he always called me by my first name. Then I heard guffaws and chuckles.

"But you showed me a list that was in Persian!" I responded.

"Yes, the list is in Persian. However, the bibliophile who donated this library to us was an Indian, and all those books are in English."

I was still defiant although defeated. Meekly, I muttered, "You should have told me."

"The next time you criticize people, have your facts straight, son."

When I returned to the Iranian school as a seventh grader, I was once again free to speak my mind. I resumed my morning speeches. I suggested founding a student newspaper. When my request was denied, I purchased a large poster board and asked my oldest brother to help me write some informational items. I added some pictures of places such as the Taj Mahal and a Chinese pagoda to make it more interesting. That was the extent of my producing a student newspaper.

In the ninth grade, we had a new teacher in Persian Literature who was sent directly from Tehran. Up until then, almost all of our teachers were either local Iranians who had been educated in and thus were familiar with the cultural environment of Karbala, or they were Iranians who had been transferred from other Iranian schools in Iraqi cities such as Baghdad or Basra. They had become acculturated and had learned the ethos of the small foreign schools in Iraq. The new teacher, Mr. Karimi, was inexperienced but very self-confident. He obviously spent a lot of time in the *zoorkhaneh*[22] for he was very muscular. He would slap and punch students who did not behave properly.

We were not used to this heavy-handed approach to teaching, and he was soon on a collision course with some of the students who complained about his methods. When he slapped two students in our ninth-grade class, one of whom was my brother, the classroom deteriorated into chaos. Mr. Karimi ordered the two to leave the classroom. When neither one did, he became angrier and used some derogatory language, calling the students "dumb Arabs who pretend to be Iranians." We were insulted. When he demanded once again that the two "troublemakers" leave the room, I jumped up and shouted, "We will all leave!" He was taken aback. He addressed me as politely as he could. "Mr. Yadegari, I am trying to

---

22 Literally, house of strength, ancient gymnasiums where men worked out. Zoorkhanehs are Iranian in origin and ubiquitous in the Iranian Plateau. However, in addition to physical sport, zoorkhanehs also provide spiritual guidance. It is incumbent upon the athletes to live upright and honest lives; in short, *zoorkhaneh* is a place for strengthening the body and the spirit. Exercise is accompanied by music, particularly drums. The teacher emphasizes spirituality, and cleanliness of the body and the soul. As the drum beats, so does the heart in the midst of vigorous movements of the body. In the total absorption and concentration of the mind, the athletes enter a meditative state. The aim of the *zoorkhaneh* ritual is to create genteelness, kindness, and humility, as well as muscular bodies. However, many people use the *zoorkhaneh* solely for exercise.

teach, and these two interrupted my instruction. It is not fair to the rest of the students."

I had no choice. I had jumped up impulsively, speaking loudly and unexpectedly. The student sitting in front of me, not expecting my sudden outburst, had also jumped up. His inadvertent reaction looked like he was in agreement with me. The class was waiting for a cue to leave. Tension was mounting. Adrenaline was pumping. I was still standing. "I am sorry, but you don't know us. You just insulted us all by calling us 'dumb Arabs who pretend to be Iranians.' You should have remembered my speech a week ago about corporal punishment. You walk around as if you're a weight-lifting champion. Even when you want to be pleasant, you're condescending. The person who should change his behavior is you, not us."

He succeeded in calming us all down, asking us to sit down, but then the bell rang. He left the classroom, deep in thought. This was not the first confrontation for Mr. Karimi. A week earlier one of the two students who were asked to leave the classroom had persuaded his older cousin to come to school and threaten the teacher. Thus, on the day of the confrontation in our classroom, Mr. Karimi was already agitated. I assume he felt his authority was being jeopardized, as he went to the principal and demanded that the students be expelled from the school. The faculty and the principal agreed to expel the two students. Oddly, the principal gave the expulsion notice verbally to the students but not in writing to the parents.

What followed was a weekend of acrimonious debate among students who gathered outside of school. Finally, it was decided that I would lead a strike against the school, demanding the reinstatement of the two students, the removal of Mr. Karimi from our school, and the banning of corporal punishment. The strike took place after the weekend. The seventh-, eighth-, and ninth-grade students refused to move into classrooms after the attendance was taken in the courtyard. The strike soon involved the elementary classes as students ignored their teachers and watched our activities through the windows.

After some time, the principal approached me in the courtyard. He was as friendly as he had always been. He notified me that the Iranian Consul in Karbala wanted to meet with me so that I could explain the reason for our disobedience. I requested the presence of another student, and we walked a few blocks with the principal to the consulate, where we met the Iranian Consul, the political attaché, my father, the other ousted student's parent, as well as some other people whom I did not know. They asked the reasons for our disruptive behavior.

It may seem strange that the Iranian consulate concerned itself with a disciplinary affair in a school. But Iraq at that time was a tinderbox of political turmoil. Abdul Karim Qasem had recently overthrown the monarchy, and the future of Iraq was extremely unsettled. Furthermore, relations between Iraq and Iran had become more tenuous. The Iranian consulate in Karbala wanted to quickly put a lid on the strike in the Iranian school. What if the strike got out of hand and students began to shout slogans or march in the streets? That would have given Iraqi officials sufficient grounds to take control of the school, turning a simple students' demand into a serious political issue between Iraq and Iran. Though, ordinarily, such an event would have been under the purview of the Supervisory Board of Iranian Schools in Iraq located in Baghdad, the consulate had intervened to immediately nip it in the bud.

As we were discussing the matter at the consulate, we began to realize the seriousness of the dilemma for the consul. Assuming an air of innocence, we explained that we refused to be taught by a teacher who beat students, who was arrogant, and who had convinced the principal and the faculty to dismiss two of our classmates, one of whom was my own brother, from the school.

At that moment, my father's demeanor changed. Looking at his friend, the school principal, he asked, "Is that true?" However, before getting an answer, he let loose a barrage of threatening verbiage. Everyone realized that he was a father who was angry that he had not even been notified of his son's expulsion. The political attaché asked us whether we would go back to our classrooms with no further disruption if they were to dismiss the teacher. We agreed.

Returning to school with the principal at our sides, we announced the successful conclusion of our strike. The fact that Mr. Karimi was going to be dismissed was greeted with applause and much delight.

The political attaché had been a recent appointee in the Iranian Consulate in Karbala, and the rumors were that he was really a member of the Iranian intelligence service, SAVAK. The Shah had set up the SAVAK soon after his return to power due to the 1953 CIA-arranged coup against Dr. Mosaddeq. The Shah received funding and training assistance from the United States and developed an effective organization that spied on Iranian citizens. He was interested in eliminating groups such as communists, nationalists, or anyone else who was against his regime. The SAVAK routinely paid money under cover to Iranians in all walks of life to report on anyone associated with an opposition group. They routinely censored the press, mail, and telephone communications of ordinary citizens. Undercover informants were so ubiquitous that citizens were reluctant to speak freely, even among their own family members.

But the attaché's extremely friendly attitude, his ability to remember everyone by name, and his astuteness in recognizing the social and economic positions of various Iranians in that city made it easy for him to attract a wide circle of friends, among them my father. Thus, I did not think it unusual when, a couple of days after our meeting in the consulate, the attaché approached me and invited me to come to his office to discuss how things were going in the school.

I went to see him a few times. He offered me tea and pastry and asked various questions about the school environment. He told me that Mr. Karimi had been transferred to Iran and was doing well, working as a clerk in the Department of Education in Tehran. I was glad that at least he had a job since we really had meant no harm to him as a person. It was his attitude and heavy-handed methods that we could not tolerate.

The political attaché showered compliment upon compliment on me for my leadership and good judgment, and I was flattered. In the course of the conversation, he mentioned that he was interested in knowing about the problems that were concerning students. He said that being aware of a problem before it became an issue would be of tremendous help to him in resolving it before it got out of control. He asked if any teacher was trying to take advantage of naïve students, attempting to indoctrinate them into various ideologies such as communism or pan-Arabism that were being promulgated in Iraq. There was no doubt in my mind that the man was asking me to be a snitch.

He crossed the room and opened one of the drawers in the desk I was sitting next to. It was full of different denominations of Iraqi dinars. He left it open and returned to his seat. I asked him what this drawerful of dinars was there for. His answer was full of implications, "To give away to people. Would you like some?"

I pushed the drawer closed and rose from my chair saying, "You know very well that if I need any money, I can always get it from my parents. I am sorry, but I am not a snitch."

I left his office and avoided seeing him again.

CHAPTER 21

A Violent Time

*I*RAQ WAS IN TURMOIL when I finished ninth grade at the Iranian School in Karbala. On July 14, 1958, Colonel Abdul-Karim Qasem had overthrown and killed the monarch, Faisal II, and his regent, Abd al-Ilah. The hated eight-time prime minister, Nuri al-Sa'id, had been in hiding but was found the next day trying to escape wearing a woman's veil. A mob beat him, stabbed him, tied a noose around his neck, and dragged him through the streets. The manner in which Nuri al-Sa'id was killed set a barbaric precedent which unleashed further violence against the royalists and sympathizers of the monarchy. Mob violence broke out in many cities in Iraq.

Much was happening almost simultaneously. Political parties that had been banned under king Faisal II were now allowed to solicit members and support causes. Information desks were set up by different parties in order to distribute propaganda pamphlets and fliers about their platforms and ideologies. The two most active parties were the Ba'ath Party (Arab Socialist Party) and the Communist Party.

Though a military dictator, Qasem was an extremely popular Iraqi leader. He was considered to be humble, genuinely interested in improving the lot of the citizenry, and a sincere Iraqi nationalist. His family affiliation to both Sunnis and Shi'ites made him acceptable to both religious groups as well. The majority of Iraqis approved Qasem's view that building Iraq's infrastructure was the most important agenda for Iraq.

It was a highly emotional time. Newly recruited National Guard members patrolled the streets of many cities with loaded guns. It was sometimes comical to see high school age students running toward a trouble scene to keep "peace and order" wearing National Guard outfits, bearing two heavy pistols, and at the same time trying to hold up their ill-fitting pants. Demonstrations all over Iraq for one reason or another were almost a daily routine. There was a lot of talk about uniting the Arab countries, but there was no consensus about the type of unity: federation or union.

Arab nationalism generated a lot of emotion and enthusiasm among the country's youth. Nasser of Egypt was extremely popular, and the union of Egypt with Syria in 1958, founding the United Arab Republic, excited the Iraqi citizenry. In Iraq, resentment of the British and their stooges was so strong that some officials and sympathizers of the old regime were threatened, beaten, or killed. In the ensuing anarchy, the crowds turned brutal. Old animosities between rivals and competitors flared up and vengeance was meted out. Mobs dragged their victims through the streets the way Nuri al-Sa'id had been dragged. There were many instances of exacting revenge on the loyal supporters of the past regime.

In one case in Karbala, it was rumored that a lawyer was dragged and killed because of old rivalries that had nothing to do with politics. One evening I was conversing with a few friends at a shop owned by an acquaintance when we heard that, a few blocks away, a crowd was shouting, "Drag him with the rope!" The shop owner closed his shop and advised us to leave because we were Iranians and the mob might harm us!

My parents, especially my father, who was aware of my tenuous situation, were extremely concerned. He had heard that some students had threatened me. When he asked me about it, I gave him an evasive answer and said that they really did not mean to harm me. It was just a case of jealousy. Furthermore, he was concerned over my curiosity in learning about the ideologies espoused by the various factions. My interest was purely academic. But those who espoused them, just like religious preachers of all "divinely inspired" religions, always hope to indoctrinate and persuade. That was another source of worry for my father: *What if?*

Most of my older siblings had departed for Iran as had been planned by my father years earlier. It was time for me to leave. Though I considered continuing my education in Iraqi schools, under the circumstances, it was out of the question for my parents. I was reluctant to go to Iran because one of my uncles was encouraging me to go to a preparatory school in Switzerland instead. He admired the Swiss. Who didn't? Switzerland was a strong but neutral country. The Swiss people had lived in peace for a long time. Two world wars had come and gone, and their neutrality was respected. They spoke three languages, my uncle emphasized. Their educational system was excellent. What better country in which to continue my studies?

My father hesitated at first but was finally persuaded. I have no doubt that his agreeing to send me to Switzerland was because of his worry and concern about the political conditions and possible negative side effects on me. He was ready to dish out some money just to get me out of the country. My interest in reading about Communism and Ba'athism was troublesome to him. Though he was well aware of the fact that I had an independent mind, he still was a father. Parents worry for good reasons. Peer pressure has a strong effect on young people whose need for acceptance makes them do many things that they normally would not do.

My uncle and I took a trip to Baghdad to the Swiss legation to inquire about preparatory schools in Switzerland. We were well received and encouraged. Promises of assistance in searching for a proper institution were sincerely given. Arrangements to be undertaken were discussed.

But nothing can remain secret once a tongue begins to wag. The word of my leaving Iraq got around, and more tongues slithered out like snakes in the sand. I told many of my friends, and before the sun had set upon our return from Baghdad, possibly hundreds of the residents in Karbala knew that I planned to go to Switzerland. Except for a half dozen genuine well-wishers, many found fault with this plan. They thought it blasphemous for a God-fearing man to send his son to *bilad-i kufr* (land of the infidels).

The more envious and hypocritical even sent "emissaries" who were highly persuasive, fabricating hadiths of the Prophet to make their points while trying to change my father's mind. The approach of these various emissaries was basically similar. It was like a well-rehearsed scenario. Don't you know it is a land of fornication and immorality? They go swimming nude or half naked. Boys and girls kiss each other anytime, anywhere. They have no shame. Don't you remember Mr. X, a thirty-year-old science teacher, who went to Washington to study for his doctoral degree and soon returned? He could not take the way people engaged in such shameless acts. And he was thirty; your son is young. And don't forget that Christians believe in the divinity of Jesus. They believe Jesus (may peace be upon him) was the Son of God, as well as God Himself, not His prophet. Do you want to see your son convert to Christianity? Letting him go would amount to losing him.

Surprisingly, my father resisted. As I said, he was concerned for my safety in Iraq.

I considered my options. There were rumors that the Iraqi government would give scholarships to study in Moscow or Beijing to any students who graduated from an Iranian school in Iraq and subsequently became Iraqi citizens. My close friend, who had changed schools with me earlier, decided to go to Moscow (whether or not the Iraqi government paid for it, I really don't know).

Before deciding upon any major undertaking, my father habitually resorted to *istikharah* (a specific form of divination which uses the Quran to predict the future).[23] This practice was repulsive to me. Not only was it superstitious and irreligious, it was a practice commonly used by the most incompetent and corrupt rulers in Persian history. The rulers of the Qajar Dynasty (1796-1925) had been big spenders who preferred to enlarge their harems and spend money on jewels rather than see to the welfare of the people. In my mind, the worst of the Qajar Shahs was Fath Ali Shah (1797-1834). His long beard had been encrusted with gems; his concubines had exceeded hundreds, his practice of divination had led to many foolish decisions that allowed the Russians to advance as Fath Ali Shah ceded one Iranian territory after another. While his capable son, Prince Mirza Abbas (d. 1833) had engaged against Alexander I (1801-1825) of Russia, the Shah himself had been oblivious to the dangers that surrounded his empire.

I made my father promise not to use *istikharah* to make his decision in this case. But ignorant "vultures" circled around me. My classmate, Hamid, who was one of my closest friends, was convinced to persuade me to seek "divine guidance." I refused; I called it a superstitious and irreligious idea.

---

23 Even though the Quran explicitly denounces the use of any form of divination, some Muslims, when confronted with difficult choices, seek guidance using the Quran or worry beads to determine the "correct" choice. This procedure is called *istikharah*.

However, Hamid was persistent and finally convinced me. He assured me that the mullah whom he had in mind had no stake in the outcome. He added that all I had to do was keep my intent secret when I asked the mullah to take *istikharah*. To put Hamid at ease, and after making him swear that he had not told him about my proposed travel, I agreed to see the mullah. Hamid and I met the mullah the next day at the shrine of Husayn after the evening prayer. Hamid explained that I was struggling with a personal decision and would like to have *istikharah* performed to assist me in making this decision.

The mullah murmured a short prayer then, with closed eyes, opened the Quran to a random page. Then he opened his eyes and began reading to himself, pretending to be extremely perturbed. He told me that my plan to go to the land of the infidels was absolutely foolhardy. My trip to a foreign land would be hazardous and fraught with failure, so much so that he felt obligated to inform my father of my consultation with him. I had no doubt in my mind that the mullah had prior knowledge of my plans, quite likely from my own "good friend." I had fallen into a trap.

Even after hearing of my consultation with the mullah, my father was still reluctant to deny my trip to Switzerland. The last straw came when my uncle took me to a tailor to have a suit made for my trip. My uncle's choice of tailor and cloth was too much to swallow. Looking back, I realize that he was foolish. I remember clearly when the tailor informed us that the material selected was going to be expensive. My uncle's response, proudly uttered, was that I was going to Switzerland, thus money was no object. The suit was seventy dinars while my father usually paid around seven or ten dinars. That was enough to make my father lose his temper and change his mind. Retrospectively, I do not blame him. The finances of a preparatory school and college in Switzerland would have cost him an arm and a leg.

I yielded and chose to leave for Iran.

Mohammad 1961

PART II

TEHRAN, IRAN

The Freedom Tower (Tehran)

CHAPTER 22

Jamsheed

IN 1959, AT THE AGE OF EIGHTEEN, I moved to Iran. Four of my brothers had preceded me over a period of approximately seven years. My father gave us each a monthly allowance for our expenses. I lived alone in Tehran, though there were many relatives and siblings around. I could have stayed with one of them, but I preferred to be on my own. I lived in boarding houses where there was no need for me to shop, cook, or do any housework. The family that ran the boarding house even washed my clothes. The other boarders and I ate breakfast and dinner together. There were six of us living with a family that had several daughters who were well trained in the art of flirtation. I smartened up quickly. I soon realized that these girls were taught to tease and smile and converse and flirt, but they drew the line if someone got fresh with them. They softly and coquettishly slapped our hands and shied away. Sometimes, though, one young man or another would fall in love with one of these girls, and I had to listen to his woes. I could not always help. How can you tell someone who has fallen in love that the previous occupant of the same room or the one next to it had had the same experience?

I enrolled in a high school in Tehran and attended the tenth grade. Rumor had it that about 30 percent of high school students in Tehran used heroin. I always thought it was an exaggeration. But then again, the rumors persisted.

Since I was not living with my family, I had considerably more personal freedom in Tehran. Even though a Muslim is not supposed to drink, fifteen is the age of manhood and consequently the age of personal responsibility before God. It was not a stranger's business to interfere. I became a heavy wine drinker. I skipped school quite often, riding buses until the liquor stores opened. Yes, in those days there were liquor stores in Tehran. On many occasions, I would go to an Armenian sandwich shop that also served wine and I would order a bottle of Shiraz wine. I would stay there until afternoon, drinking the wine and eating. The lack of parental oversight and the lure of the vices of the cosmopolitan city compared to the contemplative life of Karbala overwhelmed my common sense.

I lost two friends to heroin overdoses. Actually, they were only acquaintances, but, when you're young, everybody you know is a friend. One was Jamsheed, a handsome boy, polite, and quiet when around us.

One day he asked me to lend him ten *toman*. I did so gladly. He never offered to give it back, and I never asked him. The second time, he asked for a twenty, and I obliged him again. Another friend approached me after he saw me take the bill out of my wallet and hand Jamsheed the money. He asked if Jamsheed was borrowing money from me. I said yes and commented that Jamsheed seemed to be acting strange. He explained that Jamsheed was a junkie, hooked on heroin. "He'll do anything to get a single *toman*. Lending him money is a bad idea." I told him that Jamsheed had already borrowed a ten and had not given it back. My friend advised me that I should not lend him any more. Jamsheed was bad news.

A few months after I lent Jamsheed twenty *toman*, someone found him dead in one of the deep gutters that lined the streets. He had overdosed and fallen, hitting his head on the concrete wall of the gutter. He was found the next day. His father, who had initially done his best to straighten him out, later had given up hope. A proud man, he felt embarrassed in front of his neighbors and friends for being unable to effectively influence his son.

The story wasn't only heroin abuse. His addiction had led him to steal money from his family, then his friends, and then wherever he could. That wasn't enough. He sold his body to earn money to satisfy his habit. He would do anything to earn the money he needed. The last time I saw him before his death, I hardly recognized him. He walked by us like a ghost, emaciated and pale. He didn't even acknowledge our presence, and we pretended not to see him. Everyone felt sorry for him.

Where did the heroin come from? Rumors abounded that the British and Americans supplied it, and this engendered a great deal of ill will toward Britain and the U.S. Many believed that some members of the Iranian royal family were involved, foremost among them, Ashraf, the Shah's sister.

There was a funeral for Jamsheed. I went to the house to express my sympathies to the father. It was so crowded with mourners that there was only standing room for non-family members. Women were sobbing, and Jamsheed's father was slapping his forehead as he wept. "God, curse the Americans. They killed my child. They are the ones who brought these drugs into the country to make money. God, make them pay. Make every American father and every mother pay for their crime. Make them feel how it feels to lose a young child. My son was only eighteen!" I had goose bumps all over my body.

Years later, when I had become a father and an American citizen with two daughters approaching their teens in a culture rife with drug use, I remembered his words with much trepidation. I did not want to be the father upon whom that man put his curse.

CHAPTER 23

Sleeping on the Rooftop

IN LATE SPRING AND SUMMER IN KARBALA, the heat of the day had remained inside the house at night, so we'd slept on the flat roof, where there had been a cool breeze. Every night, we carried the Persian rugs, which covered the main floors of the house during the day, up the two-floor staircase and spread them out on the roof. A small shed stored our mattresses and blankets. These we spread out on top of the rugs at night and folded and stored them each day. My mother and our maid had done most of the work, but the children had pitched in, too.

Lying in the dark, we'd listened to a multitude of sounds: crickets, frogs, howling jackals, and barking dogs. In the morning, the singing birds and the crowing of cocks woke us. Though safe under our blankets, it seemed as though we had slept with the rest of the creatures and had woken up when they began paying homage to the rising dawn.

Nothing had been more exhilarating than the clusters of stars in the sky. The Milky Way was a magnificent highway that appeared to run across the expansive canopy above my head. The Northern Star was midway in the sky while the Little Dipper and the Big Dipper competed for my attention. A few times I saw comets in the distant domain of the unknown. There were dozens of shooting stars every night. I had seen so many of them that I gave up counting. Looking up and thinking about the wonders of the universe, it had been inconceivable to me that we were the lone creatures for whom God created all this beauty.

I had shared my thoughts with Mamdasan. His comments had been wild and hardly believable. He'd maintained that there were many earthlike planets whose inhabitants might or might not be similar to people on earth. Again, he'd quote some verses of the Quran that referred to jinn. He said that people did not understand the messages abundant in the Holy Book. The references to jinn were not to spirits like the genie of *The Arabian Nights*, but referred to other creatures of God whom we cannot see.

Mamdasan had talked of a parallel world beyond our own earth and the Milky Way. Actually, he'd said, a double that looked just like me was living on one of those planets. "He is your *shabeeh* (likeness)," he said. Intrigued, I asked if my double knew about me. According to Mamdasan, most doubles had no idea about their counterparts. However, my double knew about me and liked me. *Herebereh, herebereh,* and the conversation would change.

Much later, when sleeping on the rooftop in Tehran, my experience in Karbala was similar, but had one important difference. While Karbala was very conservative, Tehran was bursting with sexy women who dressed alluringly and wore makeup. At night on the roof I occasionally saw a naked woman slip into her blankets. Once, I saw a couple making love. It was late afternoon and there they were, unaware of my presence on the next rooftop. I got an eyeful. After they finished they walked naked downstairs, obviously to wash. But the woman gave me a glance and a smile. Exhibitionists? Perhaps.

Sometimes neighbors chatted and exchanged sweets. However, usually each family minded its own business.

One night in 1962, I was immersed in thought. Keeping an eye out for satellites that sometimes circled the earth above the Tehran sky, I noticed that the sky was moving. The sky with all of its stars was actually swinging like a clock pendulum left to right and back. Then I heard screams from below. It dawned on me that this must be an earthquake. I was well aware that earthquakes were relatively common in Iran. I had never experienced one before, but I knew I should find my way downstairs to the lower level. As I descended, I was jostled from one side to the other. Luckily, there was a handrail on the right and a solid wall on the left. By the time I reached the first floor, the earth had stopped shaking. Hundreds of people had made it out to the street and were trying to determine how much damage had been done. People were expecting aftershocks. The next day we heard that the earthquake had a Richter scale magnitude of about 7.2 and the center of the earthquake had been in Bo'in Zahra, near Qazwin, some 143 kilometers (89 miles) west of Tehran. More than ten thousand people were killed and thousands of homes were devastated. Its force was felt not only in Tehran, but also in almost all of northern Iran. In the days that followed, a great deal of aid was needed in the devastated areas. But the agencies in charge of disaster aid were known to be corrupt, so the donated materials rarely reached those in need. Therefore, people took it upon themselves to drive truckloads of blankets, food, tents, and various essential supplies to the epicenter.

CHAPTER 24

The Genius
Failed Twelfth Grade

$\mathcal{I}$T WAS JUNE 1962. Three years had passed since, in accordance with my father's plan to move the family gradually, I had moved alone to Tehran. It was a modern city of nearly two million people. There were many foreigners (American, British, European) largely because of the oil industry and the American military, as well as a boom in industrialization that required foreign expertise. The Shah was very friendly with the West. Even though he tried to move Iran toward modernization and westernization, his lust for power and his use of the secret police alienated the majority of Iranians, leading them to despise his despotic regime.

Life in Tehran was very different from life in Karbala, Iraq. Movie theaters abounded. There were cabarets and nightclubs. There were even brothels that were supervised by the health authorities, centered in Shahr-e Now, a two-block gated community in southern Tehran. The northern part of the city—where the rich resided—had its own ladies of the night, call girls who were better suited to the affluent socio-economic lifestyle.

Tehran had many shops that served wine and beer, along with a variety of sandwiches. My cousin, Jalal, and I frequented these shops. I liked shish kebab with Shiraz wine and a bologna type of sandwich called *kalbaas*.

Over the course of several hours, while sitting on a stool at the counters that lined both sides of the shop, I often emptied a bottle of wine. Around 1:00 p.m., the cabarets opened. On Lalezar Avenue, I recall Café Mash'al, Café Jamsheed, Café Baghe-Saba, and Café Suzan. The singers, mainly women, were not the best that one might hope to see, but they were the best we could find at that time of the day. Once the alcohol had worked its wonders, who cared? Most of them were, or at least pretended to be, professionals. But that did not stop us from flirting with them. Their most artful skill was the manner in which they calmed our excited hormones with polite smiles and sisterly responses and sometimes with good hard twists of our wrists that put us in our places and left us to sheepishly nurse our injuries.

One particular nightclub that my friends and I frequented, Cabare-ye Shukuf-e Now, presented various international groups of singers, dancers, acrobats, and comedians along with food and all kinds of drinks.

For a teenager like me, life in Tehran was much more enticing and exciting than the dour, deeply religious, and highly superstitious Karbala. Even the coffeehouses and teahouses were classier than those in Iraq. With no parental supervision, I was trapped by the glamour and allure of the city.

The monthly allowance provided by my father was 400 *toman,* which was more than enough for a single person living alone, and allowed me to sample all of the entertainment and delights of the city. Then, one serendipitous day about four months after I'd arrived in Tehran, I was walking on Ferdowsi Avenue and I spotted a classmate from the Iranian school in Karbala. We stopped and talked for some time and told each other what we had been doing. He confided that he, along with several other students, was on scholarship from the Pahlavi Foundation. I was surprised to hear that.

"Didn't anyone tell you about the scholarship?" he asked. According to my friend, the Shah was concerned that the new government in Iraq was trying to entice Iranian students in Iraq, especially those who had attended the Iranian schools there, to become citizens of Iraq. The Shah offered 250 *toman* per month for anyone who chose to return to Iran to finish his high school studies there. For one reason or another, I was unaware of that. The well-known plans for my departure to Switzerland may have been why no one had informed me of the Shah's offer.

The funds were to come from the Pahlavi foundation, a charity organization established in 1958 by Shah Mohammad Reza (1941-1979). Allegations of corruption had been hurled at this institution from the start.

The next day, I walked into the Pahlavi Foundation and sought to see the director of that huge facility. I opened the door to a large room, where I saw the director, Asadollah Alam (a close friend of the Shah who held many offices during his political career, among them the premiership between July 1962 and March 1964), conducting a meeting of some thirty officials, all of whom turned to look at me, the intruder who had not even knocked to ask permission to enter. Embarrassed and hesitant, I momentarily froze. But then I was pleased when that shrewd politician, who was one of the organizers of the 1953 coup against Dr. Mosaddeq, was extremely cordial to me.

"Please come in," he said, beckoning with his hand for me to come forward.

It did not even occur to me to apologize for the interruption. After relating the reason for my presence, I showed him my credentials. He looked at my grades and read them out loud. I noted heads nodding in congratulatory approval. "Seeing these grades, I will be happy to approve your scholarship. Not only that, I will tell the treasurer to pay you for the first four months retroactively," said Alam. Without hesitation, he wrote a note and asked me to take it to the proper office to receive my stipend. As I walked away from him, I felt proud of my scholastic achievement. Neither he nor I knew that my future school years in Iran were not going to be as productive as the past. Needless to say, I never informed my father of the extra monthly fellowship I was receiving from the Shah.

My father had not really thought about the ramifications of his decision to send his children, one by one, alone, to another country without supervision and without having taught them how to be prudent in their social and financial matters. I was sent alone to sink or swim. My father was busy with his business. My mother had tried to teach me to save rather than waste my money, but she had her own limitations. Karbala was not a place where she could deal directly with male outsiders. When she was in need of such encounters, she had to ask a male member of our family, such as one of her brothers, to perform the task. On the other hand, if she wished to teach me how to save, there were no banks in that city. As I recall, there was only one bank in Karbala that had opened a couple of years before I left. Private individuals called *sarrafs*, performed some of the bank's functions. If I had dealt with such an individual, he would have, intentionally or unintentionally, reported my savings to my father who would have confiscated them because, even though he was generous to others, he was not inclined to have people know how much money he and his children collectively possessed. As for myself, I was too busy having a good time with my friends, whom I habitually treated to meals and entertainment, to think of the future even in Tehran where I could have saved my money. I guess I was "genetically" generous like my father.

I did not attend school in Tehran as often as I should have. At first, I found the material and teachers boring. Comparatively, my education in the Iranian school in Karbala had been quite advanced. In Tehran, the students seemed aloof and stood around striking poses, trying to look like American movie stars. Combing their hair constantly, the boys tried to look like James Dean or Elvis Presley.

Whereas in Karbala, Iraq, women wore heavy stockings and heavy veils in public, many of them covering their faces and avoiding talking to anyone who was *namahram*, in Tehran, Iran, multitudes of females oozed with sex appeal and loved to be the center of attention. In Tehran, girls took city transportation buses back and forth to and from school. The school day ended around two-thirty in the afternoon, and both boys and girls rode the crowded buses home. Flesh rubbed flesh, and when the bus came to a halt, the intensity of accidental touches drove everyone crazy.

Dating girls was an adventure and a chore at the same time, for the whole process had to be kept secret from the girl's family. Approaching one of them to ask for a date followed a time-honored ritual. One wrong move—the sudden appearance of a brother, an uncle, a father, or even a neighbor—could invite trouble and a good beating. Many novices at the game or foreign travelers such as American hippies or members of the Peace Corps were unexpectedly attacked because they were not used to the restrictions of dating Tehran girls.

First, a boy selected a girl and followed her to and from school, making sure she noticed his existence. Then, he complimented her on her dress, her shoes, or her hair. She would usually ignore such comments. A smile was a sign that she was interested. Responding to one's greeting was a further sign of attraction. Then, the boy would get closer by walking alongside her, and, depending on his personality and boldness, he might begin to converse. Many boys were too shy or nervous to strike up a conversation. It was not uncommon for a boy's friend to speak to a girl on his friend's behalf. A couple of times, I played the role of liaison. Once, I was presented with a surprising dilemma when I found out that the girl was more interested in me than the "shy" one. The girl had seen us following her for days. She had given us the "look" and many smiles. Yet my friend had been too timid to approach her. He'd dragged me along with him in these chase games because he didn't dare to go alone. We followed her into her dead-end lane. I kept encouraging him to go ahead and ask her out. She was nearing her own house, yet he was frozen. I had had it. It would soon be too late. Though shy myself in social circles, once I made up my mind to do something, I did it. I approached the girl and spoke on his behalf. "Can't he speak for himself?" she asked. That's when I noted the disappointment on her face and her indecision. Her comments made me wonder for a short moment if this bond of camaraderie was foolish. Here I was with an unexpectedly willing date, but I was representing my friend. Regret soon disappeared, and the code of honor between friends won out. She told me to tell him that he had a very good friend and that he should be grateful for my behavior. I thanked her and introduced the young man to her. She said hello to him and smiled before she went into her house and shut the door. But the connection was made, and I was free. The rest was up to them.

In the early 1960s when I was in Tehran, several magnificent new movie theatres were built. Movies were shown every day at several different times. American films dominated the great number of movies offered. There were Iranian films, but, back then, they were mediocre at best and downright silly at worst. All of the popular American movies were available, dubbed in Persian. Movies such as *Gone with the Wind*, *Spartacus*, *Ben-Hur*, *The Ten Commandments*, and *Samson and Delilah* drew thousands of viewers. John Wayne and Elizabeth Taylor were very popular.

When Elizabeth Taylor visited Tehran, hundreds of thousands of people lined up along the streets to get a glimpse of her. She drew a larger crowd than Dwight D. Eisenhower. Iranians loved America and Americans. Even resentment about Dr. Mosaddeq's overthrow in 1953 by the CIA did not fully dampen the admiration and respect that many accorded Americans and American ideals.

Once a boy was able to find a willing date, one of the first places they would rendezvous was in a movie theatre. There, in the dark and seated in the back, they kissed and fondled each other. Those who were unable to find seats in the back were sometimes the object of jokes and pranks from those sitting behind them. Other places where the enamored couple might go were to the city park or to a coffeehouse. The coffeehouses in Tehran served both tea and coffee. They were much more modern, much cleaner, and much more sleekly decorated than the teahouses of Karbala. They were more often used for social gathering than for intellectual discussion.

I frequented many coffeehouses, drinking one Turkish coffee after another or enjoying tea in a Persian-style glass called *estekan*. First, the server poured a small amount of strongly brewed tea from a teapot being kept warm on top of a samovar. Then he diluted it with hot water from the samovar spigot according to the customer's taste. With a samovar, each customer could have tea exactly as he liked it, strong or light. Usually customers preferred light tea so that they could drink several cups without getting too much caffeine. Part of the allure of drinking this tea was its light, amber-red color in the graceful, clear glass. For Iranians, who are almost all "poets," nothing is more romantic than gazing dreamily into that rich-colored, aromatic tea. (Years later, in America, I waited a long time before I began to see the appearance of such places as Starbucks and Uncommon Grounds. But a paper cup is not the same.)

I had no wish to live in a place like Karbala again. Once in Karbala I had seen the figure of a svelte woman hidden under a black full-body covering called *abaya*. Her body was clearly curvaceous even when completely covered by that garment, and her face was extremely beautiful. I had stared at her without thinking. An accompanying male figure, probably a husband or brother, struck her with his cane on her calf. He hit her so hard that she stumbled, nearly falling to her knees, but she caught her balance, uttered no objection, made no sound, and walked straight ahead as if nothing had happened. My companion, a religious mullah wearing a turban and clerical robe, looked at me, and I looked at him. He knew what I was thinking. His eyes showed sorrow and embarrassment. "Mohammad, please don't think Islam condones that man's actions. The Muslim world has declined over the centuries, and most people have become ignorant of the true, noble faith and its guidelines for behavior. There is no verse in the Quran that sanctions such an action." I told him that the man was an Arab, and he knew Arabic. Why, then, I asked, had he not read the Quran? "What makes you think that the fool can read?" he replied. And before I could say anything further my companion urged me to read and read and read.

That was Karbala, a dichotomy, a contradiction, a place where I learned to be all that I came to be. I was a freethinker because the scholars with whom I was fortunate enough to associate had confided to me much about independence of thought and freedom to choose. One such scholar even told me that, if I were convinced that my conclusions and actions were, indeed, right, and that if I were good in my dealings with my fellow humankind, then God Himself would approve all that I did. Later, I came to recognize the existential foundation of the religious community as espoused by the learned men of that city. I was to be what I chose to be because, according to them, God had endowed me with the greatest power available to humankind, the power of intellection.[24] Goodness of the heart was the most important prerequisite for my own salvation. Mamdasan told me that God was closer to me than my own jugular vein. He quoted verses from the Quran to substantiate his point. "Think about it, Mohammad, do you understand what that means? God is here and here and here," he often reminded me pointing to my heart, my neck vein, and my head. Yet, on that day in Karbala, I had encountered a man who was so possessive that he had publicly hurt and humiliated his female companion simply because I had looked at her. In that respect, Tehran suited me better.

I passed the tenth grade without studying or even attending class on many of the school days. Eleventh grade was a bit more difficult but no

---

24 *Ijtihad* (intellection) is a process practiced by the followers of the Usuli Ja'fari Shi'ite School of Law, whereby a person who has thoroughly studied religious jurisprudence ponders a question and determines an answer. This needn't be done by an official religious scholar, but can be done by any person who has studied religious law and has pondered a situation methodically.

big problem. All I wanted was a passing grade. In twelfth grade, I began to encounter some difficulties. No problem again. I enrolled in a school that did not set high standards. But, still, I hit a wall. I failed. It was hard for me to understand why. I had been told that I was smart. I knew I was smart. I had been well read. Even in those years that I pursued carnal pleasures, I still read hundreds of books. Reading was my hobby. I was even writing, translating, and publishing articles while still in high school. How could I fail twelfth grade?

The day I learned that I had failed twelfth grade, my father was visiting. According to his plan to move his businesses out of Iraq, he took periodic trips to keep tabs on his places of business in Karaj, Iran. As soon as I entered the public bath and greeted him, I leaned against the counter where tea, coffee, and sweets were being served. He was sitting in a comfortable chair and puffing on his Kent cigarette. He asked me if I had passed. I ignored his question. He repeated it. I mumbled in Arabic (because strangers were around) that I'd failed. But my nerves were too frayed and my voice was too weak and stuck in the abyss of my throat to articulate the startling truth. He repeated again, "Did you pass?" I informed him softly that I had failed. I looked at him indirectly. His eyes were piercing. His silence was louder than screams. His disappointment was overwhelming. Then, in disbelief, he exclaimed, "YOU, MOHAMMAD, FAILED?" He emphasized and accented every word. While this seemed a rebuke, and while I was embarrassed to face him, I sensed something more. I sensed his high expectations. Never before had he expressed such confidence in me. My father was always too busy to tell me he loved me. And now, here, expressing his disappointment in my failure, he told me what every child wishes to hear, "I love you, son."

CHAPTER 25

Once a Habit, Always a Habit

TO SAY THAT IN TEHRAN I abandoned my interest in learning is false. I may not have attended school regularly, but I was interested in learning about the world. I was young, independent, and enjoying the delights of the city, and I was a habitual reader. Most of the books available in Tehran bookstores were translations of foreign works such as those of the American writers Mark Twain, Ernest Hemingway, and John Steinbeck, or those of the Russian writers Tolstoy, Dostoyevsky, and Gogol. There were also Iranian writers, Sadeq Hedayat being one of the best and most popular. I read hundreds of books.

And then, there was my intense interest in human behavior. At that time, this interest centered on different religions, not because I wanted to adopt a new religion, but because I was curious about how the human mind works and why there were so many religions. In Tehran, there were several groups promoting new ideas and new religions.

I remember meeting a young man in a barbershop who struck up a conversation with me while we waited for our turns with the barber. Afterwards, we continued our discussion in the street. In the course of conversation, I recognized the themes that kept recurring, and I asked him if he was a Baha'i. His loud and emphatic reply surprised me.

"Yes, I am a Baha'i," he exclaimed proudly. I was concerned that he was talking so loudly in the street where everyone could hear him. Baha'is were not well tolerated in Iran. Neither are they tolerated today. I cautioned him to lower his voice.

"Let them hear me. I am a Baha'i, and I am proud of being a Baha'i," he proclaimed again. His body shook as emotions overtook him. I asked him to calm down or else I would have to leave. He quickly adopted a calmer tone. He invited me to go to one of their meetings to hear the glorious message that their faith was propagating. I had some ideas about Baha'ism and this was an opportunity to find out first hand. I accepted the invitation and, after I got the address from him, we said goodbye.

I arrived at the appointed hour and found some fifteen people at the meeting. The speaker was a slender man of about thirty-five, neatly dressed in a shirt and crisply ironed pants rather than in a religious robe. His face was shaved and his hair carefully combed. He was at ease with himself and clearly calm. The members of his sect were also mostly young and clean-cut. Some of the visitors wore suits while others wore shirts and pants.

As the young man explained the views advocated by Baha'ullah, I was immediately attracted to the sect's philosophy. The Baha'i doctrines promote peace, brotherly love, internationalism, and equality of the sexes. My mother's greatest regret in life was that she did not have the opportunity to learn to read, and these people were proposing total equality for both sexes. The Baha'is not only advocated education for women, they were also active in trying to transform the attitudes of Iranian society in regard to the position of women.

I attended the Baha'i meetings for three months. While I admired their emphasis on social equality, I was less impressed with the religious dogma. The sect was strongly linked to the concept of the Mahdi (Messiah).

After a long debate at one of the meetings, I left the congregation and ended some three months of regular attendance. A gentleman who followed me out also had attended these sessions, but he had not joined in the discussions. He asked me, "Have you ever been to the meetings of Kasravi followers?"

I had no idea who the followers of Kasravi were. I thought he was inviting me to attend meetings of another religious movement. "Who are they?" I asked.

"Come to their sessions and you'll see. It is not another religion," he assured me. "They think like you."

And that was my introduction to what I began to call the "Kasravi Movement." The group was actually called the Society of Free Thinkers (*Baahmaad Azadegaan*), and was a small group of intellectuals that met regularly to discuss Kasravi's ideals and to introduce his teachings to inquisitive individuals. Kasravi had been a scholar and historian. He believed in God and considered religion necessary for human spiritual well-being. He promoted an ideal version of Islam that was to be free from superstitions and irrational beliefs. A fanatic assassinated him in 1946, after his enemies accused him of propagating a new religion.

I considered Kasravi overly idealistic because no religious society, however pure and upright, can be immune from becoming muddied in the swamps of brainless devotees and their leaders. Ideas are like trees that, with time, grow multiple branches. Many of these branches rot. Societal and situational conditions constantly create the impetus for new interpretations of their religion. Chicanery and greed also contribute to such divisions and subdivisions. Thus, in my view, regardless of the initial "purity" of a religion, that purity inevitably becomes diluted by subsequent generations through multiple exegeses.

Yet I found Kasravi's views appealing. One of his goals was to eliminate religious structures, those hierarchical and rigid organizations formed to promote the worship of God. According to Kasravi, benevolence and God-consciousness are the essence of religion, and these two attributes can be achieved without the guidance of a religious hierarchy. Indeed, the Quran teaches that each individual (male or female) is directly responsible to God with no interceder. Thus, Kasravi insisted that he was a true Muslim who rejected distortion of the original teachings of the Quran.

He rejected Shi'ite practices such as veneration of saints and belief in the Mahdi. To him, Shi'ism had been corrupted by the Safavids who ruled Iran between 1501 and 1722. Kasravi also rejected Baha'ism whose origin included belief in the twelfth Imam's occultation and return. He urged people to cleanse Islam, returning to what he believed was *paak deeni* (pure religion).

I found the Society of Free Thinkers much in line with my own thoughts. The man who had invited me to their meetings was a professor of sociology at Tehran University. We became friends and exchanged ideas in various discussions about the ills of the Iranian society and how the mullahs (self-styled clerics) had hindered the development of the nation with their obstructionism. Like the Kasravis, I believed in women's right to vote, to work, and to be treated equally. I believed that practices such as presentation of passion plays and the use of divination to guide decisions should be abandoned.

However, this group had one practice that I disagreed with. Every year on December 21, they had a ceremony in which they burned books that they felt promoted superstitious practices. They called it the "Night of Fire." In one such ceremony I attended, they burned the books of great Iranian poets such as Saadi (d. 1291), Hafez (d. circa 1389), and Rumi (d. 1273). These celebrated poets were mystics, and Kasravi rejected mysticism.

Even so, I was very impressed with this group. Its members were highly educated and thoughtful people. They espoused a rational approach while applying the lessons of the past as a basis for determining future action. They categorically opposed war and criminal behavior associated with wars and emphasized pursuit of universal peace and equality of humankind. They sympathized with the plight of the poor, not only in Iran but also throughout the world. They advocated universal women's rights and condemned mistreatment of blacks in America. What impressed me most was their tolerance for each other, their unyielding support for secularism in government, and their emphasis on modern sciences and education. Had I stayed in Iran I would have probably found my niche with this group.

CHAPTER 26

A City at War with Itself

WHEN SCHOOLS OPENED IN THE FALL OF 1962, I metamorphosed into a hardworking, well-behaved young man. I moved into my eldest brother Mehdi's house, renting an empty room on the third floor. I gave up drinking large amounts of liquor. Actually, my constitution was beginning to disagree with alcohol consumption. I no longer wasted time riding buses or stopping at sandwich shops waiting for the afternoon cabarets. Chasing girls was put on a back burner. I even reduced the number of movies I saw. However, being a movie buff, I wasn't ready to give them up completely.

I repeated the twelfth grade, but this time I made great adjustments to my previous routines. I took my books, notebooks, and pencils to coffee houses, where I drank Turkish coffee to keep me awake while I studied. Upon hearing that I had not slept for thirty straight hours, one of my uncles warned me that someday I would pay dearly, health-wise, for this kind of excess.

I wrote a note that I was studying, asking my friends not to disturb me, and taped it onto the door of the house. I was grateful that they all respected my wishes once they understood I was serious. Some of them, especially my cousin, Jalal, even helped me find tutors. I began to study day and night. I approached one discipline after another, reading the textbooks. Sometimes, I had to begin with the tenth grade for, regardless of how smart a person is, he/she may forget what he or she has learned, especially if the learning has been superficial to begin with. One can be born a genius, but if guidance and training are absent, natural intelligence is easily wasted. I passed the final exam for the twelfth grade with a 65, but that was well earned and I felt no shame.

On June 5, 1963, the day that I left the building after finishing my test, I was confronted with a city at war with itself. Wherever I turned, I saw smoke and fire rising above the buildings near and far. I heard the rumbling of tanks rolling down the streets several blocks away. Luckily, no one was rioting in the street where I stood. It was almost deserted. I could not help but know that the city of Tehran was in turmoil. I heard sirens, screams, and the chanting many streets away. Angry sounds appeared to rise up and bounce upon the canopy of the sky and echo back to earth. I knew that months and years of controversy and tension had broken out in violence.

A lone taxi drove slowly and cautiously, braking close to me as I motioned it to stop. The driver was nervous. He asked me where I was going. When I named the street, he told me to get in. I asked what was going on. "Hell on earth!" was his reply. I pressed for details. He told me that people had responded to Ayatollah Khomeini's call to revolt. "Some say thousands have been killed. Young man, go home and stay inside. That's what I am going to do. I am going to have to drop you off one street away from your house. Take the lane in between and walk fast. Don't run. You never know, a policeman or a hoodlum might get suspicious."

The taxi driver had reached the vicinity of his own house. He let me off and did not charge me, insisting that I should go home quickly. As I walked through the lane connecting the two streets, I saw some women peering out of the windows and doorways as if they were anxiously waiting for their loved ones or just curious to find out what was happening. I recognized a heavy man who was bleeding from a superficial wound on his abdomen. While he had always been neatly and fashionably dressed when I had seen him in the past, now he was in his t-shirt, pacing back and forth slapping his forehead and weeping. I quickly entered the house and went to my room to turn on the radio. Martial music blasted from the radio. I turned it off and went to a neighbor's house across the lane. The family was pro-Shah, and they were simmering with anger at the audacity of the Ayatollah. They told me that the Shah was so mad that he had ordered the military to crush the riots and restore order even if they had to roll over thousands with their tanks. When the revolt finally subsided, rumors had it that ten thousand people were killed in Tehran alone. However, the actual number was nearer four hundred. We heard that thousands more had also died in Tabriz, Isfahan, Mashhad, Shiraz, and Qum.

The animosity between the Shah and Ayatollah Khomeini resulted largely from the Shah's attempt to curb the power of the clergy. The seeds of tension in the country had been sown after the CIA-arranged coup of August 1953 had ousted the Prime Minister, Dr. Mohammad Mosaddeq, and bolstered the position of Mohammad Reza Pahlavi as Shah. The Shah then embarked on a campaign of intimidation to consolidate his power base by any means possible. Accusing his enemies of being communists, he sent some of them to jail and executed others. The Shah eliminated almost all centers of opposition, leaving untouched only the Shi'ite clergy that enjoyed the strong support of a majority of Iranians. At that time, the Shah prudently avoided a direct clash with the religious hierarchy.

However, when the most popular and influential cleric, Ayatollah Borujerdi, died in 1961, the Shah recognized his opportunity to eliminate the power of the clergy, the only viable entity remaining that could someday challenge his regime. External political forces, such as revolutionary movements in the Arab world and pressure from U.S. President Kennedy, had induced the Shah to implement some reforms. He announced his "Revolution From the Top," known as the "White Revolution" consisting of six points: land reform, establishment of a literacy corps, women's suffrage, nationalization of the forests, sale of government-owned businesses to private owners, and profit-sharing for workers in factories. In taking these liberal steps forward, the Shah hoped to placate his critics and, at the same time, break the power of the landed aristocracy and create support for his rule among the farmers and factory workers. Rumor had it that he was also planning to take over the endowment lands held by the religious institutions. Critics called these reforms unconstitutional and inspired by the West.

Long before it had become clear that the Shah's concocted reform would fail, Khomeini had criticized the Shah, asserting that his reforms would cause people to lose their moral base and look to the West as an example to emulate. In January 1963, leading an army contingent, the

Shah traveled to Qum, where Khomeini lived and taught, and delivered a harshly worded threat against religious leaders who had opposed his reforms. Khomeini was not fazed. He condemned the Shah again and accused him of being a lackey of the United States.

The first of many direct confrontations with the Shah came in March 1963 when the army attacked the Fawziyya Religious School in Qum, killing some of Khomeini's students. Khomeini's response to this savagery was vehement. He compared the Shah to the hated Yazid, the exemplar of evil who had killed Imam Husayn in 680 CE. He called the young victims innocent martyrs. Khomeini's verbal attack on the Shah was unprecedented, and the conflict between the two henceforth became more pronounced and personal.

June 3, 1963, was the annual commemoration of Imam Husayn's martyrdom. Seething from the killing of his students in Qum, Khomeini used the occasion to urge the populace to revolt. His denunciation of the Shah's regime was heeded by a great number of people, among them members of the National Front, students, and the bazaaris (the middle class businessmen of the bazaars who have always played a prominent role in the political destiny of Iran). Three days of riots began on June 5, 1963, the day that I witnessed the violence in the streets of Tehran.

Khomeini's criticism of the Shah over these issues gave voice to popular sentiment. In 1964, the Shah put Khomeini under house arrest and finally exiled him from the country to Turkey. From there, Khomeini took up residence in Iraq, initially in Karbala as a guest of Ayatollah Mohammad Shirazi. Later, he moved to Najaf.

Before the revolt of June 5, 1963, I had no knowledge of the Ayatollah who was to become even more popular and influential than the Grand Ayatollah Borujerdi. In the following years, I witnessed the continuing acrimonious struggle between the Shah and Ayatollah Khomeini who, in 1979, toppled the monarchy, established the Islamic Republic of Iran, and founded a new world order, thus changing the history of the world.

CHAPTER 27

Beating the System

HEN I FINISHED HIGH SCHOOL, the military draft was the next step. I dutifully signed up with the hope that the lottery system would exempt me, but I lost, which meant that in three months I would be ordered to report for duty. Still, I wanted to continue my education in college. Where? Iran had only a handful of universities and colleges in the early sixties. My option was to choose a country abroad. Among my choices were Israel, Italy, or the United States. Of course, the United States stood out as the most desirable. It was the dream of every young Iranian.

However, the task of getting an exit visa was not simple. There were rules to follow, bribes to pay, doors to knock on, and more bribes to pay. It would have been easier if I were a member of the "One Thousand Families."[25] In the absence of such high and mighty connections, the next best tool was *parti-baazi*. In other words, if you knew someone who knew someone who was related to a friend of your relative, doors could be opened. No problem, I said to myself. I am going to find a friend of the family, a military officer, or a member of the SAVAK, someone who could help me get out of the country. As luck had it, I found out that I was in a "closed-door period," and during such periods students were not allowed to go abroad. His imperial majesty, the Shah of Shahs, had

---

25 *Hezaar Famil*, in Persian, is an arbitrary expression rather than an accurate number. "One Thousand Families" was used to describe the powerful and "connected" families of Iran. Wealth, power, and control were ascribed to the members of that privileged group.

the habit of decreeing sporadic "open door" periods of short duration for students to go abroad to study. The number allowed to go was limited to approximately four hundred students. "When is it going to be open?" I asked every bureaucrat that I happened to know, from the police chief in Karaj to multiple other officers in Tehran who, in one form or another, were connected to the process of study abroad. The more I asked and the harder I tried, the more people became aware that I wanted to go to study in America. Almost everyone who knew me in that town of eight thousand people was wondering if I was going to beat the system. There seemed to be no way out.

It was June, and the hot sun shone sharply. My desire, my hope, my fixation to find a way to go to America and study made me hate those miserable sunny days. Going from one office to another, from one ministry to the next, and from one person to his friend had drained my energy. I could not believe that I could not beat the system. When you live and grow up in a corrupt country like that of the Shah, you know that there is always a way. I was not going to accept defeat.

I tried the education ministry, the foreign ministry, the police stations in both Tehran and Karaj, and the various offices that could give me some kind of *khorooji* (exit visa). Finally, one office kicked me out without speaking to me. They had gotten tired of me. I stood outside on the marble steps totally dejected, my brain throbbing, and my pride hurting. How insolent these people were. They didn't know who I was. I was a very important person. I kept dreaming about someday in the future when I would show them and teach them a lesson. I tried one more office. There, I was literally lifted from the floor by two security guards who grasped me under my armpits, took me out of the huge building, and dumped me on the steps next to a marble column. They left, admonishing, "And don't you come back again." Again, with hurt pride, my imagination took me to a future date when I would exact my revenge. Those fools didn't know with whom they were dealing, I told myself. Unfortunately, I had neglected to get their names. Helpless, I stood up, lonely but rebellious with a constant companion of anger inside me urging me to go back and beat the heck out of those ignorant snobs. How dare they insult and humiliate me? I imagined a scene that was going to be pow, wow, smack, crash, with sudden punches to the left and to the right. The way John Wayne did it in the movies. Slug one while kicking the other at the same time. Fortunately, I did not act on this impulse.

Still, I did not give up. I had one more place to check. A friend had given me the name of a department that arranged exit visas during the open-door period for the children of the privileged. What did I have to lose? I was also ready to pay. I was armed with several hundred *toman* (even though every eight *toman* equaled one dollar, the purchasing power of one *toman* in Iran was about one dollar at that time). I opened the door to the office, expecting to see a desk where only one person with whom I could reason would be sitting. Since this was the closed-door period, all I wanted was to find someone who would change the date of my application from June back to May when the "door" had been open. Stamp it, take a hundred or two, and I would be on my way. It all made sense to me.

What I saw made my stomach sink. The room was huge with desks only about five feet apart, and secretaries with typewriters busy at work. People were talking, walking, and looking busy. How in the world could I offer money to one of them in such an open space? Voices echoed throughout the place, as if it were a warehouse turned into an office. It was impossible to go through my planned ritual without attracting too much attention.

I approached a desk, having decided to give them the same spiel without hinting at baksheesh (a bribe). The secretary listened and sent me to the next desk. They seemed to have their game perfected. My story went this way: "Even though I knew about the open door during the previous month, my poor mother was very ill in Karbala, Iraq. I was so worried about her health that I just forgot to apply on time for an exit visa to go abroad." My lamentations did not convince them at all. I told them that even though I was studying for the college entrance exam, I still continued to write to her every single day. I asked them if there was any way that they could make an exception and let me go to America to study. They told me there was no way. Completely dejected, I left the office putting my life in Destiny's hand. That was it. I had tried everything, even lying about my mother, saying she was sick and could possibly be dying without having seen her son. How heartless people can be!

Before leaving the building, I paused to take a drink from the water fountain. Immersed in my disappointment, I did not notice a young man of about thirty standing next to me.

"Did I hear you say you were born in Karbala, Iraq?" he whispered, then pretended to take a short sip of water.

I replied affirmatively.

"And are your parents really in Karbala right now?"

Yes, of course.

"Do you know anyone in the Iranian Embassy in Baghdad or at the consulate in Karbala?"

"They're all our friends," I responded, not understanding why he was asking such detailed questions. But, I continued to talk enthusiastically. "I still remember their names."

"There is a law that many people are not aware of. The only way you can get out of Iran at this time is to request to go to visit your parents before reporting for military service. No one can deny you this right. If your parents are in another country, they have to give you a round trip passport to see your parents and say good-bye. The Shah just let four hundred kids leave Iran to study abroad. All the children of the big shots took advantage of it. There is no other way that you can go now. The only way for you to get out of this country is to ask for visitation time with your parents before reporting for military service."

I began to perk up.

"Listen to me and listen carefully," he continued. "You must ask for a two-way passport to Iraq and back. They'll give you a short time, a maximum of one or two months. You can't go anywhere else with this passport. If anyone asks you about your plan to go to America, deny it. It doesn't matter who asks you or how he asks you. People have their ways of getting you to talk by acting chummy and friendly. Don't fall for their tricks. Deny it, deny it, and deny it. Tell them you just got word that your mother is sick, and you have the right to visit your parents before you serve your country. Do you understand?"

Yes, I did.

"When you get to Karbala, as you're walking by the river, toss your passport in the river. Then go to the consulate and tell them you lost your passport. Don't tell them what kind of passport you had to begin with.

They will issue you a new international passport. You can go anywhere you want with that passport. Do you get it?"

I nodded yes. God in heaven, you do have angels on earth. That's all I could say to myself. I asked him if I could do anything for him. My hand slid down to the pocket of my pants. He tapped my arm. "No, nothing. I have one request, though," he added.

"Anything, anything. You've been extremely helpful."

"When you go to Karbala and are visiting the shrine of Imam Husayn, please pray for me." I asked for his name. "No name, no name. Just pray for me, and God will know for whom you're praying. Can you do that? Would you do that?" My eyes were damp again. My throat was dry and hoarse when I promised him that I would. We shook hands and gratefully I turned to leave.

He had finished sipping some more water from the fountain. He called me again and gave me the name and address of the office where I should go to ask for such a passport. He told me what I had to do first in Karaj, where I was residing. Then slowly, with hunched shoulders and a humble walk, he went through the door and back to the big room.

Almost all government officials in Karaj knew I was planning to pursue my education in America. It took almost a week to break their determination to stop me. In the police station, in a meeting with police officials and a couple of army staff officers, they made me sign an affidavit that if I did not return, my father would pay them twenty thousand *toman*. They even swore that they would get me if I left without doing my military service and came back years later. I promised them that I would return as soon as I had visited my parents. Even so, they were sure—and I was sure—that I was headed for America. And I had no doubt that a four or five-way division of the twenty thousand *toman* fine was already being planned in their minds. As fate had it, they did get to enjoy their dream of using their shares, and I did everything that I was advised to do by the "angel" for whom I sincerely prayed in the shrine of Husayn in Karbala and many times afterwards.

Approximately three weeks before my departure from Iran, Sorush, one of my friends, who was a SAVAK employee, approached me and asked, "Have you recently received a letter from a friend in Moscow?"

Flabbergasted, I replied affirmatively and inquired how he knew. He had read the letter in my folder at the SAVAK.

The letter was from my childhood friend who had been a classmate of mine since first grade. He was among the children who were unceremoniously moved back from second grade to the first. He was the same school friend in the Iraqi school who had decided to return to the Iranian school and had lost one year because we had decided not to participate in the demonstrations against the Iraqi government while in eighth grade. And he was one who chose to go to Moscow to continue his education during Abd al-Karim Qasem's tenure in office. All I knew about him in 1959 when I finally decided to leave for Iran was that he was interested in becoming a film distributor to Baghdad theaters, a business that was unlikely to succeed.

Sorush's advice to me was firm, "If you wish to go to the United States, make sure your answer is indignant about his choice of place to go for his education." What was I to think? Why should I insult my friend and toss to the wind years of friendship and camaraderie with someone I had known since childhood just because he had chosen to study in Moscow? In his simple, friendly letter, he had related what had happened during the four-year separation between us. He had married a Russian woman and they were happily expecting the arrival of their first child. Congratulations were definitely in order, not a sharp rebuke over his choice of location.

Life, however, is often cruel when living under constant surveillance. I did what I was advised. I wrote to Hossein, berating him for his choice by asking, "Why did you go to Moscow instead of London, Washington, or a western European country?" Knowing that the KGB (the Soviet Union's intelligence agency) would read the letter, my friend returned it with a simple note: "I don't have the time to read such rubbish." Soon Sorush told me that my file in the SAVAK now contained my letter as well as Hossein's response. All three letters were side by side. There would be no problem caused by the SAVAK when I left the country.

CHAPTER 28

Bus Trip to Baghdad

THE BUS TRIP FROM TEHRAN TO BAGHDAD gave me an opportunity to reflect on my four-year sojourn in Iran. Time had passed quickly, but life in Iran had been eventful. I had learned to rely on myself and thus I looked on my forthcoming travels with much anticipation.

I was beginning to doze off when I heard some passengers' loud comments. Opening my eyes, I saw dozens of shiny new buses being driven in the opposite direction toward Tehran. The road snaked through the mountains and the parade of buses was impressive indeed. I heard someone exclaim with patriotic elation, "The pride of Iran!" Then another sarcastically commented, "Yes but did we build the buses ourselves?" A sharp jab aimed at the ineptitude of Iran's monarchical regime followed: "No, this country can't even make a pin, let alone build a bus."

Someone chided in disgust, "Do you always have to criticize the Shah?"

"My dear brother," I heard the antagonist utter. "I am not criticizing the Shah. Our whole country is corrupt to the core. Iran has everything: iron, coal, copper, oil, and even gold. You name it; we have it. We have all that we need to be a second Japan in Asia. Why do we have to buy everything from Europe and America?"

The discussion was heating up. In the back of the bus, a man rose from his seat and his loud voice cut through the discussion, "I've heard enough of these treasonous comments. Do you want me to show you who I am?"

A pall of silence settled like a cloud of smog. The passengers hushed. Everyone knew what he meant. Rumor had it that whenever three people gather together, one of them is likely to be a spy from the SAVAK. The speaker was obviously a Savaki. His grey-haired mother and his beautiful wife accompanied him. It was clear that his display of power would have to be followed by some more bravado.

"We are still in Iranian territory, and Qasr-e Shirin (near the Iran-Iraq border) is ahead of us. I can report you to the authorities, you traitorous coward. What do you have to say now?" Obviously he was demanding an obsequious apology.

Placing his right hand over his heart and bowing slightly, the subdued man obliged, saying humbly, "I am really sorry your excellency. I didn't mean to disparage Iran and his imperial majesty. I love Iran and am ready at any time to sacrifice my life for my country and the *Shahanshah* (king of kings)." Most of the passengers sympathized with the apologizing critic because he had merely expressed the sentiment of the majority of Iranians, yet now he had no choice but to grovel.

The power and control of the *Savaki* had been established. Now it was his opportunity to flaunt his victory. "I am going to report you anyway. A few years in a jail cell will teach you a good lesson." Further apologies continued. Other passengers participated. Finally, an appeal from several passengers to the mother and wife induced them to intercede, and the *Savaki* sat down, content that his authority had been well recognized.

When we reached the city of Khanaqin in Iraq, just beyond the Iranian border, we were permitted to step outside, stretch out our legs, and rest. As the Savaki exited from the bus, two tough-looking passengers grabbed him under his arms, lifting him off the ground. Others followed them behind the back of the bus. They slapped him in the face and punched him in the stomach. Then, stretching his arms up toward the sky, they pushed him against the bus. He begged loudly for mercy. Other passengers rushed to his aid, pleading for his release. Finally, it was his mother who prevailed. She slapped one of the two assailants while admonishing both, adding indignantly, "And you asked me to intervene on behalf of the man who had insulted the Shah! I will put a curse on you when I visit the Shrine of Imam Husayn in Karbala."

The two assailants desisted and the tension of the confrontation was diffused, but the Savaki's partially damp trousers exposed his humiliation. The assailants bowed to the mother politely, uttering the usual Persian formality, *"Chashm"* ("Upon my eyes," i.e. "Yes Ma'am, I will do your bidding"), and humbly reentered the bus.

CHAPTER 29

Karbala, Again

REACHING KARBALA LATE IN THE AFTERNOON, I visited my mother, who had made my favorite dish of eggplant and chicken with basmati rice. We recalled the good times of the past years and spoke about my younger sister's forthcoming wedding. I expressed my apologies that I would not be able to attend her wedding because of my intent to visit friends and relatives in Europe and to travel to America in order to begin study in college in September 1963. When my father arrived, it was all business as to when and how I could obtain a new passport and when I should go to Baghdad to get visas to the countries I planned to visit.

The next day I went to the Iranian Consulate. Even though the clerk in Tehran had advised me to throw my passport in the river, I was reluctant to do so. Instead, I kept it hidden in my pocket. As soon as I entered the office, I encountered the same person who had originally issued my international passport four years earlier. After our usual greetings and an offer of tea that I politely refused, I reported that I had lost my passport. That was not a problem. A new passport was issued as a continuation of the original to be renewed in approximately fifteen months. From there, I proceeded to my first destination in Karbala, the Shrine of Imam Husayn. I had to keep my promise to my "guardian angel."

My planned route to America was to go through Europe to England and to sail from there to America. My father got all my tickets and the needed visas for me. However, due to political turmoil, he did not get a visa to England. On February 8, 1963, there had been a coup d'état in Iraq,[26] during which Abd al-Karim Qasem was murdered. Afterward, there was a period of violent purging of Communists—several thousand were killed and as many were imprisoned. In the summer of 1963, during our attempt to get the visa for England, my habitually cautious father was reluctant to approach the British Embassy because it was located close to the area of turmoil. We decided it would be best to acquire it along the way. With my plans in place, I spent time visiting friends and saying goodbye.

As far as I could see, nothing had changed in Karbala. Trucks were spraying water to clean the same dusty streets. I visited the same teahouses and found the same people involved in discussions and gossip. I joined in and spent hours talking and reminiscing about the old days and found that some of my schoolmates had gotten married and had children. I went to a restaurant to have *kofte* kebab with some friends. The savory ground lamb grilled with onion, tomato, and spices was one of my favorites, but I missed the beer that I'd had with it in Tehran.

Babajoon was still thin and wiry and as vigorous as when I had left him in 1959. I visited him at his hammam and was given the usual Coca-Cola from the same icebox. There were no more instructions about good deeds, good words, and good thoughts. I guess those precepts were for the very young. By then I was old enough to be responsible for myself.

I visited Ayatollah Sayyid Mohammad Shirazi (d. 2001). This Ayatollah was our family's Marja'-e Taqlid,[27] a religious authority who offered guidance on religious matters to his followers.

I was offered tea from a constantly simmering samovar, and we chatted amicably. I had known Ayatollah Shirazi for several years and had found him extremely open-minded and well read. Indeed, he was well versed

---

26 This coup d' état was fomented by Britain and America because Qasem was in the process of nationalizing Iraq's oil industry.

27 Islam, as presented in the Quran, has no officially appointed clergy. Each Muslim (male and female) is considered individually responsible to God. It is the duty of the individual to be educated, to read the Quran, and to determine for himself or herself the proper behavior for a good Muslim. However, many Muslims do not have the time or reading ability to do such an extensive study of the Quran. They have come to rely on religious scholars—those who spend their lives studying the Quran and Islamic law—to advise them. Such religious scholars are called Marja'-e Taqlid among the Shi'ites and mufti in the Sunnite world.

in both Islamic and secular sciences. During our previous conversations, his comments on Nietzsche's statement, "God is dead," a very hot topic of discussion among intellectuals and pseudo-intellectuals at the time, had left a lasting impression on me. Shirazi pointed out that Nietzsche was mistaken to consider man's moral capacity sufficient to replace God as the final arbiter of good and evil.

Since I had come to say goodbye before leaving the country and eventually heading to America, he began by encouraging me to establish a student center for propagation of Islamic religion during my stay in America. I was amused because not only did I not consider myself religious, my early rejection of many of the superstitious ideas promoted by some ignorant clerics was well known. Even though I should have kept my disdain for religious hypocrites to myself, I blurted out that, frankly, I often forgot to perform my daily prayers regularly. In addition, I had no respect for the many ignorant people claiming to be Muslims just because they prayed regularly while their lack of social concern and moral behavior was embarrassing. "Why should I pretend to be someone I am not?" I asked.

"As for your daily prayers, it is a matter between you and God. Furthermore, I am not asking you to teach Islamic religion or convert unbelievers. If you and some other Muslim students could gather once a week and spend one hour reading the Quran it would do a world of good for your souls." The Ayatollah's response to my negative reaction was stoically unemotional. At that point, I did not feel I should perturb him anymore by disagreeing. In fact, I told him that I would try. He knew me well and was quite aware of my reluctance to adhere to any of the diktat of religious orders. He was also cognizant of the fact that, theoretically, Islam forbade any coercion in religion. Men and women are looked upon as responsible beings who have to face God and account for their actions themselves. It is not anyone's prerogative to pressure another to perform the daily religious acts of worship.

Then our conversation turned toward more theoretical matters. Ayatollah Shirazi expounded upon a theory that was being promoted in the religious circles of Karbala and Najaf. As he elaborated on his subject, I was stunned by the phrase, "When we establish the Islamic government."

I interrupted him by asking, "What?"

He repeated the same phrase. Again, I asked for clarification.

"If you would permit me to elaborate, I will tell you what, how, and why," he calmly offered.

I apologized but could not hide my total surprise. "I am really sorry," I said. "It is inconceivable that a theocracy might supplant an existing nation-state government in the present day." His face was beginning to redden, and I felt guilty that I had agitated him. In a society that always emphasized humility and respect, I was definitely out of line. But I was shocked. Not only was the idea of an Islamic government ludicrous, it was not to my liking. Yet, prudence necessitated silence. In any case, I resolved to listen but muttered simply, "I find it impossible."

"Why?" he responded.

"Whose Islam?" I asked. "I am sure you know better than I that there are many schools of law and multiple factions that call themselves Muslim."

He interrupted me at this point. He explained that he was talking about an Islamic government in Iran and Iraq run by the Twelver branch of Shi'ism that would respect minorities and their beliefs. To him the two countries were very compatible, each country having a large majority of like-minded Shi'ites.

I was dumbfounded. "But how and why?" I asked.

Ayatollah Shirazi began his exposition by stating that the Hidden Imam had been absent for many years. I tried to suppress a smile. He noticed it and used it to expand his argument.

"I see you smile and that's understandable. It has been so long that the Expected One has not reappeared. I am sure some people are beginning to doubt the Imam's occultation. Let us say that he is still in hiding and may not appear for another thousand years. The question is, who is the legitimate ruler during his absence? Certainly not the Shah and his like."

His question gave me the chance to take a shot at religious authorities. "As you know, the Shah, and various other kings who preceded him, 'rent' the office of the Imam from the religious authorities in Mashhad. This political arrangement gives legitimacy to the monarchical system of Iran."

Ayatollah Shirazi continued, "This is, indeed, an arrangement that has its roots in the Safavid dynasty [1500-1724]. The Safavids claimed they were holding power temporarily until the coming of the Mahdi. That claim continued and evolved into 'renting' the office from the keepers of the

Shrine of Imam Reza in Mashhad. That is only a political ploy. No sane person could believe that the Imam would sanction such an idea."

I nodded in agreement.

"We are of the opinion that the true and legitimate interim rulers are the religious jurisprudents since they are the true representatives of the Twelfth Imam." Ayatollah Shirazi was opening a completely new line of thought in the political and religious doctrines of Ja'fari Twelver Shi'ism. "It is possible that the Expected Imam may not appear for another thousand years. In our opinion, the Shah's regime should be replaced by a knowledgeable and just *faqih* (religious jurisprudent) or a *shoura* (council) of such men. The Shah must go and justice must prevail."

I left the Ayatollah's house, and time, as usual, removed the conversation from my memory until 1979 when Ayatollah Khomeini, who had espoused and popularized the same political theory while in exile in Iraq, was able to topple the Shah and replace him with his brand of Islamic government, the very same type of government that Ayatollah Shirazi had described to me in 1963.

CHAPTER 30

European Sojourn

THE PURPOSE OF MY TRAVELS through Europe was twofold: to get a visa to the United States and to visit and see the sights. Fortunately, I had contacts in every country I visited. On my way to Italy, I stayed three days in Damascus and Beirut with friends of my father. In Beirut, I tried to get a visa to England but was unsuccessful. I went on to Italy where one of my brothers, Saheb, was studying political science at the University of Rome and lived in an apartment on the outskirts of the city. Saheb was a smart, opinionated, and outspoken person. He was extremely interested in politics and considered himself a Marxist. He had written and spoken against the Shah on several occasions. Actually, just before I departed from Tehran, my friend Sorush, who worked for the SAVAK, had advised me to remind my brother to cut down on his anti-Shah rhetoric if he wished to get a job when he returned to Tehran.

During the fifteen days of my stay in Rome, Saheb took me many places. He had been in Italy for three years and was an expert guide. We went to the Coliseum, St. Peter's Square, St. Peter's Basilica, the Vatican Museum, and the Sistine Chapel. I had a wonderful time.

One problem that most Muslim travelers had in Europe was finding acceptable food to eat. Muslims do not eat pig meat of any sort.

Furthermore, all meat must be from animals butchered in a particular manner and blessed to be acceptable (halal). In those days, my brother Saheb had no problem eating *haram* (forbidden) meat. Once, when Saheb and I were waiting for the train from Rome to another city, he bought us each a ham sandwich at the train station. He did not divulge that it was ham. I was very hungry and devoured my sandwich as fast as I could, asking for a second as I kept exclaiming how delicious it was. My brother asked with a sly smile, "Are you sure you want another ham sandwich?"

I thought he was joking. "Was this a ham sandwich?" I asked incredulously.

"Yes," was his smug reply. "There was nothing else but ham, and I didn't want you to go hungry."

I almost vomited.

From Italy I left for Germany, where another of my brothers, Hadi, and several of his friends were working in a factory. Germany was in the midst of a miraculous economic recovery due to the ingenuity of its citizens and the toil of millions of migrant workers, mostly from Italy and Turkey. There were some Iranian workers, but most of the Iranians in Germany were students.

The Lufthansa flight from Rome to Frankfurt was smooth until we hit turbulence. It lasted only a short time, but it felt like an eternity. Then, there was a sudden lifting and sinking in my stomach. We had hit an air pocket. Soon after, calm flight followed, making me feel as if I were resting in a boat with a breeze at my back.

Arriving at the Frankfurt Airport, I carried my two suitcases, one in each hand. I was slightly worried, since it was after seven o'clock in the evening and I did not see anyone there to meet me. I expected a half dozen Iranians, but I did not recognize anyone among those milling about the large rotunda. I slowly made a full-circle turn, anxiously scrutinizing the faces before me. Suddenly I recognized a familiar face coming my way.

Mahmood, an industrious, hardworking fellow of thirty-two, had tried to start several businesses but hadn't succeeded with any of them. I recall him trying to sell shoes in Mashhad in his uncle's Persian carpet shop. Then he opened a small factory-shop making parts for prefabricated houses. My elder brother, Mehdi, had provided the capital while Mahmood managed the business. It lasted only a few years because there was little demand. One of his other ideas was to build a garage for automobiles, which would have required a great deal of investment and would have been risky in Tehran because such facilities were not common then.

Thus, Mahmood had decided to go to Germany to work, save some money, and experience a different culture. At the time I was there he was working in a company that made pens.

Mahmood was pleasantly sycophantic, showering his companions with praise and compliments. He was always polite and friendly, yet not overwhelming. It was a pleasure to see him at that moment.

I dropped my bags on the floor and, opened my arms to greet him. We hugged and exchanged the usual cheek-to-cheek kiss of friendship. I also kissed him lightly on the lips. While that's not unusual in the Middle East, it's not done often. However, I was happy to see him, and we were close friends.

I saw a beautiful woman with a curious smile sitting near the gate. I stared at her with interest.

Mahmood chided me, "Stop ogling that woman. You never change! Besides, she is older than you."

"No harm in looking at a beautiful woman who is smiling at me," I said.

"Yes, she is smiling, but not because you're handsome. She is amused with our embrace and you kissing me on the lips. God, I was so embarrassed! You're something else."

"But I was nervous, Mahmood, and really glad to see you. Why was she so amused by our greeting?"

"Because this is probably the first time she ever saw two men kissing. Germans are very interested in other people's customs and cultures. Luckily, they are also well aware of foreign habits. This was an opportunity for her to observe Middle Easterners hugging with such emotion."

"No one was here to meet me. I was afraid that you didn't get Saheb's telegram from Rome, so when I saw you I was really glad."

"We got it," he said shaking his head incredulously. "But Saheb didn't indicate whether it was 7:00 a.m. or 7:00 p.m. Since it was just one sentence indicating your arrival at 7, we thought it was in the morning. Your brother, Hadi, and three other Iranian friends were in the welcoming party, but no plane arrived from Rome. After a long wait, we inquired and found out that your flight would arrive at 7:00 p.m. I stayed, but the rest drove back to Heidelberg. We'll take the train."

Mahmood looked tired, for he had gotten up a couple of hours before 7:00 a.m. and had stayed in the airport until I arrived. I felt bad for the misunderstanding and baffled by the mistake. We took the train to Heidelberg where Mahmood shared an apartment in the suburbs with my brother Hadi.

During the first month of my stay in their apartment we ate a lot of eggs because there was no halal meat available in the markets. I suggested that we buy the meat sold at the butcher shop. To convince them that it would be religiously acceptable, I recited verses from the Quran that explained that, when there is no alternative to consuming "what was forbidden," there would be no harm in doing so. Unfortunately, they were obstinate in maintaining the appearance of piety. I was tired of meatless meals. I finally suggested that Mahmood find either a butcher or a farmer from whom we could buy a live chicken. I volunteered to slaughter it in a halal manner. To slaughter an animal in a halal manner, a person must face Mecca, recite *"Bismillah al-Rahman al-Rahim"* (in the name of God the Most Gracious the Dispenser of Grace), then slit the animal's throat and hold it upside down to allow the blood to drain. This undertaking turned out to be one tragic comedy of "chicken killing."

Mahmood was successful in locating a local German farmer who raised and slaughtered chickens to distribute to small shops. When we arrived at his farm and saw a bloody wooden chopping block set in the middle of a yard, I felt nauseous. I had never before slaughtered an animal. I was getting cold feet, so I was pleased that neither of us had remembered to bring a knife.

"Good," I thought to myself. "This is my way out."

But Mahmood, who was anticipating a warm and delicious chicken stew, was persistent. I had promised to kill a chicken, and I was obligated to do it, especially when Mahmood pointed out, "Your poor brother is sitting in the kitchen peeling carrots, potatoes, celery, and tomatoes, and anticipating a chicken stew." I was trapped. He chided me loudly, "We were so happy when you volunteered to kill the chicken, and now you're chickening out?"

"What's wrong?" the farmer inquired, interrupting our heated discussion.

"We forgot to bring a knife," said Mahmood, his face as red as a lobster.

The kind farmer produced a very small knife.

But I was still looking for an excuse to be relieved of my obligation. The poor chicken, which surely knew her life was in my hands, started wriggling and squawking. I tried another approach. I complained about the chicken's uncooperative behavior saying, "We should just let it go. I can't control it."

Then Mahmood grabbed the chicken with both hands and shouted, "Just grab her head and say *'bismillah'* before you cut it off."

I had no choice. I made an attempt. I can swear that, if a chicken could laugh, she would have burst out in a loud guffaw, making a mockery of the two of us. The knife was so dull that it would not pierce the poor bird's throat. Again, I thought I was off the hook. I shouted that the knife was too dull. The kind farmer understood and rushed into his shed to find a sharper knife. As I looked around, I suddenly came face to face with several women who were watching us from the window on the upper floor of the farmer's house. They were not laughing and did not seem dismayed, but they looked curious. I froze in my place just looking at them as they watched one of God's creatures struggling to escape the hands of destiny.

Finally, we finished the job. We returned to the apartment, plucked the feathers, cleaned the chicken, and made the stew. It was delicious. The experience, however, had been so disconcerting that I immediately wrote a letter to Ayatollah Shirazi in Karbala. I complained that my roommates did not believe me when I told them that, in difficult situations, exceptions could be made. The Ayatollah wrote back that, if and when halal meat cannot be obtained, traveling Muslims might eat the meat that is available. They must not allow themselves to become undernourished and sick. God is indeed much forgiving, a dispenser of grace.

Heidelberg was another beautiful city, and I found the German people extremely friendly and welcoming to foreigners. There was so much to see and enjoy in the city. Mahmood told me that some 20 percent of the Heidelberg University enrollees were from abroad. I visited the University often during the days that my friends were busy working or attending classes. I had lunch at the University and then strolled along Philosophers' Walk, a walking path along the Neckar River near the University that offered great views of the old section of Heidelberg and of Heidelberg Castle. The path is said to have inspired many poets and philosophers from the University who walked there often, seeking solitude and inspiration. I had plenty of time, and I enjoyed the beauty of it.

Because my request in Beirut had been denied, I anticipated that getting a visa from the British Consulate in Frankfurt might be a long process, and that I might have to remain in Germany longer than I had expected. I might even have to abandon the idea of reaching the United States as my final destination. I decided I might as well begin to learn German. I selected some elementary books to learn some of the language on my own, and I often sat in the student union and studied. I had the habit of practicing my German out loud, especially when I was with friends. I used them as sounding boards, and they corrected me if I pronounced a word incorrectly. On one occasion when I had finished reciting my numbers from *ein* to *zehn*, sounding like a boy three years of age, one very impressed German woman started clapping and smiling. It was a bit embarrassing, but she was flushed with patriotic delight to see my enthusiastic attempt to learn her mother tongue. She invited my friends and me for dinner at her house. Upon learning that we were Iranians, she explained that the word "Iran" meant "land of the Aryans," noting our shared ancestry.

"Ah, you know exactly what it means," Mahmood said with a wide smile.

"Of course I do," she said.

When we commented on Germany's impressive progress, she beamed with pride. Pointing to a nearby street she predicted, "Do you see all those little boys? They're all going to be future Hitlers when they grow up."

We were startled. We smiled and nodded respectfully, waiting until after we left to express our astonishment to each other. Of course, the meal she'd prepared had been enjoyable, and we were thankful for her hospitality.

On another occasion we met an elderly German couple whose lunch table was very close to ours. Upon hearing us chat in Persian, they asked about the origin of our language. Our conversation continued, and, since their pronunciation of German words was slightly different from what we were used to, we asked what region of the country they were from. "East Berlin," was their response. Before we said goodbye, they gave us their address and invited us to their place. We had our doubts whether we should accept their invitation but finally decided there was no harm in it.

Their apartment was fairly modest, but they had done their best to prepare a good meal. Their slightly sad demeanor convinced us that they might be among those who had escaped East Germany by climbing the wall that separated East Berlin from West Berlin. Judging by the look of their ages, they could have possibly left sons or daughters with young families back in East Germany. Vicariously, they were experiencing a "family" supper with us.

I had stayed a month in the apartment rented by Mahmood and my brother. The landlady had permitted them to have me stay there for free until my departure to England. The accommodations were fine, though I missed the daily routine of going to a public bath and getting a *keeseh* to exfoliate my body. Swimming in a pool had been a daily luxury for me in the Middle East. During winter, when business was slow, I could often swim by myself in one of the pools in my father's hammam.

The apartment had a big bathtub, and one day I decided to fill it to the rim and have a nice soak. As I slipped into the tub, it immediately overflowed onto the bathroom floor. I did not notice since the radio was playing loudly. The landlady, however, lived directly below. She became livid as the water dripped through her ceiling. When Mahmood and Hadi returned from work, they were politely but firmly told that I had to leave within one week. We searched for a room in the neighborhood.

I rented a room from a woman whose husband had passed away a couple of years earlier. Apparently, as we found out later, she was more in need of company than of a tenant. The room was magnificent and large; the bed was clean, comfortable, and the sheets were changed often. As soon as I awoke, I went back to the previous apartment to eat breakfast and supper with Mahmood and Hadi.

When I returned to my rented room to get a good night's sleep, the woman of the house was waiting with a tray of tea and pastries ready to offer me. At first, I gladly accepted her hospitality and found it a warm gesture of kindness. We sat together in the living room, chatting in broken German supplemented with broken English. She asked me about Iran but soon drifted into a sad conversation about her beloved husband who was taken to his eternal abode at the young age of fifty-five. The two years of loss had been very hard on the woman, and she missed him a great deal. I began to dread those nightly conversations.

One day, I took the train to Frankfurt to the British Consulate to try to get a visa for England, but I was told that I should have gotten it in Baghdad. I took three trips from Heidelberg to Frankfurt, each time hoping to deal with a different person who might give me a visa. After the third rejection, I concluded that the British Embassy in Beirut must have used invisible ink to make a notation in my passport about my appearance there and their rejection of my request for a visa. They must have suspected that, for some reason, the British Embassy in Baghdad had also refused to issue me a visa. In actuality, I had never been to the British Embassy in Baghdad.

As luck would have it, my father had connections with someone in London. He had become friends with Ayatollah Muhsin al-Hakim (1889-1970)[28] from Najaf. Since there was a sizable community of Iranians in London, Ayatollah al-Hakim maintained a representative there to facilitate the religious life of his followers by leading prayers and performing rituals such as weddings and funerals. Britain's policy was to afford special status to such religiously and politically influential personalities.

Al-Hakim's representative in London in the early 1960s was Mr. Mehdi Khorasani, also my father's friend. When I left Iraq to travel in Italy and Germany, my father had made arrangements for me to stay afterward with

---

28 Ayatollah Muhsin al-Hakim (1889-1970) was a renowned Marja'-e Taqlid who succeeded Grand Ayatollah Borujirdi in 1961 after his death. His sons were also religious scholars, but they were politically active. Ayatollah Mohammad Baqir al-Hakim was the head of the Supreme Council for Islamic Revolution in Iraq. He was assassinated by a bomb attack on August 29, 2003, in Najaf. His brother, Abd al-Aziz al-Hakim, was selected by the United States to head the Iraqi Governing Council in December 2003 after the U.S. invasion of Iraq.

Mr. Khorasani in London, and he had given me letters of introduction that I carried with me.

I finally wrote Mr. Khorasani and asked for his assistance. He wrote a letter to the British Consul in Frankfurt, Germany, and assured the Consul that I would be his personal guest, live in his own house, and that as long as I was in England, he would be my personal sponsor.

To the total surprise of the Vice Consul in Frankfurt, I got my visa. His grudging comment to me was, "If my boss had not ordered me to give you a visa, you'd never go to England."

I flew to London Heathrow Airport, thinking that my problems of entering the "Land of Fog" were over. Unfortunately, that was not so. At the airport, many questions were hurled at me. Glances were exchanged between the officials as they showed my passport to one another. More questions were asked. "And where are you staying in London?" I showed them the address and the letter Mr. Khorasani had written to the Consul in Frankfurt, Germany, a copy of which he had forwarded to me. I saw the dilemma begin to dissipate. Heads were shaken, less suspicious grimaces were exchanged, and my passport was stamped. I was respectfully allowed to enter the country.

Among the first things I discussed with Mr. Khorasani when I arrived at his house was the problem of getting a visa for the U.S. I had hoped to leave for America right away to start my studies in the fall of 1963, so that I would not lose another year of my educational life. But it appeared that I might not be able to begin until the fall of 1964. I asked if he thought I would run into the same roadblocks I had experienced when I had applied for a visa to England in Germany. He advised that it was likely.

"Don't worry," he reassured me. "If need be, I know the Ambassador, but I don't think it'll get to that. For now, enjoy staying in London. We'll worry about these matters later." He tried to console me by pointing out that at least I would have a chance to study English at the University of London for a few months.

I signed up for English for Foreign Students at the University of London. In those days, students wore jackets and ties. However, heading for the English class, I was overdressed in a formal black suit, carrying an umbrella, and wearing a well-polished pair of black shoes.

As I left the underground station walking toward the University, I saw an Englishman with a dog regarding me with a smirk. He unleashed his big dog on me. The dog's sudden charge startled me; I backed up, mumbling gibberish. The man immediately called his dog back and watched as I gingerly skirted around them, trembling uncontrollably.

Still anxious and half-terrorized as I entered the classroom, I became even more anxious when I realized that the class had already begun. Some forty students were silently listening to a grey-haired woman who was obviously the teacher. Immediately spotting an empty chair in the back of the room, I slid into the safety of its embrace. The class was quiet, the woman cheerfully smiled.

"Good " said the congenial teacher, "you finally showed up."

"I am lost." A roar of laughter filled the air.

"So, you are lost and suddenly decided to join the class?"

"There was a dog out there," I stated indignantly. This time the laughter stung and sweat drenched my body.

"Why are they laughing?" I asked myself. Everything I was saying was true. I was late because I did get lost for a short time and there was a dog out there blocking my way. From the laughter, I could tell that I was expressing myself poorly. Having noticed my frustration and meager ability in language, she asked my name, my country of origin, and welcomed me to her class. I found myself relaxing.

The students were friendly, especially a pretty French girl who showed me where the cafeteria was and then ate lunch with me. I really liked her, and we spent a few days having lunch together. However, I realized that since I would be going to go to America and should be learning English using American pronunciation, the class would not be beneficial. But since I was stuck in London, I decided that I might as well enjoy my stay in that impressive city.

I spent the next several months sightseeing alone and sometimes with young Iranians who, possibly for similar reasons, were seeking refuge from their own aloneness. I visited all the interesting sights: Hyde Park, Big Ben, the Tower of London, Buckingham Palace, Piccadilly Square, Soho at night, and of course the British Museum. I visited them again and again. I went to movie theaters to see *Lawrence of Arabia* and *West Side Story* and many other movies. In the course of approximately four months, I got to know London and its landmarks almost like a guide.

Of course, I also visited the American Embassy to try to get a visa. The same problem greeted me. "Why do you want to go to America?"

To visit.

"Are you looking for work?"

No.

"Sorry I cannot give you a visa."

I would try again the following month.

For lunch, I often ate in a cafeteria near Putney Bridge, though it was always crowded, especially on Sundays. Rarely did I find an empty table to enjoy my meal alone, but I did not mind. I struck up conversations with whoever was sitting at the table. Many people were friendly, perhaps drawn by my own friendly attitude.

One Sunday noon, I asked a woman and her twenty-year-old son if I could join them at their table. They had just finished their Sunday worship. I asked if they were members of the Church of England. "We're Quakers," said the nice woman. She introduced herself as Mrs. Barlow and her son as Dudley.

"Followers of William Penn," I exclaimed with delight because I happened to have read about William Penn and was familiar with the concept of "inner light." Mrs. Barlow corrected me, stating that George Fox had founded Quakerism, but I could tell she was delighted that a Muslim knew of her religion. Thereafter, I saw her and Dudley at least once a week. I attended their meetings and was impressed with their contemplative life, their silent meditation, and their calm, relaxed demeanor.

After my third visit to the American Embassy, I was told not to show up there again. They were not going to give me a visa to visit the United States. It was not until Mr. Khorasani waved his magic wand that I was allowed to buy a ticket and board the RMS *Queen Mary*, from Southampton, England, to New York City.

Mohammad 1972

PART III

ALBANY, NEW YORK

The Egg Performing Arts Center (Albany)

CHAPTER 31

First Day in the USA

ERTAIN EVENTS IN HUMAN LIFE leave indelible imprints and, though insignificant to others, remain chiseled in the minds of those experiencing them. I doubt that anyone ever forgets his or her day of arrival in America. Mine was April 28, 1964.

I had selected America as the place to continue my education after considering many possible destinations. Italy or Germany would have been reasonable choices, and I did have several friends in England where there was a large Iranian community.

Yet I must admit that I had become enamored with America in the fourth grade when I read biographies of Lincoln and Jefferson that had been written for children. I didn't come to America to find a job. I came because America was the land of idealism and freedom. What better place to continue my studies than the United States?

Upon arrival in the U.S., the RMS *Queen Mary* passed by the Statue of Liberty. I was elated that I was finally going to see the land that had graced the earth with so many good men. To be honest, I didn't know much about the women who had also set their marks slowly but deliberately, and sometimes stubbornly, on the destiny of this country. Neither did I know much about the racism in the hearts of many Americans.

The ship slowly docked at the pier. Preparing to disembark, all passengers were to meet briefly with an immigration officer. Standing in line, each traveler showed his or her documents. When my turn came, the officer appeared irritated. He was big and fat. I mean *big* and *fat*. His stomach, at times, would lift the table at which he sat.

Looking at my passport, the fat officer barked at me, asking why I had come to America.

"To visit," I said. After all, that's what my visa had been issued for. What else could I say? I had learned long ago not to tell people about my dreams. And in this case, I wasn't sure how my dream would turn out. I couldn't say, "I am visiting America, but I am hoping to change my visitor visa to a student visa after getting accepted in a university." I wasn't about to tell the officer my life story or my future dreams. He didn't seem interested in that, anyway.

"Are you planning to work?" he asked. Apparently, he thought I had come in search of a job.

I laughed at the question, thus making him angry.

"How much money do you have with you?" the officer barked again.

"Six hundred and fifty British pounds," I answered.

"Do you have the money with you now?"

Of course I did. It was in my pockets.

"Let me see it," he demanded.

"Right now, here?" The line behind me was silent. I looked at the queue that snaked around. His demand was not proper with all these people watching. I had been drilled again and again not to show my money publicly. Some people might try to steal it. Pickpockets are quick. They might even use a knife. So I was supposed to be careful not to display my money openly.

Again, he barked his demand. I detected a sound of victory in his voice. Obviously, he didn't believe that I had the money with me. "Yes, show me the money!" He paused for emphasis after every word. He thought he had trapped me, especially when I hesitated a bit longer by looking around at all the people who listened and fidgeted as they were being held up by this nuisance. The fat officer looked triumphantly down his nose at me. His eyes and nose and ugly lips and his whole flabby body told the story of his encounters with many hundreds if not thousands of stowaways and hungry people doing everything possible to enter the Land of Opportunity, who had been grasped and smashed in his paws.

Reluctantly, I took out my money and started separating it into piles of like denominations on the table.

"Is that all?" At first, disappointed, but still persistent, he asked if I had more in other pockets.

"Do you want to see everything?" My smiling face did not help the situation.

He scowled in response. Loudly, he demanded, "Yes, everything. I also want to see your watch."

I emptied all the change that was in my pockets but was not happy about showing him my watch. It was my mother's last gift when I'd left Karbala on my way to the U.S. "Here, son," she had said, "this is for you. It is solid gold. Haji Ali Akbar, a religious and honest man, made sure it was worth a lot of money. I bought it for three hundred dinars. If something happens and you are in dire need of money, sell it. As long as you wear it, no one will notice how much it is worth." When I took off the watch now, I thought it was going to be the fat officer's baksheesh.

The fat officer counted the money, slowly, deliberately, and sure enough it was 650 pounds and some change. Still, he was looking for an excuse to detain me. Suddenly, he found it.

"Bursar!" he yelled loudly.

The financial officer approached him and was admonished for not looking at my passport carefully. My passport was five days short of the required six-month extension period. I had missed the deadline by five days. According to the fat officer, I needed to have six months or more to enter the United States of America, not six months minus five days. At last, he had won, and the passengers who had been unhappy with the delay would now blame me and not him.

The bursar looked at me sadly and said, "Why did you do that to us, sir?"

By then I had understood what the whispered discussions were all about, and for the first time, I was beginning to think that the fat officer was going to send me right back to England. A flash of inspiration suddenly crossed my mind. The day I had shown my passport to the bursar was five days earlier when I had boarded the ship. I blurted out that fact loudly. "If you add the five days on the seas it would be exactly six months."

The quiet passengers burst into loud laughter that embarrassed the fat officer greatly. He had no reason to delay the ordeal any longer.

"I am going to give you a ten-day permit to stay in New York," he said. "You must extend your passport at the Iranian consulate and go to the immigration office to extend your stay in the United States. Do you understand?"

Yes, I did.

As I left him, a few hands touched me on my shoulder and wished me good luck. I walked onto the pier and the clock said 10:30 a.m. An acquaintance of my father, Mohammad Kazemi, was waiting to drive me to the YMCA somewhere close to Macy's where he had reserved a room for me.

After settling me in my room, Mr. Kazemi left. I went out to look around. I spent some three hours in Macy's. I walked up and down the aisles, past men's clothes, women's attire, the perfume section with beautiful women sampling Channel No. 5 and other perfumes. Hunger overtook me. Chock Full o' Nuts invited me in. I sat at the counter and looked at the waitress.

"What will it be, honey?" the middle-aged waitress asked.

I knew very little English so I pointed to the menu listed on the wall.

She realized I did not know English. "How about a chicken salad and some milk?"

I nodded yes and held out my hand with a ten-dollar bill, a five-dollar bill, and some change all in my palm.

"That's too much money, hon." the waitress explained and gently took the cost of the sandwich from my hand.

For several days, chicken salad sandwich became my favorite. Not only was it tasty, it was the only sandwich I knew how to order.

During that time, I spent a lot of time strolling in the streets. Two physical features of the people I saw struck me most. First, many of them had crooked teeth and second, a great number of them, men and women, were thin. Being tall made their slim figures look attractive.

Walking the hallways of the YMCA each time I approached my room, I had to cover my nostrils. The accumulated odor of human sweat over the course of decades had added an invisible layer on the walls and the floors. The room itself, though more tolerable, was still nauseating. I hated every moment of the six days I stayed in that smelly room. I remembered my seventh-grade science teacher's excuse for returning to Iraq from the United States. Not only was the odor of the YMCA nauseating, I did not like the fact that men bathed in a communal shower room. I made it a habit to take my showers very early in the morning or late at night. I also was taken aback watching men fill the sinks with water, shaving their beards and washing their faces exactly as the science teacher had described it almost a decade earlier in Karbala where religious instructions insisted that washing must be done under running water. I watched carefully and noticed that after their routine they did, indeed, turn on the faucet to clean their faces and hands with running water before drying them with towels. Still, the process was dismaying.

CHAPTER 32

Albany, Here I Come

SOON AFTER I ARRIVED IN NEW YORK CITY, Mr. Kazemi helped me enroll in a ten-week course at the American Language Institute (ALI) at New York University. The program taught English to foreign students to prepare us for the Test of English as a Foreign Language (TOEFL).

One of the teachers and I became friends. Professor McNaughton was religious and interested in spreading the message of Christianity, and I was very interested in learning about various religions. From early years when I'd been in the elementary school and had begun reading voraciously, I had learned about many religions and orientations and had become fascinated with the various religious denominations and their multiplicity. I am afraid that my genuine interest in learning gave him the wrong impression. He thought I was searching for answers and was seeking to find the Ultimate Truth. He had decided to bring me the True Light patiently and carefully. I tolerated his proselytizing mindset. We developed a very friendly and respectful attitude toward each other. I didn't actually realize the extent of his religious zeal until much later, when I decided to marry a woman who was Christian and he adamantly opposed an interfaith union. However, until we parted on unpleasant terms, Professor McNaughton and I tolerated each other's approach. I had a purely philosophical interest in religions while he had ulterior motives that compelled him to show a great deal of patience with me.

On one occasion, though, he essentially chastised me when I unintentionally questioned the concept of the Trinity. It was in a Bible study session and Professor McNaughton was discussing the core of Christian theological doctrine that God the Father, that unlimited, undefined being, manifested Himself in Jesus. The topic prompted me to ask, "Isn't this statement contradictory?" Silence followed my curious questioning.

Professor McNaughton, his voice rising, demanded, "Speak up, Mohammad."

I was totally surprised. I was not accustomed to the Professor's abrupt and challenging tone. I said nothing.

Again he commanded, "Speak up!" He had an unusual look on his small face. I detected drops of saliva on his lips and was fearful that he would start foaming. I realized that I should have kept quiet in the first place. But, now, I was caught between a rock and a hard place. I had uttered what I should not have uttered, and he was demanding an explanation. On the other hand the contradiction was very clear to me. Why didn't he understand it?

"If God is unlimited and undefined, then His manifestation in Jesus would make Him limited as well as defined. That is a contradiction."

Silence sometimes is more powerful than words. It breaks into you like a thunderbolt leaving you cold and sweaty. That's how I felt. No one was looking at me except Professor McNaughton. It was my turn to say, "Speak up," but I didn't dare. At least in the presence of the Ayatollah in Karbala I had found the courage to interrupt him and smirk when he espoused the idea of Islamic Government. He had tolerated me. But here, no one responded to my audacious statement. Then again, it was best that I kept quiet because my English was too weak for me to be able to articulate my thoughts clearly.

In any case, it was Professor McNaughton who directed me toward a small city in upstate New York. He said Albany was beautiful, and the college had a small population of students. He also had a friend who taught in the area, an elementary school teacher in Altamont. He promised he'd visit me and would take me to Bible school sessions where there were many highly qualified religious scholars who could help me in my "search."

By that time, the summer of 1964, I was sharing an apartment in the Bronx with Mr. Kazemi, who had received his bachelor's degree in Business from Indiana University and was starting a company in New York City to import *zereshk* (dried barberries). I paid him half of the monthly rent but was directed to sleep on a sofa bed in the living room. He allocated the spacious bedroom to himself, while using the smaller one for storage. He reminded me that when his bride arrived from Iran, he'd need the whole apartment, and I would be obliged to leave as soon as she made her appearance. Not knowing anyone else in the city, I had agreed to his terms.

When Professor McNaughton suggested the State University of New York at Albany (SUNYA), I looked up the name of the college in the dictionary appendix. I still have the dictionary. The cover is torn but I keep taping it. It was the first book I purchased in this country, and I rarely throw a book away. I remember that I had been happy and grateful that I had bought it so cheaply from Mr. Kazemi. Five dollars had sounded inexpensive to me. Since he had used it for several years, I thought I had struck a bargain by buying it secondhand. Alas, later, I saw the same dictionary, completely new, for the same amount in a bookstore. What a letdown. By then, of course, I had found out that my "friend" had had some shabby dealings with other fellow businessmen, mainly buying things cheaply and selling them expensively.

While professor McNaughton touted the charming city, what attracted me most to SUNY at Albany was the ratio of girls to boys: five to one. That was it. I did everything I could possibly do to enroll as a student at SUNYA. At first, I received a negative response. I called them and put my shyster friend on the phone to talk to them. What a dumb thing to do because they were wondering why I hadn't called them personally. Mr. Kazemi told them that my English wasn't good, which was enough for them to say no, again. Do you blame them?

Realizing my big mistake, I decided to take the bus and go to Albany personally. Yes, the city was perfect. On a sunny day in August, a slight breeze was blowing in my face. I looked everywhere and found no garbage thrown in the streets, not like in New York City. It was as if the people of Albany knew I was going to be in town and had swept the sidewalks and even the streets. During the bus ride from downtown Albany to the campus at Draper Hall, I kept looking at the stores and the buildings and the maple trees lining the sides of Western Avenue with their leaves weaving and waving back and forth, touching each other softly and changing direction and then leaning back again as if hugging, caressing, and kissing. Everything was so beautiful. I fell in love with the city.

I met with the admissions officer, the foreign student advisor (Dr. Frank Carrino), and another fellow who looked at me sternly and curiously, as if trying to discern why I was determined to come to Albany. The only thing that gave me courage and hope was the friendly smile of Dr. Carrino.

"Do you know how much the tuition is?" he asked.

Of course, I knew. It was $250 per semester.

And "Do you have the money?" Oh yes.

"Why do you want to come to Albany?"

Foreign students usually chose bigger cities and bigger universities. I had chosen this small college in a city typically unknown to foreign students. Dr. Carrino asked how I had learned about SUNYA.

"Professor McNaughton recommended it. He is a professor at the American Language Institute in New York City, and we have become close friends. He'll come and visit me often because he has a friend in Altamont. That's a town close to Albany." At that moment, I saw the atmosphere changing. Dr. Carrino, whose perpetual smile was reassuring, said he was sure I was going to like it here. I was in. But they reiterated that the tuition would be $250 per semester and that I would need to pay it two weeks later on registration day.

I returned to New York City, packed the two suitcases I had purchased in Tehran, and headed back to Albany. It was my second trip on a Greyhound bus and my second on the thruway. I had time to reflect as the bus roared out of Lincoln Tunnel. Everything seemed modern: the wide roads and multiple lanes, the trains passing by carrying cargo from one end of the state to another, the trucks whizzing along.

These were all exciting to see but not totally unexpected. When I'd been in elementary school, our geography teacher had taught us a lot about America. He told us that many civilizations had risen and fallen: the Greeks, the Romans, the Arabs, the British, the Spaniards, the French, the Babylonians, the Chinese, the Iranians, and many other people had built great empires that had been eclipsed. However, two nations had gone through successive periods of rise and fall: China and Iran. "Look at history," he'd pointed out. "These two peoples have risen from the ashes of decline several times. Remember that the reasons for their rebirth were because they had a strong merchant middle class and sense of nationhood. Until modern times, when nationalism as a concept began to emerge, only China and Iran had developed a sense of belonging to and nurturing the motherland. But most important, their strong economic backbone and know-how helped them make a comeback after falling from greatness.

"America, however, is different. Just observe what they have done. They did not build an empire. They brought many people together and melded them into one nation. They had a revolution, but the leaders of the revolution were not selfish people. Can you believe that George Washington was given the chance to become king and he refused?" Our geography teacher had not only taught us about American geography and history, he made us memorize a lot of facts: the names of the rivers, mountains, national monuments, the length of the Mississippi River, and the height of the Empire State Building. We learned statistics about the ratio of paved roads in America compared to the rest of the world, the number of cars compared to the rest of the world, the number of railroad miles compared to the rest of the world, the number of universities and colleges compared to the rest of the world, and most important, we learned the ratio of middle-class businessmen to the population. Nowhere in the world, at any time in history, had there been a country with such a large middle class. America was new and strong and like a sailboat with the wind at its back. America was *taze nafas*, a breath of fresh air. Sitting in the bus on my trip back to Albany, I saw America parade before my eyes. What I had been taught about the roads, the buildings, the cars, the trucks, the trains, and everything else was true. I loved every minute of it.

I had no idea that Albany, New York, would become my final home. I had promised my mother that I would return. When I'd said my final good-bye to the family in July 1963, leaving the city of Karbala, Iraq, to go to Europe with the simple intention of continuing my education in the United States, I noticed that my mother had stood apart, leaning against the living room wall, just looking. There was no smile. There were no tears, no advice, nothing, no expression on her face. With both hands folded against her abdomen, she just kept looking at me. Our eyes met and I was puzzled. Why was she looking at me with no expression whatsoever? She did not move forward to hug me. She did not even show any sadness. It shook me. "*Maadar* (Mother)," I said. "Please tell me what is wrong?"

She replied slowly, each word a separate entity, emotion quietly rising from the depth of her being, "I am not going to see you again!" The sentence was simply said, but it pierced my heart.

"Yes, you will," I said laughing. It was unbelievable to me that I would never go back. She repeated the sentence again. "I'll never see you again." I extended my arms to touch her, to hug her, and continued to refuse to believe her. She did not move. Her head bent slightly to one side and her eyes still focused on me. She did not come forward to hug me or kiss me. She looked as if she were storing that short memory of my face in her long-term memory. I was a bit taken aback. I laughed again and said, "You'll see, I am going to prove you wrong." Of course, mothers know best. She knew it, but I did not even give it a thought. She was right. I chose to stay in America, and I never saw her again.

But long before I knew that, as the taxi maneuvered through the streets of Albany, I was filled with exuberance and enthusiasm. The capitol building and the education department on Washington Avenue looked so impressive that they made me joyfully giddy. What is the name of this building and that park and this other one with the big marble columns? The middle-aged taxi driver answered patiently, narrating as if he were a tour guide. I had given him the address of my dormitory. He had looked at it carefully but doubtfully.

"Are you sure this is a dorm?" he asked.

I replied affirmatively. The school officials had selected that building, which they referred to as the "White House." I distinctly remember one of the officials smirked whenever anyone mentioned the "White House." In 1964, we were called foreign students, not international students, and there were only seven of us. We were given the red carpet treatment by being assigned a huge house as a dormitory of our own, the White House.

The taxi driver continued to look a bit dubious, but my constant questions seemed to help him forget whatever he was thinking. And for the next fifteen or so minutes he was extremely forthcoming in naming the streets through which he was wending his way. "Albany's streets are very simple to understand," he said. "There are about four or five main streets in this city. Once you learn their names and directions you'll never get lost. Right now, I am driving from east to west. This wide street is called Washington Avenue. See, it branches off at the corner. On the right is Central Avenue, we'll continue on Washington but look straight ahead where the fire department is located. By the fire station the road splits into Western Avenue and Washington. I can take either one to your place. I think I'll drive you on Western Avenue to show you the main entrance of the college. Here we are. See that beautiful statue? It is called Minerva. She represents a Roman virgin and Greek goddess who personifies many things: wisdom, poetry, arts." So the West was also hung up on virgins! How interesting. I found out, later, that yes, indeed, virginity was a prize kept as a gift for the husbands. In those days, a girl's number-one priority in going to college was to find a husband.

I saw the full firm breasts of the Goddess of Arts. Though concrete, I imagined them soft and tender. The taxi driver went on. To our left was Washington Park. My immediate question was whether people picnicked in the park. He nodded saying, "Sometimes."

I recalled the city of Tehran emptying every Friday while its inhabitants would desert to the suburbs by the thousands, carrying pots and pans of stew and rice and skewered shish kebabs and blankets to sit on and everything else they could think of, gathering together in the lush greenery of the countryside. Families who had never seen each other before would become friends and tell stories offering each other sweets, tea, and food. They would become one community, a sea of humanity, individuals who, once every week, became "related" to one another.

The driver's voice cut into my musing. "If you turn left on the street ahead of us, which is South Lake Avenue, it'll take you to Madison Avenue, which is kind of parallel to Western Avenue, the street that we're driving on. On our right is Washington Avenue. That's it, just five main streets." The driver had said something about Clinton Avenue farther north of Central. He made it simple for me. "You can say they are kind of parallel. But for now, as far as you're concerned, you need to know Washington Avenue and Western Avenue because your college lies right between the two. The building we passed with the statue of Minerva is called Draper Hall. You can enter it from either Washington or Western avenues. All you need to know is that Draper Hall is the central location of the college. If you get lost, try to head for that building and you'll have no problem."

The taxi stopped by an older two-story building. "Here it is, your White House." I thanked him profusely. The fare was $3.50 but I felt generous. I gave him his fare and a $5.00 tip. He took the money with a puzzled look. "That is your tip," I said. He was not impressed. He shook his head, wiping his forehead with his hand. I could read his thoughts. It was a big tip for a $3.50 fare. That must be a lot of money. I was still counting in *toman*. It would have been much smarter to give him the five to cover both the fare and the tip. Deep down, I knew what I had done was pretty dumb.

Taking my two suitcases, I walked up a set of three or four steps. This White House did not have marble columns like the one in Washington, D.C. As I entered the house, I saw a big room on the left. It was easy to see that it was a lounge or a large living room. A couple of old chairs were placed clumsily around it. An old sofa, worn and torn with cat scratches, was situated across from the chairs. The uneven floor was solid wood with dark varnish that made it look dirty. No one seemed to be in the house but there was a staircase in front of me. I dragged my two suitcases up some thirty creaking narrow steps to the second floor looking for someone who could show me my room. There I met my first housemate, a very friendly Korean. He was much shyer than I was.

"Very nice meeting you," he said upon seeing me.

Kim Minsu was extremely helpful. He showed me my room, and I left my luggage there while he took me for a tour of the White House. Kim had been there for two days, alone, and had had to learn everything by himself. There was a kitchen with an old gas stove on our floor. Kim told me to light the match before turning on the gas. Otherwise, "Boom!" Everyone and everything would explode. The refrigerator had been subdivided for the seven foreign students of the school. "There are only seven students here?" I asked Kim. He laughed and nodded affirmatively. The total number of foreign students at the White House in that year was, indeed, only seven. One was from Korea, another from Poland, a third Lebanese, another from Kenya, I was from Iran, and there were two others, much more bashful than the rest of us, whom I never met. They were always in their rooms, pretending to read.

The bathroom turned out to be a spectacle of its own. The faucet spat air and rusty looking water right into my face. Kim laughed and covered his teeth. "It no work." The bathtub was an old style tub on four legs, but there was no hot water. The toilet didn't flush properly, and it took an eternity to refill.

"Why is this dorm in such bad shape?" I asked Kim.

"The plumber is supposed to come to fix it," he replied.

I must admit that when I lived in Iraq and later in Iran, we did not have a bathroom in the house. There was a toilet but we didn't take baths in the house. Full showers or bathtubs in houses were uncommon in many parts of the country. But there were public baths in every city, some good, some not as good. People went there to bathe, some weekly and some every other day. In my father's public bath, I used to take a long shower every day, sometimes twice. When I was touring Europe in 1963, before coming to America, I had gotten used to the new, modern bathrooms in Rome, Heidelberg, and London. The house I lived in while in London was in a middle-class neighborhood by Putney Bridge and had a fairly acceptable bathroom, but there was no heat in it. There was an electric heater that ran when you put a shilling in the coin slot. Well, I had gotten tired of getting out of the bathtub and sticking a shilling in every few minutes. Shivering and wet, looking in my pants pockets to find more shillings was no fun. I had remedied the situation by going to a public bath, but I didn't like the small stalls. They looked like some of the stalls I later saw in public state campsites in America, but at least they had hot and continuously running water.

In any case, I could not accept the conditions in our White House "dormitory." I stayed through the weekend and went to register on Monday. I was told by the admissions officer to go to a particular line and wait my turn to pay my tuition. I eagerly complied. He kept coming and going from his office and watching as I inched slowly but patiently in line toward the tuition payment window. As I was ready to hand in my money, a gentle hand touched me on my shoulder. It was Dr. Carrino. "Mohammad, come with me please." I politely objected. I had waited in line for half an hour to pay, and he was taking me out to talk to me! He put his arm around my shoulder and directed me to his office.

Filling out papers delightedly, he was very happy and too nice for me to be angry with him. He smiled; I smiled back. He told me that he had been right about me. He knew I was sincere. Then he said that foreign students were exempt from paying tuition. I was dumbfounded but pleased. I told him that I hadn't known. He replied he had guessed that I hadn't. The entire charade in the admissions office was because the admissions officer had suspected I knew and was applying only for that reason.

It was then that I brought the conditions of the White House to Dr. Carrino's attention. He was very understanding and sympathetic. He sent me to see the director of Waterbury Hall. The director listened to my complaints and did his best to persuade me to stay in the White House. He said that foreign students had a lot in common and were usually older than the American students. Therefore, it made a lot of sense to provide a separate house for them. As for the plumbing, as we were talking, it was being taken care of. The serviceman had been called, and it would be corrected by that afternoon. My voice went into high gear, not because I was angry, but because I always talk loudly, even today.

"The White House dorm is a sty," I said. "And all these students speak English as bad or worse than me. I came to America to learn English, not Korean or Polish."

Apparently, that statement, which was true to the core, impressed the director. He was delighted. "Let me see. I have a room that is occupied by two juniors. We can put another bed and desk in it for you. They may not like it because they are good friends and probably would prefer not to have a third person crowding their space. Come, let's go see them anyway."

I had made my point. I was moved into that room. Unfortunately, I had problems with the food in the dorm. The university cafeteria served hot dogs and beans almost twice a week for dinner. One day, I contracted an unbelievable stomachache. Air moved in my stomach like a hurricane, but I did not know it was due to gas-producing beans. I thought I had appendicitis and, one of my new roommates took me to the emergency room at Albany Medical Center Hospital. By then, of course, the pain had slowly dissipated. I was checked and probed. The doctor was puzzled but in his routine questioning he asked me what I had eaten for supper that night. "Hot dogs and beans," I replied. Having eliminated other possibilities, the doctor confidently diagnosed that it was the beans that had caused the pain. My roommate was sincerely relieved, and I was very grateful to him for the favor of transporting me to and from the hospital.

Regardless of the initial kindness of my roommates, as time went by, it became obvious that we could not get along. They did not like to hear me talk about American foreign policy which was, in my opinion, lacking in foresight. They thought that criticizing the CIA was tantamount to not liking America. The roommate with a goatee, a professorial manner, and a fake British accent kept nodding while sucking on his pipe and responding to my comments by saying, "Um" all the time. The other was a know-it-all. "Where are you from, Mohammad?" Iran, I would answer. "Where is that?" In the Middle East, I would say. "Next to Israel?" No, it is not next to Israel. Not knowing how little these two young men, who were both juniors, knew about geography, I would name all the countries in the Middle East and elaborate on the differences between the Turks, Iranians, Arabs and Hebrews. My explanations would fly over their heads. They had no idea what I was talking about. "Who is the ruler of Iran?" they would ask. The Shah, of course, thanks to the American CIA that overthrew the democratically elected prime minster and returned the Shah to power.

They would then look dumbfounded, as if I had uttered a blasphemy. I was becoming suspect in their eyes. With my limited English, I seemed sardonic and sarcastic. Didn't I realize that the American government donated millions of dollars to improve the lives of the miserable poor in the Third World? On the other hand, I erroneously assumed they knew that the CIA, in a covert operation, had ousted Dr. Mosaddeq, a popular democratically elected prime minister, in order to bolster the teetering rule of the Shah, the egomaniac dictator who catered to the whims of Britain and the United States. I was not connecting to my roommates at all. It took many years for me to realize that most Americans had no idea what kind of political intrigues the U.S. government had played throughout the world. "Well," my roommates persisted, "if the people of Iran don't like the Shah, why don't they overthrow him?" That was a stupid question, and I would tell them so. But when your vocabulary is limited, you often sound blunt, curt, or dumb. That's an unfortunate fact of life.

Then there was tension between us, and their reactions and cold shoulders exacerbated the situation. Their constant smoking and loud music got on my nerves. One of my roommates had just purchased a new record album, *The Hallelujah Chorus*. He blasted it loudly, and I liked it at first. However, after hearing it again and again, I had had enough. Their heavy smoking, though, was the most bothersome problem. I had tried smoking at age eighteen but had become dizzy every time I smoked, so I gave it up. Secondhand smoke was just as bad. I requested that they cut down on their smoking, but they just laughed at me. I explained that the pall of smoke in the room made me cough and saturated my clothes with an intolerable cigarette smell. The pipe smoker countered that he used the best tobacco available, and that it had a special aroma that acted as a "freshener." That sent me to my dictionary to look up "freshener." Worse yet, right after supper, they had so many friends dropping in and staying for hours that it really disturbed my sleep. My physics class was scheduled for 8:00 a.m. But they did not wake up until 11:00 or 12:00. Life became intolerable.

I devised a plan to counter the thoughtless behavior of those uncouth, inconsiderate roommates whose ignorance and arrogance drove me crazy. I gave them an ultimatum to stop their late night shenanigans or else.

"Or else what?" one of them asked me with a smirk.

"You'll see," was my reply.

The next night some five boys came to our room to chat. I slowly slipped into my bed and waved good night. Pretending to be asleep, I treated them with a loud burst of flatulence. The room was silent. I heard one of them whisper about the loud passing of gas. I could not help but laugh. When they heard me giggling under the sheets, they knew it had not been accidental. I heard one of my roommates mutter something about the odor. Peeking from under the sheet, I said, "Much better than your aromatic tobacco!"

Several weeks later, against the wishes and pleas of the dorm director, I found an apartment on Madison Avenue and left the dorm. The director knew that my roommates were the cause of my departure. He called me in to his office and insisted that I tell him it was they who had made life difficult for me, and he swore he would penalize them. All I had to do was to tell him so. I persisted in my denial.

Other than the dorm situation, I was very happy at SUNYA. I walked through the halls looking at that old but cozy university with awe. Apparently, it had recently changed its name from Albany Teachers College to State University of New York at Albany. Originally, the college's main task was to prepare students to teach. There were lots of students, some five thousand of them. I could tell that they were as nervous as I was. But they all spoke perfect English. I had just gone to a ten-week school for foreign students at the American Language Institute at New York University Heights. I had passed my TOEFL (Test of English as a Foreign Language) but did not know English well enough. How would I communicate with the fast-talking young kids who had learned to speak English from their infancy? I had guts and was able to get along. Yet, as a newcomer to America, I had a lot to learn.

One of the first cultural shocks that confused me occurred the very first week. Here I was, still euphoric, walking down the big hallway in Draper Hall, a constant smile painted on my face. A young man was coming my way. There was no one else in the hall; apparently, the others were either attending class or working in their offices. The doors were shut. I saw him looking curiously at me. We were some distance apart. My imagination took flight. "He must know me," I said to myself. "He must know I am very smart." After all, many people had called me a genius from the time I was a young boy growing up in Karbala, Iraq. Here at SUNYA, my perception was that many students knew it. This boy must have heard about me. Who had told him? The imagination is creative.

The smile on my face brightened, as I got closer to the six-foot-tall kid. He kept his piercing eyes on me, as he asked, "How short are you?"

Even though I heard him, I had to inquire, "What?"

"How tall are you?" He was not polite. I daresay he was rude, condescending, and uncouth.

I answered, "One hundred and fifty-nine."

It was, obviously, his turn to ask, "What?"

I repeated, "One hundred and fifty-nine." I was talking in centimeters and no doubt he was used to feet and inches.

He didn't get it, but his facial expression was not simply bewilderment at my answer but more obnoxious. His lips and eyes revealed many emotions: hate, disgust, and arrogance. We parted our ways but it suddenly dawned on me that whatever he was thinking had nothing to do with my genius. His height had made him think that he was superior to me.

I turned around and shouted, "Half of it is under the ground." I had translated a common Persian joke, *"Nisfish zeer-e zamineh."*

He looked back at me but speeded up his pace. Probably he did not understand my joke, either.

For the first time in my life, at the age of twenty-three (I was older than other freshmen), I found out I was short. What a crime! It did not dawn on me that I had just been "classified" in America, the country that, years later, I would choose to call my home.

CHAPTER 33

On Probation

$\mathcal{I}$T IS A COMMON HUMAN FOLLY to repeat the mistakes of the past, and there I was in Albany, repeating what I had foolishly done in Tehran. This time, it was not through my own initiative.

Moving from one apartment to the next, alone and lonely, life had been suffocating and depressing. Thus, I sought refuge with Kim and his Lebanese roommate, Philippe, the same foreign students I had first met at the White House. They had rented a large apartment on Lark Street, and they invited me to move in with them. Dividing the rent and the cost of telephone and utilities by three was beneficial to all of us. So I joined them. The apartment easily accommodated three occupants. There were three bedrooms. The kitchen was large with a good stove, a refrigerator, and a dining table. As I climbed the stairs and entered the foyer, to my right was the kitchen; to my left, a decent size living room; and across from the entrance door, there were two bedrooms. The third bedroom was adjacent to the kitchen. That one belonged to me.

The refrigerator was sub-divided into three sections. Since Philippe told us he'd eat out often, there was more room for Kim and me, who attempted to prepare our own meals by cooking. Kim was a good cook, and I did my best. Our relationship was basically formal because he kept to himself and displayed a high degree of self-discipline. He was habitually neat and clean. We agreed upon a schedule whereby each of us was designated to sweep the floors of the kitchen, the bathroom, and the living room on specific days.

Philippe had met a young woman from the Syrian Orthodox Church who did his chores. Kim did an exemplary job, strictly fulfilling his duties on time. I did a halfway decent job but occasionally was lax. I had not done housework before, and thus I would forget. However, Kim and I had only one squabble, when he interrupted me and my date as we sat talking in the living room, and he demanded that I do my specific chores of sweeping and cleaning right then and there. He wouldn't accept "I'll do it later" for an answer.

Instead, he went into a rage and began a litany of complaints, declaring that I was lazy and never did my assigned chores. Since he had a heavy Korean accent, I could not help but laugh, which only served to infuriate him.

"So, you laugh, ha?"

That made my date and me chuckle and led him to become a bit rude to her, too. However, gentleman that he really was, he immediately controlled himself and quieted down. Adding insult to injury, though, he silently picked up the broom and started sweeping the kitchen floor adding, "I'll do it for you this one time only." I thanked him, feeling pretty embarrassed about forgetting my chores.

We were supposed to make our own food. Except for the chicken that I helped cook in Heidelberg because Mahmood and my brother would not eat non-halal meat, I had never done much cooking. In Tehran, I had lived in boarding houses that provided breakfast and supper. For lunches, I had either eaten out or at relatives' homes. Now, in Albany, New York, I had to learn how to cook. Breakfast was easy and for lunch I made sandwiches. But supper was difficult.

I started with chicken legs. I'd buy three chicken legs, and planned to eat two for supper and one for the next day's lunch. Initially, I boiled the chicken with onions, tomatoes, and carrots. Later I thought of frying slices of eggplant and adding them to my dish. This meal became my specialty and even now, I occasionally cook it for old-times' sake. That chicken dish served with rice became my usual repast. I cooked it for anyone whom I invited to my apartment. People who ate my "specialty" were very polite, thinking that this was, indeed, a much prized dish in "my country."

Miss Helen Mayo was an older woman, maybe fifty-some years old, who had replaced Dr. Carrino as the Foreign Advisor. One day, I invited her to come for lunch. With the intention of being generous, I filled her plate with several cups of rice topped with a chicken leg, vegetables and two large slices of eggplant. She ate as much as she could but no matter how much she consumed, the plate still appeared full. Finally, I heard her sigh as she pleaded, "Mohammad, do I have to finish this whole plate?"

I had been eating with gusto and paying little attention to her dainty approach to her large plate of food. When I noticed her dilemma, at first I didn't understand. Then it became clear that, in an effort to be a good host, I had overfilled her plate. What I thought was a reasonable serving had become a Herculean task for this small woman, who was stuffing herself to please me. I laughed but apologized for my carelessness.

"I am really sorry, Miss Mayo," I said. "I shouldn't have filled your plate so full. You don't have to eat any more. This dish is my own concoction because I don't know how to cook or what to cook. Please stop eating if you are full. After all, I was the one who filled your plate. It was my mistake."

"What other dishes do they cook in Iran?" Miss Mayo asked, trying to be conversational. I described several wonderful Iranian dishes with relish, adding that I wished I had learned to prepare them myself. Thereafter, I was much more careful in dishing out food.

In the apartment with Philippe and Kim, I was continually in the process of "perfecting" my recipe. Kim made his Korean recipes for dinner and rarely ate at the table with us. When I would start eating my usual dinner, Philippe would sit right across from me, watching. I'd ask if he had already eaten. He'd say that he was not hungry. However, when I finished eating my supper, he'd ask if I minded if he finished the rest of my plate. He'd pull the plate around to his side and finish it. Then he'd ask if I didn't want the extra chicken leg in the pan. He'd finish that, too.

In those days, I shopped on Lark Street at a small grocery store that was owned by a mustachioed Italian immigrant. He had noticed me coming in almost every other day to buy frozen spinach, bread, rice, chicken legs, and six or seven large, ripe tomatoes. Apparently, tomatoes were considered expensive, and one day the owner asked me why I bought so many tomatoes.

"How many tomatoes do you eat every day?" One or two was my response. "Then why do you buy so many every time you come in and what do you do with the extra ones that rot?"

"I throw them away," I answered. I don't know why I bought so many tomatoes. Maybe because when I was in Karbala, my mother had a large vegetable garden with all kinds of vegetables in it. I would often pick several tomatoes and eggplant to fry with eggs for my breakfast each morning. The owner of the store advised me to come in every day and buy one or two tomatoes for that day only, then come again the next day and buy one or two more. "They are expensive and you're a student, you shouldn't buy so many that they may rot," he would say. "My store is right across from your apartment," he would add. I would agree with him, but then I would purchase three of the largest tomatoes I could find. He finally gave up advising me about what I should do, but he was extremely cordial and friendly and often struck up a conversation with me about Iran and the ancient military expeditions between Persia and the Roman Empire.

I liked Philippe's company, especially because, after I had related my first attempt at dating, he taught me not to be insistent when asking American girls out.

I had called a girl whom I had met at a foreign student mixer. The college occasionally organized social gatherings for foreign students. At one such social occasion, I met a student, a junior, who had been given the task of talking and socializing with us "lonely" students, far away from our homes, with no friends. Her extreme friendliness prompted me to call her. She had given me her telephone number and asked me to call her if I needed someone to talk to. I didn't think there was anything wrong with calling and asking her out.

She said no. But no in my mind meant maybe. I did not know that the Mediterranean custom on the one hand, and my experience in dating Iranian women on the other hand, were totally opposite from what I was supposed to do in America. I continued to insist, and she continued to say no. I really don't know how long the conversation lasted. It was long enough that I must have sounded pathetic. I was perspiring when I left the phone booth.

Philippe later explained the dating principle of "Don't insist." "Never insist." he said.

He taught me that this was not the Middle East, that in this country, yes means yes and no means no. I subsequently followed his advice. If a girl said, "Not this Friday or this Saturday," I accepted her refusal graciously and added with a smile, "I am not really in the habit of asking again." Several times I was surprised when I was encouraged to call again. The girl would explain that the day that I suggested was taken because of family or other reasons, and she would insist that I call her again.

Emigrants, foreign students, or even tourists are really "blind" to the social mores and customs of the countries they visit or choose to stay in. Furthermore, slight mispronunciation can totally change the meaning of a word. It is both funny and depressing when I think of all the words I would pronounce incorrectly. For example, in mathematics class in 1967, our methods professor, who was preparing some thirty-five students for student teaching, asked me, "And how did you do this problem?" My quick and very loud response was, "I fuctored it." The entire class hushed. The professor hesitated. Putting his hand behind his ear, he asked, "How?" For the second time, I replied, "I fuctored it." But this time, the deadly silence evoked the idea that I was saying something wrong. The professor's face was slightly red. He put both hands behind both ears. Turning around and looking straight at me, he asked again, "What did you say?" This time I noticed my mistake and immediately corrected myself saying, "I factored it," making sure that my emphasis on the letter "a" was truly and clearly understood.

My stay on Lark Street with Philippe and Kim lasted only a couple of months but was highly effective in my social development. Those who have traveled to other lands know how it feels to be alone, with no familiarity with the native language, and trying to make a fresh start in education or business among people whom they do not know. My stay in that apartment was a transitional move from loneliness back to independent living and regaining my self-assertion.

While helpful in some ways, Philippe had a bad influence on me. He was into going to nightclubs, though there weren't many of them in Albany. A couple of bars had belly dancers as entertainment. There was a bar on Delaware Avenue near Spectrum Theatre that featured such dancers about once a week. Philippe chased girls, especially those from among the Syrian Community that had its own small neighborhood and Syrian

Orthodox Church. I joined him during his escapades and began to drink again but did not overdo it. However, the end result was harmful to our grades. Both Philippe and I were put on probation. This was a déjà vu of the Tehran experience, and I was not about to let failure take hold of me again. So I repeated the same thing I had done in Tehran: I rented an apartment of my own and taped a note on my apartment door reading, "I came to America to study, not to go to bars or nightclubs. If you're my friend, leave me alone and permit me to study." My Lebanese friend just tore up the note and walked in, making a joke out of it. I realized I had to be more forceful. He was more persistent. The third time, I locked my door and kept quiet as he knocked and knocked. That did it. Of course, one "vice" I did not abandon was dating the many beautiful girls SUNYA had to offer.

Neither did I abandon my interest in learning about the many different Christian denominations, and I found many people interested in showing me the "Light." A number of them were also interested in giving me a ride to various churches. All I had to do was pick up the phone, call one of the willing drivers, and ask to be picked up at my apartment and taken to church. These people were enthusiastic in introducing me to their beliefs. They were patient and seemingly tolerant. Prejudice against my religion presented itself later in the workplace when I started teaching mathematics at RCS Central School.

Sometimes an African student, George, joined us for worship. He was a quiet and polite fellow from Nigeria. A man named Mr. Rice picked me up before stopping at George's place, then going to Loudonville Community Church. The discussion on the way to and from the church was always centered on salvation through Christ. After the service, Mr. Rice would ask us if we felt the spirit of the Lord. "I feel like my whole body is warm and relaxed," he'd say. "The Reverend's sermon was mesmerizing. It just transformed me, especially as time passed into the second half of our session."

George agreed constantly. I was quiet. Mr. Rice continued, "Didn't you feel it, Mohammad? Didn't the holy ghost enter you?"

I would sigh and say, "I did feel relaxed, but I really think it was the result of an hour of sitting and contemplating, letting my anxieties evaporate. I have had similar experiences before, when I sat still and tried not to think of anything and not to worry about intrusions of irrelevant thoughts encroaching upon my meditation. I have experienced it also at many other meetings when I was absorbed in contemplation and meditation."

"You've got to give it time, Mohammad," he'd respond. "You definitely have felt the power of the Holy Spirit trying to enter your body. It will awaken you when it finally touches you."

One day George was not able to come with us to church. Mr. Rice and I were alone in the car, and he began to talk about his hopes that George would soon accept Christ as his savior.

"George?" I asked.

Yes, he replied.

"But he is already Christian!" I added with total surprise. Apparently Mr. Rice hadn't realized that George was a Christian to begin with. He knew I was a Muslim but was not aware that George had been born into a Christian family. It didn't occur to me then that George's extremely black skin had made Mr. Rice think that he was not one of his own co-religionists.

I attended many churches. Among them were, to name a few: the First Presbyterian Church on State Street; Friends Meeting of Albany on Madison Avenue, where I really enjoyed the contemplative life; the Unitarian Universalist Society on Washington Avenue, which seemed to be open-minded; Loudonville Community Church; and the Pentecostal Church, a small but loud congregation.

CHAPTER 34

Love at First Sight

ONE WINTRY DAY IN 1964, I had just finished eating my lunch in the cafeteria at the State University of New York at Albany. I was in a big hurry to get to my class. I made my way through the hallway, weaving between students toward the classroom. My eyes fell upon a very skinny, shy woman of about nineteen standing in line to purchase a ticket for a concert. Her dirty-blonde hair was fixed in a bun above her head, making her face look smaller and narrower than it was. Her eyes were soft blue. I passed by her, speeding toward my destination when, impulsively, I began to backtrack with relative agility. I had a premonition that I had found a lost treasure that belonged to me.

I was always a happy and carefree young man. My smile rarely left my face. Laughter brought me joy and made my friends laugh with me. From my early childhood, many people had told me that the sound of my laughter was music to their ears, and they joined me. I knew that it was an asset. I made many friends. But now, I was not smiling. I was immersed in a serious, absorbing moment of contemplation.

I walked backward till I reached the vicinity of her presence. Even though she was beautiful, my interest, at that moment, was not her physical appearance.

Not only she did not notice me, she didn't seem to notice anyone else. She seemed too shy to look people in the eye. Was she teasing, holding a secret? I did not think about anything. I only felt things. I looked at her blue eyes that appeared to move up and down and sideways, staring at the walls, the ceiling, and the floor as if flirting with inanimate objects but not with the people in the hall. I leaned against the wall with my left shoulder inspecting her thin, innocent face and crimson lips. I felt a sense of certainty that this woman would be my wife.

Immediately and impulsively, I started scurrying to my class again. All was forgotten. She had appeared to me for that moment only like a flame rising from a burning bush, brightening the surroundings, and quickly being extinguished in the void. I didn't think about her again for a long time.

Weeks later, I had just gone through the cafeteria line, performing for the workers who laughed at my jokes. I was in the habit of opening conversations with almost everyone who was receptive. Most people liked my unabashed demeanor, my friendly face, and mostly my perpetual smile. I was boisterous, always proclaiming loudly how much I loved America. "Why?" the cafeteria workers would ask, pretending that they had not heard this before. I would shout back, "Because America has so many beautiful girls. I love them all." The cafeteria workers would laugh heartily. The students looked curiously at me. Some girls would smile. Many boys would look peeved. My English, in those days, was extremely broken.

I took my tray of food and headed toward the seating area. It was full. Everywhere I looked I saw that the tables were occupied. I stood there in the middle of the room looking for a booth or a table, to no avail. Then, I noticed that right where I was standing, there was a table with a blonde girl sitting alone, eating her lunch quietly. I asked if I could join her. She said, "Yes." I sat down and introduced myself. She said her name was Priscilla. Looking at her face, I suddenly recognized the same woman I had seen a few weeks earlier in the hall. She was proper and shy but had no difficulty talking to me. I told her about myself and asked about her. She was a sophomore studying biology education. I asked what that meant. As she explained, I realized for the first time, that, if someone wished to teach, he or she had to obtain a teaching certification in the field he or she had chosen. My student advisor had enlisted me in the general studies program. I was also fond of teaching. I had tutored many students in Iran and I was good at it. The first thing I did after lunch was to go and switch my course of study to the education program.

I did not ask Priscilla to go out with me that day, not because I was prudent enough to wait, but because, as I was thinking about asking her, she told me that she had to go to her class. That skinny girl had finished her lunch before I could even eat half of my food. I guess I had done most of the talking, as usual.

Again, I thought nothing of it. All that had happened that day was a simple conversation with a girl named Priscilla. I went on with my work in school and my activities with my friends.

The university had outgrown its campus and was building a new one, but it was not yet operational. In the meantime, SUNY at Albany had arranged to hold classes in several commercial buildings. There were buildings called English Annex, Biology Annex, and another called Detroit Annex where history and social science classes were held. These annexes were on Central and Washington Avenues, and we walked several blocks from one building to the other to attend classes. It was a cozy and homey college. I liked it because, wherever I went, I saw many people I knew among the students and faculty. The foreign student office was nearby. And the library was within walking distance.

In Brubacher Hall, there was a Student Union where students could get short-order foods such as sandwiches and hamburgers. Priscilla worked at the counter, usually as a cashier, under the Work-Study Program. One night I saw her seated at the cash register. Paying for my hamburger, fries, and Coke, I asked her if she was free Friday night (February 5, 1965) to go out with me. She said yes. As fate had it, she was the last woman I ever dated.

I don't recall how long it took me to fall in love with Priscilla and ask for her hand in marriage. All I know is that it was just a few weeks, five, possibly six. You see, I never thought I would get married at all. But when you're young and exuberant, once your heart urges you to do something, logic and reason vanish. As I recall the events, it feels that the moment I asked for Priscilla's hand in marriage was the most outrageously awkward and silly one. Yet two months later when I met her parents, those funny moments metamorphosed into sobering ones.

I don't know if others have had such an experience; I don't know if I should write it down; I don't even know whether I should laugh about it now. All I know is that it happened the way I am reciting. We were kissing, touching, and fondling when, unexpectedly, I forgot everything. I forgot where I was, what country I was in, and what the future held in store for either one of us. All I knew was that I loved her. I had never loved a woman before.

I stopped for a moment, thinking. I slid off the couch to the floor, ran my fingers through my hair, and heard myself speak. Words sputtered out of my mouth: "I love you. Would you marry me?"

She looked at me quizzically. She was not in love with me. Yet, she thought that she might end up loving me. Within minutes she said yes, and within weeks she was in love with me. How did I know? It was easy to see. She asked me to go with her to visit her parents the last day of classes on June 24, 1965.

Mohammad and Priscilla 1965

It didn't take long to drop the bombshell that we were engaged and were planning to get married after graduation, two years later. Her parents put up a good front. However, they were churning inside. Who was this stranger who'd come from *I-ran*, four years older than their daughter, who couldn't speak English well, a head shorter than her, and worse yet, dark? Priscilla's mother, Susie, did not say much, though she mumbled and sighed again and again. She was a southern belle with the heaviest southern accent I had ever had the pleasure of hearing. Albert, her father, who was from New York and proud to be a white, Anglo-Saxon Protestant, did not see anything good coming out of this marriage.

Religion didn't seem to bother him. He had his own theories about Jesus, that Jesus was an alien who had come from another planet to teach human beings how to live together peacefully. As far as I know, if Albert ever became concerned about the differences in religion, it was his friends who might have influenced him in that regard.

My relationship with the foreign student advisor, Dr. Carrino, had been extremely cordial, and that familiarity and friendliness continued with Helen Mayo, who replaced him in February 1965 when he took a sabbatical leave. He later went on to accept another position. One day, Miss Mayo called me in to offer me an application for a fellowship. The International Institute of Education (IIE) was looking for foreign students who had demonstrated leadership qualities to be in what was called the Leadership Training Program, and she had selected me to be the one student to apply from SUNY at Albany.

This turned out to be a wonderful opportunity. The Leadership Training Program provided training for some two dozen students selected by various foreign advisors of different universities simply for demonstrating leadership abilities. The members of our group represented approximately two dozen universities throughout the country. The diversity of our gathering was educational in itself. There was financial support consisting of any tuition and a generous living stipend.

Also, the Institute of International Education (IIE) organized a summer program at different universities every year. At these summer sessions, each student took a course or two of his or her choice, the credits of which were transferred back to his degree program. In addition, a weekly seminar was offered by IIE. Since foreign students did not work during vacations and didn't have families to visit at these times, the summer session program worked out well.

In the summer of 1965, the International Institute of Education (IIE) Program was holding its seminars at Cornell University in Ithaca, New York. I took a physics course. Priscilla decided to attend the summer session there on her own. She took a course in microbiology, and we both stayed in the dorms.

Ithaca is one of the most beautiful areas of New York State. The campus sits on a hill above the town and is traversed by gorges, waterfalls, and a stream that empties into Cayuga Lake. Today I might have difficulty climbing up and down the hilly parts of the city. At that time, we didn't mind walking the steep streets and roads in and around the college. We enjoyed the many coffeehouses, pastry places, and small restaurants in the town. At one of the jewelry stores, we selected and purchased Priscilla's engagement ring. The beauty of Cornell and Ithaca impressed us so much that for many years thereafter we returned to the Finger Lakes region to camp in the various state parks.

We had no inkling of what Priscilla's parents were doing behind our backs. Bear in mind, this was June 1965, two years before the U.S. Supreme Court legalized interracial marriages throughout the United States (*Loving v. Virginia*, June 1967), and two-and-one-half years before the movie *Guess Who's Coming to Dinner* was released. In that film, Katharine Houghton invited Sidney Poitier to her house to meet her parents, played by Spencer Tracy and Katharine Hepburn. Interracial marriage was the main subject of the movie, which, though legal by then, continued to be very uncommon.

The first sign that something was amiss was when one of Priscilla's high school classmates, who was also attending the Cornell summer session, called her to ask her out on a date. When she declined, the young man was honest enough to meet us and tell us that Priscilla's mother had asked him to ask her out. We thought it odd but did not dwell on it. However, when we went back to college in the fall of 1965, we became aware that a stream of letters had been written to the president of the State University of New

York at Albany, and thus the dean of undergraduate study, Miss Mayo, and a host of others, including my academic advisor, had been informed.

We were called in to meet with the dean of student affairs. After an hour of discussion, we assured her that we intended to wait until after graduation to marry. She pretended to be delighted at our engagement. However, it occurred to me that something was amiss because, every time I went to see Miss Mayo, she was too busy to meet with me. And my I-20 form, which was necessary to extend my student visa, had not been issued. It was clear that the university officials had conspired to delay providing me with the needed documents and thus force me out of the country. Evidently, we had to make a decision or else I would have to leave the U.S. with my tail between my legs. Elopement solved the problem. It occurred just before Christmas, December 22, 1965.

I became bitter, though, and remained bitter for many years afterward. How dare they consider me inferior? What was wrong with being from Iran? What was wrong with being dark and a head shorter than my wife? Why did her father drag us to Binghamton for consultation with a minister of the Presbyterian Church who had been in Iran as a missionary? The man was obnoxious, rude, and sarcastic, using the few Persian sentences he had memorized while in that country. Those remarks, uttered in a ridiculous accent, were caustic and mean.

Then, there was the intolerable insult when Priscilla received several letters of "advice" from her father trying to explain his objections. When we went for a visit, he handed her a letter from the American embassy in Tehran that detailed the hodgepodge of information they thought they had gathered about me. As often happens, the embassy had the wrong Mohammad Yadegari (which is not an uncommon name in Iran). As described in the letter, I was in America being trained as an air force pilot. The Iranian government had supposedly provided me with a scholarship. I found the content of the letter ludicrous.

My bitterness began to subside when, a year and a half after being married, we were blessed with the birth of our daughter, Shireen. It dawned on me that if anyone ever came from an unknown land, with a peculiar background, suddenly expressing that he wished to marry my daughter, I might be as intolerant and impatient as they were.

It was some nine years later, when my father-in-law's brother died and we were attending his wake that Albert, with a tight throat and teary eyes, confessed to me, "I want you to know that I could have never asked for a better son-in-law!" At the time, I said thank you but kept wondering why in the world it had taken him so long to feel that way. As time went by, I realized his reticence had been "genetic." Darn Englishmen, they can look so stoic and staid outwardly, yet inside they are often self-conscious. Sometimes I feel like slapping them in the face, urging them to open up, to show some emotion, to laugh like children laugh. It just doesn't work. They can be tight-lipped and tight-assed with pent-up emotions and guilt inside. God, why did you create this austere, Calvinistic attitude?

During Christmas vacation of 1965, the IIE organized a seminar held in New York City. Priscilla and I had just eloped, and the IIE officials had no objection to her attending the lectures and other events. That week in New York City turned out to be a very enjoyable honeymoon.

Several sessions were offered about how to tackle economic problems, if and when we encountered them in the future after returning to our respective countries. In addition to the lectures, IIE gave the entire group of students the red-carpet treatment. They took us to Lincoln Center, to Radio City Music Hall, to a Broadway theater to see *Golden Boy* with Sammy Davis Jr., and to Wall Street to tour the New York Stock Exchange. We had lunch in the Chase Manhattan Bank with David Rockefeller as our main speaker. Then we visited the United Nations, where a representative from Jamaica spoke to our group. Yes, this select group of international students was being well groomed to have a good opinion of the United States.

In 1966, the summer session was offered at Michigan State University (MSU) in East Lansing, Michigan. We stayed in the married students housing, and I took two courses, anthropology and history, while also attending a half-dozen seminars sponsored by IIE, again, mostly dealing with economics. One seminar I particularly enjoyed dealt with how to succeed in business. It brought back memories of my father's philosophy and management style. Not only did I learn the ways of improving business skills, but I was also reminded of all the advice and suggestions my father had taught my siblings and me while we were growing up in Karbala.

I had taken my driver's test in Albany, New York, and I received my license in the mail while I was attending MSU. We looked at second-hand cars in Michigan and found a 1960 Valiant for two-hundred-fifty dollars. We decided to sell our return air tickets, buy the car, and then drive back to New York.

We then drove all over the state of Michigan. We bought some camping equipment (a pup tent, sleeping bags, a small pan for cooking, and a cooler) and went to Albert Sleeper State Park in northern Michigan. We set up our campsite with our minimal equipment right next to some experienced and well-equipped, middle-aged campers. The couple seemed very interested in helping make our first camping experience successful, and they kept offering to lend us equipment. As we foraged for campfire wood, they brought over an axe, and they lent us some more pans for cooking. The weather was warm, and we didn't need much. We had a wonderful time.

Mohammad on first Valiant

Another place we visited was Mackinac Island on Lake Huron. The island itself did not allow cars. After taking the ferry over, we rented bikes to tour the picturesque place. Seeing the horse-drawn carriages reminded me of Karbala, but of course Karbala was very stark in comparison.

I took two courses at Michigan State University: Anthropology and History of Western Civilization. I found both enlightening. However, I was dismayed with the attitudes of some students in the classes. In anthropology, the teacher was a plain-looking Egyptian woman with slightly dark skin. Some of the male students smirked and referred to her as an *A-rab*. I found the students rude.

One of the topics my anthropology teacher talked about was female circumcision. She had spent six months in a Nubian village in Egypt and, since she was a woman, knew Arabic, and could speak the Nubian dialect, she had been allowed to observe the ritual as performed by women of the village. Her firsthand observation and commentary on the subject was extremely intriguing and enlightening. She asserted that the practice went back thousands of years and had nothing to do with any religion.

The professor who taught us Western Civilization was a tall, hefty, bearded man whose shirttail always pulled out of his pants as they slid down his hips, exposing the top of his underpants. In those days people were careful about their appearance, and I think that was the reason some students laughed and secretly made comments behind his back when he turned toward the blackboard. The poor man didn't realize what was happening. He was so enthusiastic about his teaching that he did not pay attention to his appearance. Again, I found the lack of respect distressing.

The yearly fellowship of $1,000, the full expense of the summer session at Cornell University in 1965, the red-carpet treatment in New York City during the month of December 1965, and the full expense for the summer of 1966 at Michigan State University made me curious as well as suspicious about who or what organization was spending so much money for nearly two dozen international students gathered from various universities in the United States. Furthermore, why was it called Leadership Training Program? I decided to ask.

After making an appointment, I entered the office of the man in charge of the program. I met with three gentlemen. I thanked them for including me in this remarkable group of obviously talented and well-qualified students. Then, with my total honesty and naiveté, I bluntly asked my question, explaining that I was curious about who financed the whole thing.

The director nodded and thought for a short time, then said, "Well, you have raised a question rarely asked by others. I feel that you are entitled to an honest answer. The money comes from the CIA."

"What for and why me?" I asked, slightly surprised.

"Again, to be honest with you, because we feel that you and other members of the group have leadership qualities, and we assume that, when you go back to your respective countries, you will quite likely be in leadership positions. We would like you to have a good opinion of us at that time. And, by the way, I feel that in your case we did not make a mistake. You do have leadership qualities because your very question today indicates it."

I laughed, assuring them that I loved this country, and after some short niceties, I left.

That summer and the summer before it at Cornell University were fun as well as educational experiences. Priscilla and I frolicked in the grass by the rivers, in campsites, and on beaches, two carefree lovers with no worries but excited at the beauty of life and love. We went everywhere, we saw everything, and had a tremendous time enjoying the scenes and sounds of nature.

When the summer session ended, we drove our 1960 Valiant all the way to Albany, New York, stopping at state campsites along the way. At Lake Erie, I hesitated to go in the water because it looked dirty and the shore was awash with dead fish, Coca-Cola and Pepsi cans, and broken bottles. Priscilla went in just for a moment, exiting with sludge dripping from her body. It was a disgusting scene. That's when I learned that the beautiful lakes and rivers of the United States were sometimes depositories of sewage. People were dumping everything in their water resources. "How could anybody do that?" I wondered. In those days, highways and byways were often dumping grounds for whatever people consumed in their cars. Cigarette butts, empty beer cans, Coke bottles, and broken glass were all over the roads. When steep fines were put in place for littering, things began to improve.

We also began to see drunk drivers weaving back and forth on the road. On one occasion, we observed some five passengers stopped by the side of the road vomiting and making a joke of it. Worse yet, we saw some other cars passing the scene laughing and joking about the young people throwing up.

Drinking and driving and even occasionally running over an innocent bystander were not out of the ordinary in America. Many were killed or maimed until more serious penalties for drinking and driving were put in place. At least twice, we were in accidents where drunk drivers did not apply their brakes fast enough.

The car we had purchased had a Michigan license plate. We had to change it in New York, which meant we had to have the car inspected. I took it to a garage on Central Avenue. After the inspection, I was presented with a list. The car needed shock absorbers, brake pads, and had several other deficiencies. The repairs would be expensive. I did not think it was wise to do such costly repairs on a car that was purchased for $250. I told the manager that I was a foreign student and the cost of the car was $130 cheaper than his charges. He was so "kind and gracious" that he suggested, "How about just two dollars a week?"

"That would come to three and a half years. I can't pay that money. My father sends me only $200 a month." A smile crossed his lips. Obviously, he thought he had found a "turkey" that didn't even know that interest would also be added.

"I am sorry," he said. "That's the price. Go home, think about it, then come back, I'll fix it like new in a jiffy."

"You mean I can drive the car even if it doesn't pass inspection?" I didn't know that I could take it to another dealer.

"Sure," he said. "I'll give you up to ten days to decide what you want to do. For now, I have to fill out this form that says the car did not pass inspection."

As I was driving home, it occurred to me that Chrysler manufactured Valiant. If I could find a Chrysler dealer and talk to the boss, he might tell me what to do. The first Chrysler dealer I found in the Yellow Pages was Armory Garage. I drove there the next day. It was noon, and all the mechanics were eating their lunch. I slowly approached them, not knowing who I should speak to. My English was poor, and this was only the second time I had entered a service station.

"What can I do you for?" asked a tall, slim, gentleman of about forty.

"Who is the engineer here?" I asked. I wished to talk to the person in charge, not just a mechanic. There were bewildered looks because they didn't understand why I was looking for an engineer in a garage. The gentleman, whose name was Ernie Bacon, suppressed a very soft, friendly smile, saying, "Why are you looking for an engineer?" I related the story and showed him the previous estimate and list of what was needed to pass inspection, adding that I had purchased the car for only $250 and that the garage mechanic had asked me to pay over $380 for things I knew nothing about. "Is that really the price for inspecting my car?"

Ernie Bacon said that he was the foreman of the garage, not an engineer, but he was the boss, the "chief." Pointing to all others, he continued, "I supervise this bunch of guys."

Then, without hesitation, he ordered a couple of mechanics to set the car up for inspection. Both jumped up, put their sandwiches down, and sipped some Coke, saying, "Yes sir, we'll take care of it."

They checked everything thoroughly while I answered Ernie's questions about what my name was, where I was from, and what I was doing. After thirty minutes, they finished reporting to their boss that nothing was wrong with the car. The inspection cost me three dollars. Ernie told me, "From now on don't go anywhere else. Just come here, we'll take good care of you." And so I did. I don't really remember how often I visited him with car problems. Later, he helped me buy another secondhand car that he personally inspected by test-driving. Then he helped me buy a new 1970 Valiant that pulled our trailer all over the state of New York. We put 130,000 miles on it, but still it did not quit. Ernie Bacon was, indeed, a decent and honest man.

When we got married, we had been planning to return to Iran. By 1968

our daughter, Shireen, was one year old, and though I had received my bachelor's degree in mathematics, I still intended to continue for my master's degree and, ultimately, a doctoral degree. I decided to become a permanent resident in the United States, teach mathematics part-time, and continue studying for my master's degree.

In 1968 when I became a permanent resident, I wrote to IIE, thanking them for awarding me the fellowship and informing them that I would very likely remain in the United States rather than return to Iran. Thus ended a three-year period of wonderful experiences.

CHAPTER 35

Pseudo-Pseudo Intellectual

ONE OF MY FAVORITE TEACHERS at SUNY at Albany was Bob Garvin. He taught philosophy, and I came to know him when I took his course, Philosophy I. Ever since, we've been friends. I recall having great difficulty in any course that required reading. My English was good enough to converse and handle subjects such as mathematics. After all, mathematics itself is a "language," and, fortunately, with its use of the same symbols all over the world, it is an international language. But reading a textbook, like *An Introduction to Modern Philosophy*, was not as easy for me. I had to look up almost every word in my English-Persian dictionary, so it took me about an hour to read a page. I am not exaggerating. I really timed myself. Many times, I hoped for a day when people of the world would speak one simple, easy, and comprehensible language. Some people say that music is a universal language, so I thought it should be possible. As time went by, I began to change my mind. No matter what the language, geography and the passage of time corrupt it. Just listen to the various people who speak English across the world. Their accents are so diverse that Americans have a hard time understanding them. I have trouble understanding accents in British comedy let alone Indian, Australian, or South African accents in reports on the news.

In any case, I almost dropped the philosophy course. Imagine being in a classroom or a discussion session where everyone had an opinion and some were very bold in expressing their points of view. In Professor

Garvin's class, I also had opinions and wished to express them but couldn't. I was a naturally loquacious person, and it was really difficult for me to sit quietly and listen to other students who seemed sophisticated and spoke fluently. My classmates not only talked and argued with one another, they assumed airs of being much more knowledgeable than they actually were. The male students mainly dominated the discussions. Girls in those years were meek and demure. They did not speak much, if at all.

In the 1960s, smoking in public was common, and pipe smoking was a fad among male college students. Some of my classmates smoked pipes in class and others pretended to smoke by sticking an empty pipe in the sides of their mouths. I thought it was funny to see young men of eighteen imitating older adults sucking on pipes. Once, before class started, I struck up a conversation with one of them, complimenting him about his ease in speaking and comprehension of the material. He replied that he was a "gifted" person. Philosophy was really his hobby, but his actual major was psychology. "Hobby" was a new word for me and, as per my usual habit, not only did I ask him what it meant, I also requested that he spell it for me. A condescending smile followed, but he spelled it out. I also asked him why he pretended to smoke a pipe while there was no tobacco in it.

"I don't smoke; I suck the pipe," he said confusing me further.

"But why?" I persisted. He said that if I knew psychology, which I did not, I'd know that, according to Freud, the first psychotherapist . . . I interrupted his dissertation.

"Freud was not the first psychotherapist, Ibn Sina[29] was." My classmate looked perplexed. He didn't bother to ask me what in the world I was talking about. He continued his narrative. According to Freud, it was natural for human beings to suck. As babies, we sucked milk from our mother's breasts and later sucked our thumbs. We shouldn't forget that most babies love to suck on pacifiers. As we grow, he continued, we stick anything we can find in our mouths and suck on it. That's why children like lollipops. That was another word alien to my limited vocabulary, but I restrained myself from asking him what it meant or how it was spelled.

---

29 Ibn Sina (d. 1037) was a renowned Iranian physician and philosopher, known in the West as Avicenna.

Even though I never liked Freud's ideas, I was impressed with the man-boy student classmate and his domination of the class discussion. Professor Garvin was very liberal and looked interested as he listened to the students speak their minds.

One day during a class discussion, the aforementioned student and another classmate, who took opposite views in an adversarial tone, got into an argument that hushed the class. The student antagonist asked the pipe-man, "What you are saying is that you are a pseudo-intellectual, right?" The "psychologist" was silent for a moment fidgeting with his pipe. Then, I heard him reply that he was a pseudo-pseudo intellectual. Luckily, I had looked up the meaning of the word, "pseudo." I was vexed and puzzled. Why didn't I understand the great debate between the gifted one and his adversary in philosophy, a subject that interested me greatly?

As soon as I entered my one-room apartment, I consulted my English-Persian dictionary. There was no such word as "pseudo-pseudo." Consternation overtook me, forcing me to consult the professor. After all, if I was good at one thing, it was going to my professors for help. Most teachers like students who ask for help, and they remember the face, the discussion, as well as the fact that the student is, at least, trying. In my case, there was an added incentive. If my professor knew how poor my English was and that it took me such a long time to read a single page of the textbook, I hoped he'd be more sympathetic to my problem.

Professor Garvin was extremely sympathetic and tolerant. He seemed very interested in foreign cultures. Years later, I found out he was particularly interested in Buddhism and meditation. When I asked him what a "pseudo-pseudo" intellectual was, he was baffled, and he wondered where I had heard the term. When I reminded him of the discussion in class, Professor Garvin started laughing, which indicated that he was amused by some of the shallow discussions his students carried on in class. That was when I confessed that my English was weak. He said at least I'd caught on to the "pseudo-pseudo intellectual" part, again laughing. He suggested that I visit him once a week in his office and discuss any philosophical topic that interested me. He said that he'd grade me based on those discussions as well as my class performance. Our conversations took the form of one-on-one discussions regarding the philosophies of Descartes, Nietzsche, Schopenhauer, and Kant. He realized that, though I could not write about them or talk about them in a class discussion, at least I was familiar with them. Muslim philosophers such as Ibn Sina and al-Farabi and Sufi masters such as Rumi and Ibn Arabi also became common subjects of these personal discussions.

Professor Mathew Elbow was another teacher with whom I had established a very amicable relationship. I took his Middle East History courses in the first two semesters of my stay at SUNY Albany. He'd been to Lebanon for two years under a Fulbright Foundation fellowship and was completely enamored with the region. For several years afterwards, he gave talks and showed slides of his trip in churches and schools. He was sympathetic to the Palestinian refugees living in squalid conditions in various refugee camps in the Arab world. He did, however, get a lot of flack from his colleagues for what they termed his "lies and innuendos." They accused him of being an "anti-Semite."

I must admit, however, that my sentiments at that time lay with Israel. To me, the Israelis had performed a miracle, having turned a desert region into a country with many resources. Many Jewish students were really impressed with my views. I had gathered a circle of friends who were Jews and we ate dinner together in the college cafeteria until one day one of them asked if I liked Nasser of Egypt. I replied affirmatively. He immediately became angry. He started shouting and swearing and uttering some words, possibly in Hebrew because I didn't understand what he was saying. His spate of temper made his mouth foam on the sides of his lips and his rice splattered across the table onto my food. I was shocked. What possessed him to get so upset?

"What's wrong with you?" I asked. He asserted that Nasser was a liar and a dictator who didn't care for the welfare of the Egyptian people. To me, this was completely false. Nasser was very popular and respected by the Egyptians and most of the Arabs. He was one of the founders of the Non-Aligned Nations[30] (today, called Non-Aligned Movement) and thus

---

30 The idea of non-alignment was discussed between President Tito of Yugoslavia, President Nasser of Egypt, and Prime Minister Nehru of India in 1956. President Sukarno of Indonesia supported the trio's initiative, and the first summit of the Non-Aligned Nations consisting of some 25 countries was held in Belgrade in September 1961; today, it boasts of 120 countries and nearly 24 observer nations and organizations. It is the second largest international body after the United Nations.

well known in the Third World. But the boy was vehement that Nasser was the devil incarnate and that, by saying I liked Nasser, I was anti-Israel. I told him I did not dislike anyone. I liked Khrushchev as well as President Johnson and Nasser and many others. What was wrong with saying that I like Nasser of Egypt? To make a long story short, I did not finish my food because, in his emotional outburst, he had spat in it. No longer did I see the few Jewish friends I had come to know except for one cute Jewish girl from Morocco. Her smile was always like a fresh breeze soothing my nerves.

Professor Elbow took a personal interest in me, inviting me to his house for Thanksgiving and Christmas. A friendship began to develop between us. We even taught a course together and appeared in panel discussions side by side. He was a genuinely good man.

CHAPTER 36
Cultural Differences

*L*EARNING THE SUBTLE NUANCES of a new culture is a slow process. In terms of social attitudes and customs, I was like a child.

Dr. Ethel Cermak, a physician at the University medical clinic, enlightened me about some of these facts. I had talked to her there several times. Every time I visited her at the clinic, she inquired about Iran and the working conditions of women doctors and dentists in that country. How many women were there in the medical field compared to the number of men? I didn't know the exact answer, but I had seen many signs in Tehran that indicated women doctors and dentists. My dentist in Iran was a woman.

In addition to her work at the clinic, Dr. Cermak had a private office where she treated patients. When my daughter was born, I asked Dr. Cermak to be her pediatrician. I went to see her with my daughter, and her curiosity about Iranian society was as strong as ever. I asked why she was so interested in the ratio of educated women compared to men. She explained the difficulties she had encountered in medical school when she had finally broken the social barrier that kept women in America locked out of many professions. When she went to medical school, her classmates, all male, had shunned her and occasionally played tricks on her. The highest status "allowed" for women in the United States, she said, was to become a teacher, nurse, or secretary.

"Ah," I said to myself. My apartment was close to Albany Business School on Washington Avenue, and I remembered seeing many well-dressed, business-like young women typing their days away behind the large glass windows of the school that faced Washington Avenue. I liked to look at them. They were pretty and chewed gum so gingerly that it was amusing. They never looked up to see me or other passersby. *"Now is the time for all good men to come to the aid of their country."*[31]

Dr. Cermak explained that she was interested in how other societies looked at professional women. According to her, the majority of Russian physicians were women. I remembered that in Iran, people didn't mind having women doctors. Girls and women preferred to be examined by a doctor of their own gender. Women were entering higher education by the thousands. Often, they surpassed their male counterparts in hard work and intelligence.

"Why do they go to school?" Dr. Cermak asked me. I shrugged. I didn't understand why she was asking. To get educated and advance. She explained that women entered college here in the U.S. mainly to find a husband. Again, I had heard that too. "And what do you want your daughter to be?"

"A doctor, of course."

As for sex, I found most Americans conservative and lacking in knowledge. I, myself, had learned about sex when I was twelve, not from my peers in the streets, but from reading the religious treatises authored by the Ayatollahs. At the time, my father followed the dictates of Ayatollah Sayyed Mehdi Shirazi. It is customary for every Ayatollah to spell out his religious dictates in a treatise (*resaleh*). I used to read all kinds of books I could find, and the *resaleh* was available in our house. One day, I opened it and found that there was a chapter on marriage. In reading it, I had to ask my mother what semen meant. The reason for the discussion of sex in the *resaleh* was to describe proper behavior and to spell out what was allowed and what was forbidden in sexual relations. For example, following intercourse, *ghosl* (ritual washing) is required. Masturbation is forbidden. However, if a person does indulge in such an act, *ghosl* is

---

31 An expression that used to be typed repetitively by students practicing to improve their typing skill and speed.

still required. I remember a friend of mine who was Ayatollah Borujirdi's *muqallid* (follower) told me that when and if he visited a whorehouse (another forbidden act) or masturbated, he was instructed in the Ayatollah's *resaleh* to perform his *ghosl* in cold water. I had laughed, thinking Ayatollah Borujirdi to be cruel.

In America in the 1960s, virginity was still a big deal. If a woman got pregnant without a husband, families were torn apart. Parents blamed each other, and some early pregnancies were terminated with clothes hangers. Women often feigned ignorance because they didn't want to upstage their male classmates. After all, one of those young men might be a prospective husband.

In the early 1970s, Priscilla and I bought a house in a blue-collar neighborhood in Colonie, a suburb of Albany. It was an old house, and I never liked it. But teachers were poor and we had to do what we had to do. It took our neighbors some two years to open up to us. At first I thought they were racists. By then I had come to know what bigotry meant. Then I realized it was not racism. It was something that I could not put my finger on. Later we did become friends with some of the neighbors and were accepted by them. Under the influence of several cans of beer, one of them revealed the reason that the neighbors had ignored us at first. "Well, when you guys moved into the neighborhood, you were a teacher and had ambitions of finishing your doctoral degree. Your wife has a masters' degree in biology. Then we saw your nephew who was studying at RPI (Rensselaer Polytechnic Institute) in civil engineering. We all thought you were a bunch of educated snobs. As time went by, we realized that you were really down-to-earth people." Apparently, almost all the neighbors thought that way.

CHAPTER 37

The Hebrew Academy

RECEIVED MY BACHELOR'S DEGREE in mathematics in 1968. My goal, however, had been to achieve a doctorate. It never occurred to me that I would stop at the bachelor's level. It also had never occurred to me that my field would be mathematics.

When I came to the United States and enrolled at the university, I was convinced that I had the ability to study any subject I chose. In my mind, physics was the most difficult, but I had done well in memorizing all the scientific theories that had been taught in the Persian language in high school in Iran. I decided to study physics. On the day of registration, I hurried from one advisor's desk to the next. The advisor's job was to determine what level was suitable for me. At the mathematics desk, the advisor asked me, "Do you know how to take the derivative of a function?" Of course, I did. It was a piece of cake, and I could even calculate second derivatives. "What about integrals?" Oh yes. That was anti-derivative. All you did was apply the reverse process for derivative. That meticulous advisor was dubious. "Here," he said to me. "Do this problem." He handed me a function to integrate. But he had drawn an elongated S ($\int$) in front of the function.

I kept staring at it. I had no idea what in the world that symbol meant. I looked at him, dumbfounded.

"Well, go ahead," he prompted.

"I have no idea why there is an S in front of the function," I said. "Why do you draw the letter 'S' so big?"

He mumbled some curse under his breath. I didn't understand what "Goddamn" meant but he kept using it often. "You better start in Calculus I."

But I knew how to find the anti-derivative. He had been unfair to me. I belonged in Calculus III not Calculus I. He didn't ask me any more questions, insisting that I sign up for Calculus I.

"The physics advisor signed me up for Physics III," I told the mathematics advisor.

"He did you a disfavor," he replied. "Probably you fooled him the way you're trying to fool me now."

That added insult to injury. I reflected that while almost everyone had been pleasant and helpful, there were some very haughty people around. I had told the good fellow at the physics table that I had studied sound, electricity, and atomic theory, all about the nucleus and protons and neutrons. I even had drawn a circle correctly showing the locations of these particles. And when I told him about the concept behind the musical notes do, re, mi, fa, so, la, ti, the man was impressed. He signed me up for Physics III (electricity and some other fancy title). He never asked me what kind of lab experience I had had. I was to attend three classes and one three-hour laboratory period every week. I thought the lab work was a continuation of the class lecture period. What a wonderful system they had here! I go to class, I learn the theory, and then another person, a graduate assistant, would review and reinforce that theory back to us. I had no idea that I had to do lab work with a partner, working on some experiments where we collected data, drew charts and graphs, and analyzed the information by presenting a conclusion. Needless to say, I failed that course terribly. My English-Persian dictionary was limited to simple language, not scientific words and terms. Getting a tutor did not help either. I complained to the graduate student in charge of our lab, and he spelled it out accurately.

"Do you see these little kids?" Yes. They were bigger than me, but I understood what the lab supervisor was trying to say. "From fifth grade or earlier they were taught to do experiments in school. You read about them in books. You memorized what your teachers taught you, but, as for lab experience, you have none."

Boy, did that hurt.

The gruff man at the mathematics desk had been right. I knew how to take derivatives and anti-derivatives but had never used the mathematical symbols for those two operations. Since I was put on probation right after the first semester, I switched my major to mathematics, keeping physics as a minor. Soon, I found out that they had enrolled me in general studies and not the education program that would lead to getting a certificate in teaching. The New York State Department of Education had strict rules. I had to take education courses, a methods class, and then do some eight weeks of student teaching to get my temporary teaching certificate. Changing my major made it easier to do well, and the probationary period was lifted. Still, the innate genius failed to shine through when it came to philosophy, English, and history. My English was appalling, but mathematics and easier courses saved me. Using a bit of sycophancy did not hurt either. A lot of teachers were very understanding, and I was good at talking my way through. Grades of C or B- began to appear on my records and kept me going. Grades of A and B+ in mathematics saved my credibility. As time went by, I graduated on time.

Now with a one-year-old baby and a wife, I found it necessary to look for a job, a part-time teaching position. I wanted to finish my master's degree in two years instead of the five that was common for many public school teachers who studied part-time. Securing National Defense Loans and New York State Higher Education Loans would help to finance my study. Still, I needed a job. I looked for a part-time position in teaching. Public schools did not hire part-time teachers, so I looked into private schools. The Hebrew Academy and Kenwood Academy of the Sacred Heart were both looking for a part-time mathematics teacher.

In 1968 and for some years thereafter, mathematics teachers were in short supply. Whenever a school found an enthusiastic teacher with zest and energy, they immediately grabbed him or her. I went for an interview at Albany Hebrew Academy. It was not long after the Six-Day War between the Arabs and the Israelis, when the Israelis had smashed through the Arab defense lines and had taken full control of the Sinai Peninsula. America was euphoric, or so it seemed. My perceptions, like anyone else's, were colored by the television reports. The Israelis were proud; Americans were proud; the magazines were full of the bravery of General Moshe Dayan. The patch on his eye had become a symbol of courage and bravery all over the country. When I entered the school and passed through the halls to go to my interview, I could see students during their lunch hour shouting in unison, echoing the powerful voice of a teacher who encouraged them to shout slogans in Hebrew. All I could understand was the word "Africa." I assumed they were hyped up about entering the African continent victoriously. I was neutral. I just listened.

Before my interview, the principal took me to the class taught by the teacher they needed to replace. I was impressed by the students' attitudes and their enthusiasm for learning. The students did not talk to each other during class. They were well dressed, clean, attentive, and the teacher was treated politely. They raised their hands when they had questions, and the questions were substantive. The students were obviously sharp. After class, the teacher approached me and advised me not to take the job. He told me the students usually were unruly. They had been ordered by the principal to behave themselves. They knew I was applying for the job and that they should behave. I asked the teacher why he was leaving. He replied that the students drove him crazy, always talking, always laughing, and throwing chalk.

The principal escorted me to the interview room, and I was faced with about five members of the board of trustees. After the introduction, I underwent some grilling, but the questions were reasonable. I knew I had the job. They didn't have to tell me. After a half hour of discussion, a man I will call Mr. Skeptical introduced himself and asked me where I was from.

"I am originally an Iranian," I responded.

"What do you think of the Six-Day War?" he asked.

"The Arabs deserved to lose," I said and continued, "They constantly agitate. What has Israel done? They want to live in peace but the Arabs keep threatening them. The Israelis have the right to defend themselves."

Mr. Skeptical pursued the question. "But, you're a Muslim!"

"So? I have always supported Israel. Most Iranians, especially the young, are highly supportive of Israel.[32] Iranian Jews have not felt the need

---

32 During the 1960s, this was true. After the Shah was replaced by the Islamic Republic of Iran in 1979, attitudes toward Israel changed.

to leave Iran, nor were they deported. They do good business, and many work in government. They are respected and they love Iran."

Looking at the expressions of the rest of the board, it became obvious they were not comfortable with the "interrogation." I was beginning to suspect that Mr. Skeptical opposed my employment.

I was surprised that he was not fully aware of history. I continued, "Historically, the Jews were not persecuted in Iran. After all, who saved the Jews from captivity? Cyrus the Great [580-529 BC] conquered Babylon in 538 BC and sent the Jews who wished to leave back to Jerusalem. He issued a decree to rebuild their temple. Though the construction was delayed, his successor, Darius, completed it. It's in the Bible." I received many nods of approval. There were some gestures and signals to Mr. Skeptical to stop this line of questioning. The principal was really rooting for me. Others were impressed by my sincerity. I was telling the truth. That was a time when, regardless of what anyone thought, I really was pro-Israel. Many Iranians were. The Europeans were responsible for almost all the pogroms, massacres, persecution, building of ghetto walls, and discrimination against the Jews. Muslims, specifically Iranians, had protected them in their adversity. Both Jews and Muslims had been tortured and killed by the Christians in Spain and other places. To Christians, Jews were "Christ Killers." To the Western church, Muslims had a false prophet, Orthodox Christians were heretics as well, and the Jews were nefarious. Inquisitors had condemned them to die in the name of Christ, who had preached, "Love thine enemy!"

I had no doubt that this line of questioning had no place in the interview. My diction and my credentials impressed the other members of the board of trustees. Besides, they really needed me. Mr. Skeptical continued to ask one irrelevant question after another while the other board members looked genuinely irritated. Yet etiquette plays a part. They had to sit silently, tolerating all questions and insinuations.

"Yes, Cyrus the Great was indeed a great king, but what about the persecution of the Jews by Persians in the story of Esther?" he asked.

Even though I had read the Bible in Persian, the English name of Esther did not ring a bell. I looked puzzled. I thought about the question and dug into my brain to see if there was a Persian word for Esther. I could not retrieve it. Exasperated, I asked, a bit annoyed, "Who is Esther?" He narrated the story of Esther, concentrating on the discriminatory acts of Haman, and I suddenly remembered the annual feast of Purim as celebrated by the Jews in Iran. I also remembered the parts Mr. Skeptical had left out about the massive retaliation of the Jews against those who had wronged them.

As I remembered the story and noticed his intense interest in this incident from Biblical times, I began to weigh the immensity of the undertaking I was about to accept. I was an Iranian, proud of the history of the Persian people who had shown time and again their great tolerance, not only toward Jews, but also toward various other ethnic and religious groups such as the Nestorian Christians (now called Assyrians) who were persecuted and massacred by their own Christian brethren after the Council of Ephesus in 431. I could not make sense of the nonsense I was listening to. The Persian King, Ahasuerus, had married the Jewish Esther, saving her relative, Mordecai, from eminent death. Ahasuerus made Mordecai the prime minister of the kingdom and allowed the Jews to take revenge upon those who had intended to harm them. Still, Mr. Skeptical's main interest was in the fact that some Persians had previously persecuted a group of Jews. Even though other members of the board of trustees were visibly uncomfortable and unhappy with the insinuations of their colleague, I decided that the Hebrew Academy was not the place for me.

The principal was obviously unhappy. But we all sat in silence, listening to the narrative. At the conclusion, I sighed deeply and blurted out, "You're telling me a story that happened some three thousand years ago. Didn't you say that Esther married the king? So, what's the problem?"

Mr. Skeptical's face was red.

I got up from my chair. "I don't want your job," I said and left the room.

The principal ran after me. "Please don't be offended," he said. "Everyone loved you. Right now they're giving him hell. Take the job. It's yours."

I was standing by the staircase, waiting for the students to clear the hallways so that I could leave the building. "I am really sorry; I can't take this job." I said calmly. I left the building and drove to Kenwood Academy of the Sacred Heart (later, Doane Stuart) on Route 9W. Kenwood offered me a job on the same afternoon.

CHAPTER 38

The Night I Returned to Myself

IN 1970, MY FATHER CAME TO AMERICA to consult a doctor about his periodic chest pains. Doctors in Iran had suggested that cardiologists in America might help diagnose the cause and suggest a remedy. I took him to see a specialist in New York City. Priscilla and I sat in the waiting room under the watchful eye of a middle-aged secretary, who had a bouffant hairdo and a face full of wrinkles that she had done her best to hide behind heavy makeup. She smoked several cigarettes at her desk during the time we waited.

After about an hour, the doctor called me in. My father couldn't speak English and, in those days, doctors didn't tell patients how bad their conditions were anyway.

"Your dad has what is called angina pectoris. Unfortunately, there is no cure for it. I think that the Europeans have developed some kind of pill that might be helpful. If you know someone in England, you might be able to get him some of those pills. The FDA (Federal Drug Administration) has not approved the drug for use here yet. I am sorry to tell you this, but your father has somewhere between three and five years to live. Don't tell him what I told you; he'll worry about it and won't enjoy his life during the last few years he has left."

Though sad, I did my best to keep my composure. I thanked the doctor for his diagnosis, ignoring my father's constant badgering of whispered questions. What is it? What's wrong with me? Is he going to give me some

Abbasali Yadegari 1970

pills that will stop the bouts of pain? I said that I would tell him when we left. He became quiet and patiently waited. As we drove to Albany from New York City, I told him everything in the car except that he was facing the prospect of death soon. He must have suspected something, though, for he blamed his condition on the rich food he had consumed all his life. He used to refer to it as "the good and fatty food, full of energy." My father used to eat a lot of meat and poultry and was fond of cream and fatty lamb. Most of the aches he felt in his chest occurred after eating lunch or supper. "You know I love shish kebab and *pollow morgh* (a rice dish with chicken). I eat a full course and then some. Soon after, I feel the pain. Also when I pray, I feel it during *ruku'* and *sujud*.[33] Then, the pain slowly goes away. All I need is a bit of rest. I didn't have to come to America and pay a

---

33 The process of bending down and prostrating during the daily prayers are called *ruku'* and *sujud* respectively.

lot of money for the doctor to tell me what I already knew. And what kind of doctors are they? He didn't even give me a pill to ease the pain." I said nothing, pretending that I was concentrating on my driving.

The next day, I took him around and showed him the city of Albany. He was surprised at how clean the streets were. We walked along Central Avenue with him asking questions about how business people fared in their sales. I didn't really know, but I had surmised, right or wrong, that most of the shop owners were independent, middle-class businessmen, and that they did fairly well. They were not rich, but they made a decent living. I told him that America's economic backbone rested upon the shoulders of small independent businessmen. I related what my geography teacher back in Karbala, Iraq, had said about what made America so rich and powerful. The percentage of the middle class and independent bourgeoisie was high compared to other countries. My father agreed with me. But he also said that if he were to come to America to stay, he'd open a store that sold things like *sangepa* (pumice stone), loofas (exfoliates), *keeseh* (scrub glove), and *wajibi* (powder-like mixture of calcium oxide and arsenic sulfide used to remove hair). I started laughing. Americans didn't even know what these items were, let alone shave their pubic hair or sit in the bathtub scrubbing their feet with pumice stones. He was puzzled, really puzzled. "You mean men don't shave their pubic hair?" We both had a hearty laugh. Between bouts of laughter, I related that women didn't shave either. He could not believe it. As far as he and I knew, in the Middle East, most people shaved. Actually, it was said that the ancient Egyptians were the first to prepare and use *wajibi*, that pasty substance that dissolved hair.

In Karbala and some other parts of the Middle East, the use of *wajibi* was a sign of physical maturity. Teenagers who started growing dark hair followed the adults' tradition of applying *wajibi* to remove unwanted hair. It must have been a very ancient custom and no one questioned it. I remember, when I was about fifteen years old, I kept anxiously looking for hair on my arms and legs to give me a reason to apply *wajibi*. One of the elder workers in my father's public bath advised me that it was too early to do that. "Your hair will begin to grow fast and you will look like a gorilla soon. Wait a few years." I did.

"What about the hair on their legs?" My father asked.

"Oh, yes, women shave but not men. But some women don't shave their underarms often." We both laughed. It was the first and only time that I had such a conversation with my father. He didn't treat me like a kid any more. He was fascinated by the country and its progress but also repulsed by the poor grooming habits of the people. When it came to business and social life, he had no inhibition about asking questions. Not having seen me for so many years, he was treating me as one of his friends.

It was very disturbing to a man who started as a public bath owner to think Americans were not clean. I assured him immediately that they were clean. I told him that they took baths daily, and that only the very poor in shantytowns didn't take showers as often as they should. Not shaving, however, was hard for him to accept. I also told him that some Americans had misconceptions about the Middle Eastern habit of washing with water instead of using toilet paper after defecation. I told him that one of my history professors, who had been to the Middle East, related to his class that Muslims poured water from an *aftabeh* (water pitcher) holding it with their right hands while cleaning with their left hands. Hence, he cautioned us jokingly to be careful only to shake hands with the right hand of a Muslim, implying that the left was filthy. My father asked me why I did not correct him. I said my English was so bad I couldn't explain it, and the humiliation was too much to bear, so I had just slouched down in my chair and felt terrible.

He was angry. "Hopefully," he said reproachfully, "when you improve your English, you'll try to educate them." I agreed.

"You see, Baba [papa], America is not like Europe. Europe's geographical proximity to the Middle East and the rest of the East has provided its people with a fairly common history. In many European countries, public baths are common. Some have had contact with North Africans, learning from them about loofa and exfoliation. In America, the pilgrims had a rough and tough life, constantly challenged by nature and hard conditions. It is a new country, just about two hundred years old. In comparison, Europe, the Middle East, China, and other places are old countries. But, let's face it; America is the greatest country in the world, so what if they don't shave their pubic hair? It's not a big deal." Again, we both laughed.

"To be honest," I told him, "I don't shave anymore either. We should learn from the Americans and build our infrastructure, be self-reliant and self-sufficient. See what an amazing world they have built?"

But my father had a one-track mind. He was thinking of business and the only thing he knew was something new and novel. After all, teaching, a profession that paid a very low starting salary, was therefore not an acceptable occupation to him. Since he had no plans to stay in the United States, he really felt he could help me start a business that would pay off and save me from a life of "poverty." Teaching never made anyone rich. He knew it; so did I. In his own way, he was trying to be helpful.

"But I hear there are public baths in Europe. Why is there no public bath here?" He still was thinking about his kind of business.

"For one thing, at this time, Americans don't need public baths. Every house has a private bath, and people here don't need to go to public baths. However, Americans do like mineral baths, and they pay good money to use them. There is a famous public bath in Saratoga Springs, close to Albany. It is well known for its massages and its mineral waters."

My father had a devilish smile on his lips. I knew his mind was on sex. To him, it was not sexually stimulating if people had lots of pubic hair. It was unheard of!

"Wouldn't it be wise for someone, say yourself, to open a public bath in this city and try to educate people about these things? One way to promote this venture would be to concentrate on the sexual benefits. You know, sex is part of life and a condiment of marriage. When it comes to the glue that binds marriages, it is sex between husbands and wives that really does much to keep them together." My poor Baba had given me the opening to take my shot.

"You mean husband and many wives, don't you?" He was taken aback for a short time.

"But, son, I didn't do anything wrong. Islam allows it."

I didn't let him continue. "No, it doesn't. If you read the Quran carefully, it states that a polygamous man must treat his wives equally. One aspect of this equality, in my view, is to love them exactly the same. How can a man love and treat two or four women equally? It is impossible. And, while we're at it, let me ask you this."

"What?" he asked defensively.

"You proudly count the number of descendants you have so far. At this point, you have dozens of children and grandchildren and great-grandchildren, as well as in-laws. We know about our half-brother and half-sister. If, God forbid, you suddenly pass away, are we going to have any more surprises?" He looked puzzled. "I mean, are we going to see some other kids showing up saying, 'Hi, I am your brother or sister?'" I said it smilingly with no malice.

He took it that way and we both laughed again. He assured me the answer was negative. My mother had made his life so miserable over the second wife that he had given up his dalliances.

I was feeling a bit guilty for having put him on the spot. I broke his silence by adding that there were no *zoorkhanehs* in America either.

"I couldn't believe that there were no such places where I could go and exercise, either. We grew up with *zoorkhanehs* that are so common throughout the Iranian Plateau, but Americans have no idea what I am talking about when I ask about gymnasiums. When it comes to these things, they just don't know. There are places called the YMCA, but the human body odor there is intolerable."[34]

"So, where do they exercise?" he asked dumbfounded.

"When they're young, they exercise in schools and universities. And to them exercise is playing football, basketball, and baseball. Some schools don't even have running tracks. Ping-Pong is not considered a sport. People think it's a game for amusement. By the way, their football is not what we call football. They call our football, soccer. Their football is completely different."

Later, in the 1980s and 1990s when I taught history of the Middle East in college, my students were very interested in learning about the differences

---

34 It must be noted that this discussion took place in 1970, when fitness centers and spas were extremely rare. Today, such places are widespread and easily accessible. In 1970, my only experience with the YMCA had been in New York City. Later, I became a member of several YMCA's that were clean and well-equipped facilities.

in culture and social institutions in the Middle East and America. For one thing, in the 1990s, young people had no idea that fitness centers were a recent development. Some young students thought they always existed. When I told them the story of my experiences here, especially the part when I first signed up for the European Health Spa on Wolf Road, they were fascinated. I told the students that, when I found out there was a place with treadmills, rowing machines, dumbbells, stationary bikes, a pool, and a steam room, I walked in and signed up immediately. Even though the exercise equipment was less efficiently designed than it is today, I liked the place. However, most of the people who frequented the European Health Spa came in for the steam room and to rest in the whirlpool rather than to exercise. But the swimming pool was so small I could hardly swim in it, and it was filled with numerous fat men wading in the pool. They were so heavy that when they took their clothes off, their body fat hung down. I mean down, down to their knees, covering their genitals. When I told this story a roar of laughter would burst out among my students.

The businessman in my father was still at work. He was facing an empty lot on Central Avenue where a couple of buildings had been torn down. The size of the lot was not too large. My guess is that it was about 50' x 100'.

"How much do you think this lot is worth?" he asked. His abacus brain was shifting beads in his head. "Listen to me, son. Teaching will not make you rich. As I have told you many times, money is the filthiest thing in the world, literally and figuratively, but it is necessary and it would be better to have it than not have it. Buy this small lot. Open a store and fill it with pumice stone and loofas and all the other stuff. Sell them. You'll make some money. Then, you build a small *zoorkhaneh* on the second floor. According to what you tell me, these items are not popular in this country. If Americans are as concerned about their health and appearances as you're telling me, then, believe me, they will frequent these facilities. A combination of gymnasium and something like a public bath where these products and masseurs are available will become popular. Once you open such a place, people will start frequenting it. Word of mouth will spread the news, and you'll be rich. And remember the rule I taught you and your brothers: always respect the customers regardless of how much they spend. The person who spends a dime can only afford that dime. That person and the one who spends a dollar should receive the same kind of courtesy and respect. That's the secret in being a successful businessman. I can even lend you some money to get started." (It was years later when fitness centers and spas became popular that I realized how visionary my father had been. He had stayed in this country approximately ten days, but he could see the future trend. Not only did I not see it, I daresay I could not have made a go of it.)

Sitting in the car on the passenger side, my father was the traffic light "director." When the light turned green, he'd say, *"Boro bereem"* (Let's go). I still can hear the echo of his voice. *"Boro bereem, boro bereem."* He'd also nudge me with his finger on my knee or my thigh or my shoulder. Every time he touched me, I cringed. He was a man and was touching me. You see, after living for some six years in the United States, I had already assimilated completely, and I knew that men were not supposed to touch each other. Long gone were the days that we held hands walking in the streets or even hugged when we saw each other or kissed each other's cheeks when we returned from trips. Oh yes, I had become American. And the thought of another man touching my thigh was unsettling. At every intersection, when the stoplight turned green, he poked me. I was becoming tense. Automatically and uncomfortably, I moved my leg to the left away from him until I could stand it no longer. I decided to tell him the truth.

"Baba, in America men do not touch men."

Again puzzled, he looked at me waiting to hear more. What preposterous story was I going to tell him about this American tribe? I did not say anything. I heard him say, "So?"

I had no choice; I had to explain.

"They consider it intimate," I said. I added that people thought only homosexuals showed affection toward the same sex. I gave him the whole spiel about homophobia. I said it was okay for him to remind me verbally that the light had turned green but there was no need to touch me.

I saw him looking at me askance. I saw his face begin to color. He was hurt. I was afraid that he might have a heart attack. O God, what a stupid, idiotic thing for me to have said. Then I heard his hoarse sad voice rising from a deep abyss. "I AM YOUR FATHER, SON. YOU HAVE CHANGED."

That night, after I told Priscilla the story, she was very understanding of my father's feelings. She scolded me for saying what I had said: How could I be so insensitive? My father was being a loving father. He had not seen me for years. That was his culture. It was his way of showing affection. I thought about it and regretted being transformed into such a tense and intense person. I turned around in bed, and tears poured down my cheeks. I cried my heart out. Then, I remembered something else I had long buried among the ashes of my memory. I had not cried for many years, for that was also forbidden for the American male species. The gentle human part of me had died.

Assimilation had its positive aspects, but I was losing my cultural identity and, if not careful, I would have become alienated from my own soul and my very being. It was time to return to myself.

CHAPTER 39

Teaching at RCS

B Y 1973, WE HAD A SECOND DAUGHTER named Nasrene, just as lovely as her sister. I was no longer thinking of going back to Iran, and I had come to love this country. Actually, since 1968, when I received my Green Card and became a permanent resident of the United States, for some reason, I had begun thinking of myself as American. It was, thus, natural for me to apply for citizenship and change my nationality in October 1973.

By then, I had been teaching mathematics at Ravena Coeymans Selkirk Central School (RCS) since 1969. RCS was a suburban school of about 2,400 students ten miles south of Albany. The junior and senior high where I taught housed approximately 1,100 students in seventh through twelfth grades. At that time the schools served students from the three small towns and surrounding areas but was located in the town of Ravena, where a majority of the residents were of Italian descent. As for the faculty of some eighty in the building, there was a mixture of mostly Italian, Irish, and German backgrounds. Until the late 1980s, many teachers were local people who had been born in the three towns and surrounding areas and had returned to teach there after college. Many of the teachers were "old timers" who had proudly served in the Korean War. In late 1980s, an effort was made to hire more nonlocal applicants.

When I started teaching at RCS, I did not know anything about the culture that pervaded among the high school's faculty members. There were multiple centers of power. Among them were the department chairs: mathematics, science, business, shop, English, and social studies. When it came to the academics, their words were law. Most of the board of education members valued their suggestions. They were good people who cared for the students. But no one dared to cross them.

The chairwoman of the mathematics department was extremely fond of me. In fact, during the interview, I had no doubt that the presence of the superintendent as well as the principal was only a formality. It was the department chair who was in charge of the interview. The superintendent and principal both asked questions, true, but she was the one who offered me the job, stating, "I have been looking for years for such an enthusiastic and knowledgeable math teacher. Glad to have you on board." And that was it. They helped me fill out the form and sign it. I was hired on the spot.

There were other centers of power such as the officers of the local teachers' union. Their words were also the "law." If they ostracized someone, he or she either had to leave or endure being the subject of innuendo and chatter.

There were five immigrants teaching at RCS: a Lebanese woman who left for greener pastures a year after I was hired, two middle-aged sisters from Czechoslovakia, a Greek, and myself from Iran. The Czechoslovakian sisters both had earned a doctorate in their own fields: business and mathematics. The Greek fellow, who taught foreign languages, was multi-lingual, speaking French, Spanish, Latin, and Greek, as well as English. Additionally, he was athletic and had competed for Greece in the Olympics.

I was told that the sisters' doctoral degrees were bogus. "Why do you say that?" I asked.

"Where would they get a doctorate? What kind of university? Czechoslovakia? Look at them and tell me if either looks like someone who has a PhD?"

The mathematics teacher was teaching eighth grade. Being of short stature, she was not an imposing figure. However, she was a good disciplinarian and knew her subject well. She was extremely helpful to me when I taught eighth grade. I asked her for assistance in making lesson plans, and she generously offered me her full binder of lessons. Her sister was slightly taller, and I heard that she was an excellent business teacher.

They both had brains. I saw no reason to doubt their qualifications. Really, I asked myself, "Why should these teachers be subjects of such gossip?"

I just could not understand. Few teachers talked to them. Most snickered when they saw one of them. If one of the sisters greeted a teacher, a condescending attitude accompanied the reply. They were talked to as if they were children. What I find ironic today is that I did not realize that I was treated in the same way. If ever someone responded to my greeting, the entire conversation was uttered in the same manner. "Oh, hi, Moe! How are youuuu? Haven't seen you much. Hey Jack, did you see Moe? Here, he isssss."

I did not pick up on the superiority complex. I had to wait several years and learn it the hard way. But as time passed I realized that, in their eyes, foreign teachers came from the Third World and thus were inferior. Even if the sisters had earned doctoral degrees from Prague, for example, they were the product of an inferior educational system so they didn't deserve to be called doctors. As for me, years later I was told that some of my colleagues thought I had completed my elementary and secondary education in tent schools.

The man from Greece was treated similarly. The teachers bad-mouthed him behind his back.

Well, the sisters tolerated the jokes and gestures, showing no sign of disapproval. When they retired, one of them gave a final farewell address that really broke my heart. She thanked the listeners from the math and business departments who chose to attend the retirement lunch (we numbered no more than ten) for their hospitality and generosity and for welcoming two lonely women who had come to America seeking refuge and freedom from the Communist rule in their native country. She shed genuine tears and asked forgiveness for their shortcomings, if any.

As for the Greek, he tolerated all the whispers with smiles until the coterie found a new misfit to pick on. They found me.

Small town life was too complex for me to grasp. I had been in the United States for only five years, having spent almost all of it at the university dealing with many wonderful people, students and professors alike. But at RCS, I was culturally ignorant about the nuances of American society. Therefore, just like a child, I constantly asked why. During the first five years of teaching, my English sounded good, but my vocabulary was limited. I had a lot to learn about the United States and its people. Now I understand the meaning beneath the gestures, the askance looks, the narrowing of the eyelids and the slight, almost invisible, smirks. They all tell a story. And in these gestures, each society is different from others.

I have come to learn how people communicate without words. I knew these things back in Iraq and Iran and in the larger Middle East. America was different, though. I could not discern the meaning of the unspoken words. The ethos, the values, the general knowledge of a society with its intricate symbolism must be learned to really comprehend what lies in the hearts and the minds of people. I had difficulty discerning the implied along with the verbal, the covert, as well as the overt, and in differentiating the smiles from the smirks. If I greeted someone and he passed me by without "seeing" me, I never realized I was invisible to him. I thought he had not heard me. I'd turn around calling his name saying, "Good morning, Mike." He'd continue walking and would not answer. I just walked on thinking that he definitely hadn't heard me. I thought that the next time I would greet him more loudly and wave at him. Yes, really, I am not kidding you. I had not yet learned to recognize a snub.

I was a tyro, naïve, and, yes, shy too. More than that, I was humble, proud but humble. I remember my mother warning me again and again: "Son, don't be so proud. Being sensitive can get you into a lot of trouble. Pride and sensitivity do not mesh. They're like oil and water. The first one gets you into hot water and the second makes you sink in self pity." Humility was a sign of strength where I grew up. However, I had to learn the hard way to peel it off my soul. It was not an easy task.

In conversations around the teachers' room, a Polish person was a Polack, a Jew was a Hymie, and an Italian, a wop. Victims of these slurs would also laugh at such insults. Apparently, American culture actually required it. I was told, "In America, all immigrants go through these rites. The Irish went through it and the Italians went through it, and they both came out on top. Everyone knows it. So, don't fret when someone calls you A-rab. No really, now, tell me this. Did you ever eat a desert rat?"

During those years we had no African Americans teaching at RCS. More than a decade later, the district hired an African American woman in the middle school that was built in the early 1970s across from the high school. By then I had undergone their rituals, fought my battles, and signed an informal truce. But, the culture had not changed.

Did I have a good life in America? Of course I did. Why do you think I survived? I learned from my friends how to fight back. With all the rotten apples I found among the RCS High School faculty, I also found teachers who stood by me, encouraged me, and lent a helping hand. That's the beauty of America. My allies showed me the way. They taught me to be less humble and more combative, to stand up for myself.

Teaching was one social skill that I had mastered. Being a good teacher does not come from taking a few education courses in college and acquiring a certificate that indicates you're certified to teach. Having a tremendous amount of knowledge does not necessarily make one a good teacher. Teaching is an art. And a good teacher is a good artist. Teaching is the ability to impart knowledge to students with such clarity that the students can absorb it with no difficulty. And teachers must know that the first and foremost requirement is to get the respect of their students as well as their attention.

What other qualities make a good teacher? Consistency, firmness, and honesty are foremost in importance. Additionally, a teacher must keep in mind that what works today might not work tomorrow. A teacher must change tactics and style at a moment's notice. Life bends and twists, and a good teacher must sharpen his or her skills in order to deal with those variations.

Most teachers' problems had their roots in the attitudes of the teachers themselves. Some of them, though calm in the morning, became tense as the day proceeded. I used to joke about it. "It must be the coffee and doughnuts." Then I came to realize that almost all teachers with discipline problems were inconsistent and unreasonable.

Teaching was easy for me. It came naturally, but my relationship with some teachers was tenuous. One teacher called me "Mr. U.N." And then the barrage of jokes about *A-rabs* was getting stale. I laughed along with all the other teachers during the first three years. They may have been surprised that I was so docile and didn't stand up for myself. At first, I actually found

Mohammad and fellow teacher at RCS, 1975

their jokes funny. Sometimes, I tried to educate them. I would address them all, "Don't you guys know that there is a difference between an Iranian and an Arab?" More laughs. One teacher said, "Don't they all look alike?" I replied, "Not really." It was so frustrating that even social studies teachers could not understand that Arabs were different from Iranians. "Iranians are Aryans," I would say. "Arabs are Semitic." That made them laugh more. "The Hebrews are Semitic as well," added a somber Jewish fellow. There weren't many Jews in our school in those days, and they had to deal with the same kind of jokes behind their backs. I would agree with my Jewish colleague and continue my explication. "Arabic and Hebrew are related because both derive from a common origin, the Semitic languages. Iranians speak a completely different language, though their alphabet is mainly Arabic. As a matter of fact, the Iranian language groups, including Persian, are more closely related to European languages such as German and English because they derive from a common origin, namely, Indo-

European. Turks are linguistically related to the Mongols and Manchurians. What is the matter with you guys? You're teachers and really should know these facts. Some of you even teach social studies, for God's sake."

I had almost given up trying to educate my colleagues about the differences between Arabs and Turks and Iranians. Or that Hebrews and Arabs were more related than Iranians and Arabs. They just didn't understand.

Soon after the 1973 Arab-Israeli war and the resulting oil embargo, some of us started a car pool. One day, a teacher I'll call Michael was sitting in the back seat with me. He never stopped laughing. Joke after joke passed his lips, and he was the first to laugh at his jokes. He commonly picked on minorities. One day the phrase "clip cocks" slipped out of his mouth. I had never heard the expression before. I stopped laughing. I asked him what "clip cock" meant. He almost choked on his own laughter as his face turned red.

"Moe, you of all people in this car, should know." Our two companions, both Italian, were dead silent. I knew I had stumbled upon a new discovery related to the many nuances of culture that I had not yet learned.

"No, really, I don't know."

Michael looked at me again. "Of all people, you should know that Jews are clip cocks. You're a Muslim and an *A-rab*. You should know that."

"No, I don't." I really did not.

"Circumcised, Moe. Circumcised."

I saw that Tony, the driver, was a bit embarrassed. I felt like I had been hit by a ton of bricks.

I must say that during the first four or five years of teaching at Ravena, I was very naïve. I accepted all the racial insults as jokes because they were accompanied by much laughter and amusement. Those teachers were masters at telling jokes. What really started waking me up, slowly turning me into a stubborn and outspoken adversary, came in slow steps. There were several teachers who, directly or indirectly, approached me and said I should not put up with the racist remarks of some bigots. Harold Miller, the athletic director and a well-respected teacher, commented casually, "I hear they're giving you a hard time." I began to take notice. Shrugging my shoulders, I said, "They don't really mean it. I think they're joking." He looked at me askance, trying to discern my inner feelings. Then he cautioned, "No, Moe, they're not joking. Tell them, 'Go kiss my ass!'" Of course I knew what an ass was, but I did not know the full implication of the expression. I had to ask my wife.

The problem was that I had been instrumental in making them think I was docile. When you go along with people's sarcasm and cold shoulders and racist remarks, you turn into a passive character. It is then very hard to break out of the mold.

During the summers, I had ten weeks off. We saw a lot of my wife's aunt and uncle, who came from Florida in their travel trailer. Her seventy-year-old uncle, Vic, was Italian and married to her aunt, Kathryn. He used to be part owner of a car dealership in Binghamton, New York. Retired, he was a master fisherman, and he liked to talk. We spent a lot of time together. My best catches came from the Susquehanna River near Unadilla, New York, where the small rock bass were always biting. But when we went trout fishing in a stream near Oneida Lake, I would watch with fascination as Vic caught one trout after another with ease. We were near a shallow stream with fast-running clear water, and I could see more than a dozen trout swimming, but I could not even get a bite. Vic, on the other hand, kept reeling them in.

It was the summer of 1975, when I confided to Vic about some of the sarcastic remarks made about Arabs and Muslims that had been directed at me. My frustration and inexperience were obvious. He listened patiently and intently while chewing on his cigar and, occasionally, scratching his head. He looked up when I finished my discourse and said, "You've become passive."

I nodded.

"Do you know who is the most belligerent person in the group?" he asked.

Yes, I did.

"You should start with him."

But how?

"Simple. Do you know where he parks his car?"

I nodded.

"Find a heavy metal bar or a pipe about one and a half foot long. Leave school after dismissal just a minute or two before he does. Stand by his car, as he approaches, look straight at him and rotate the bar slowly in your hand. Keep gazing into his eyes. Your eyes should be talking, not your tongue. Stay firm, quiet, resolute, with the iron bar turning slowly. He'll get the message."

"You want me to scare him? What if he calls other teachers?"

He stopped me. "No. He won't. He'd be embarrassed to call his colleagues for help and even if he does, it will be a plus for you. Walk away without a word. See what happens. I promise he'll leave you alone. Bigots are cowards. They bark when they feel safe, but as soon as you confront them, they run away like dogs with their tails between their legs."

It was then that Vic told me about his own experiences growing up in America as a "wop." He further warned me that this would be the first of a series of steps I must take to be able to hold my chin up. Because the seventy-year-old man knew that neutralizing one person would have to be followed by a full-force assault on the rest of the pack.

Did it work? Of course, it did.

Vic and Mohammad 1975

The most important tool at my disposal was following the slogan: "Success is the best revenge." That was accomplished by studying hard to receive my doctoral degree, by fighting for my right to take religious days off, by returning my colleagues' jokes with sarcasm and open resistance. I got a lawyer and made it known to them. I took my grievances to the New York State Union of Teachers and, later, publicized my action. I sent a verbal message to the board of education. (I really don't know if the message was delivered, but the messenger spread it to his colleagues.) By 1977-78, everyone was very careful and circumspect around me.

My standing among the faculty had changed. I was no longer ignored. The bigots of the early and mid-1970s had either retired or were silenced. No more "Mr. U.N." and no more "*A-rab.*" Many incidents were left on the back burner to simmer. What the racist element could not comprehend was why a "foreigner" acted the way I did. I was too proud to kneel before the mighty bullies. Once I realized that racist remarks were not harmless jokes, I went on the offensive. I dished it right back at them. It took them several years to recognize how contentious I could be. I challenged them. I worked harder. I pursued my education beyond what was necessary.

Of course I always treated my friends with the utmost regard and respect. The faculty was clearly divided. They either ignored me, or they liked me and befriended me. As for the students, they had always respected me. So did their parents and most of the community who were decent people. My quarrel had not been with the community or the students. It was with a group of cliquish, childish, and racist teachers. And, to be honest, the racists were a dying breed.

However, in the late 1970s I was so engrossed and entrenched in my adversarial stance and routine that, when a member of the Cold Shoulder Camp decided to change his attitude, I was unable to respond positively. He was a good man by nature but had gone along with the backstabbing of the Cold Shoulder Camp. One day I walked into the faculty room as usual and sat across from a group of teachers who were assembled at another table. This man, who had ignored me for some two years, greeted me. By then, my success as a teacher was quite well known. I also was teaching part-time in a local college and had begun to publish little pieces of work here and there. For these people, this was success.

When the fellow greeted me, contrary to everything I had been taught growing up, I did not respond. I looked squarely at him with a sharp, cutting gaze. His face reddened. He repeated his greeting, looking at me. "God forgive me," I said to myself. "I should not act this way." But silence echoed from my side. The Clique had noticed. They also became silent. No one looked at either one of us. When the man greeted me again for the third time, I was thoroughly angry with myself. I was not taught to ignore other people. I was taught to smile and to acknowledge people's presence with all sincerity and honesty. But here I was, in America, where humility invited disdain.

I had come to learn that the way to put a bully in his place is to corner him and to push him back. I had come to learn that a bully is only a bully if you allow him to be one. Against everything I had been taught, I still knew that if I were to live in America and keep my dignity and self-respect, I had to fight dirty sometimes. I looked at him and the rest directly, calmly asking, "How does it feel to be on the other side of the fence?" I knew I had made my point.

CHAPTER 40

Graduate Studies

$\mathcal{I}$N 1970, I RECEIVED A LETTER from my older brother that his son, Saleh, wished to come to America to continue his undergraduate studies. He asked me to get an acceptance for his son from a college in the Albany area. Saleh was interested in engineering, but his high school grades were not outstanding. Rensselaer Polytechnic Institute in Troy (RPI) was an excellent school for engineering. However, I knew that Hudson Valley Community College nearby, which offered a math-science program in cooperation with RPI, would be easier for him to get into. The purpose of the RPI-sponsored program at Hudson Valley was to prepare pupils for entry into RPI if they were capable of rising to the challenge of a rigorous program. The department chair of that program assured me that their teachers were RPI professors and that successful students in this program had a good chance of receiving scholarships from RPI. Saleh came, worked hard, and succeeded in receiving a scholarship and a loan to study civil engineering. He graduated with a master of science in structural engineering in 1975.

Saleh lived with us for the first year in Albany. His time with us had several positive effects on our lives since he was our link to Iran. After seven years of not having the opportunity to speak Persian, it was indeed a pleasure to converse in my mother tongue. Saleh himself was a loquacious storyteller who loved to laugh, the same as I. He and I enjoyed many hours reminiscing about people and happenings in Iran. Amidst the laughter and tears running down our cheeks, I translated the stories for Priscilla.

In addition, Saleh could cook some Iranian foods. While Priscilla and I usually ate American foods, Saleh began to cook some meals such as stewed lamb with eggplant and rice. Priscilla learned to cook the dish from him. Occasionally, Saleh would get a lamb's head from a local butcher shop and cook *kalleh paacheh* (stewed lamb's head and feet), that specialty I had enjoyed so often in Karbala and Tehran.

Saleh had become engaged before leaving Iran. By the time he finished his undergraduate degree, he had officially married, and his wife, Tayebe, came to the United States. Tayebe was an even better cook and prepared a much more diverse variety of Iranian foods.

Saleh was very close to his family in Iran and went to visit each summer. He brought back Iranian handicrafts and news of who got married and how our extended families were growing.

Being an engineering school, RPI attracted many more Iranian students than SUNY at Albany at that time. After seven years of being in Albany without associating with anyone from Iran or the Middle East, we began to meet several Iranian students through Saleh. A small community had been gathering momentum in the area. I knew none of them, and when we met Saleh's friends I held back. We just didn't click. I had come to assimilate into the American lifestyle while most of them had not.

Saleh's friends were all religious, as was he, and thus our lifestyles clashed. I drank alcohol; they did not. I had no problem buying meat from the supermarkets; they went to great lengths to find halal meat. They insisted that women wear hijab; I knew well that it was only a custom and not a religious injunction.

They occasionally came to our house with Saleh, and we enjoyed talking with them. However, some of their attitudes irked me. Two young men who attended RPI befriended us, and one day they called asking to talk to me. We met one afternoon. One of them was writing his master's thesis in engineering, a topic we had no knowledge about, and he requested that Priscilla read and edit his work. Now, mind you, we had seen each other only twice. We did not know each other very well and were not even friends. I found him to be too presumptuous. The other had brought some magazines extolling the virtues of women who wore hijab. He had the temerity of asking me to teach my wife to wear hijab. I must say, as much as I am hospitable to a guest, I cannot tolerate meddling in our business. It did not take long before I directed them to the door.

I was teaching mathematics at RCS High School in 1970 and studying full time for my master's degree in mathematics at SUNY at Albany. In 1966, the new campus at SUNY Albany had opened. The university had set aside a substantial amount of money to attract well-known professors, one of whom was Dr. Martin Levey, a respected figure in the study of history of science and mathematics.

Martin Levey's prestige was such that his arrival was expected to enhance SUNYA's reputation and also attract grants for his proposed department. He brought in Professor Jack Bulloff, a brilliant chemist who was endowed with a keen analytic mind and was interested in modern technological trends, while Martin Levey was an expert in the history of sciences. This diversity of interests was expected to lend balance to a proposed history of science department.

I was interested in the history of sciences because Muslim scholars in the early centuries of Islamic history had studied the sciences of antiquity from Greece, India, and Persia and had greatly advanced and expanded them in their universities, colleges, hospitals, and pharmaceutical facilities. It was a perfect opportunity for me to pursue my interest under the aegis of a top-notch scholar.

After I took a general course in the history of science with Professor Levey, we became very close. One of his specialties was translating ancient manuscripts from Hebrew and Arabic into English. As soon as he discovered my background, especially the fact that my command of the Arabic language was nearly as strong as my Persian, he asked me to translate Abu Kamil's[35] *On the Pentagon and Decagon* from Arabic into English. Since this was a treatise on geometry, my translation was accepted as a thesis for my master's degree in mathematics.

Dr. Levey sent the work to the History of Science Society of Japan to be published. He had great plans for me. We were to embark on translations of a number of treatises in physics, mathematics, medicine, and astronomy.

---

35 Abū Kāmil, Shujāʿ ibn Aslam (c. 850–c. 930) was an Egyptian mathematician whose mathematical techniques later influenced Leonardo Fibonacci.

Professor Levey encouraged me to quit teaching at RCS and assist in his research full time while pursuing my doctorate in the history of science under his guidance. I was excited at the possibility but reluctant to do so, for my family responsibility was above all ambitions I may have had for myself. He asked me how much I earned as a teacher in high school. My salary was under six thousand dollars annually at the time.

As was his usual habit, he used a piece of scrap paper to jot down some numbers. He added cost for tuition, books, and an annual fellowship. He showed me the sum and asked if that amount was enough to convince me to quit teaching and devote my time to research and translation of ancient texts into English. It was August 1970, and the History of Science Department was to begin under his leadership that fall. The total amount of money Dr. Levey was offering me was close to ten thousand dollars. A doctorate in the history of science with several published works that were already planned between us would have definitely landed me a good position in academia. I almost submitted my resignation to the RCS administration that same week but decided to mull it over a little longer.

One evening soon after, Dr. Levey called to let me know that he was going into the hospital for a minor medical procedure. The surgery and the hospital stay were to take only three days. We made an appointment to meet soon after he was released from the hospital. As fate would have it, Professor Levey entered the hospital but never came out.

I had no idea of his sudden demise when I went to his office at the agreed-upon time and told Professor Bulloff that I had an appointment with Dr. Levey. Professor Bulloff was beside himself, and I was dumbfounded when I heard of Dr. Levey's unexpected death. A man had died, and two dreams were shattered. I sometimes, nostalgically, wonder about the outcome of the other "road" had it not been blocked in my destiny.

My dream of getting a PhD in the history of science went up the chimney. Yet my desire for a doctorate was still burning. I applied to enter the PhD program in mathematics at SUNYA. One of the requirements was taking the GRE (Graduate Record Examination). Not knowing what GRE even stood for, I signed up and took it. My grade was in the third percentile, extremely low. The result was shocking not only to me but also to the mathematics department's faculty that subsequently refused to admit me into the PhD program.

I didn't have to ask anyone why my results were so bad. I knew the reason immediately: I had never in my life taken a multiple-choice exam. A weak vocabulary, no preparation or familiarity with multiple-choice questions, and my slow reading ability, all had contributed to a dismal failure. "I had never taken a multiple-choice exam before," I told everyone.

"Unacceptable," they thought.

Insanely, I applied to one department after another in the university, and one by one they rejected me. Being married with a child would not permit me to spread my wings to apply elsewhere.

One night in 1973, I was experiencing my usual insomnia. It was one o'clock in the morning, and I was unable to fall asleep. I turned on the television and saw a professor from New York University teaching history of the Middle East in what later came to be known as "distance learning." In his concluding remarks, the professor credited the learning program at NYU's Near Eastern Studies. It was then that I realized there were such departments in several large universities across the country. I applied to New York University, Columbia, and Princeton.

Princeton did not accept me, pointing out that its scholarship and fellowship would not be sufficient for the needs of my family. Columbia University had assured me that I would be accepted but required that the Graduate Record Examination be taken anyway. New York University offered full tuition and thirty credits transferred from my master's degree work but did not require the GRE. While I was leaning toward NYU, I wanted to take the GRE anyway. I had never accepted my previous grade as being reflective of my knowledge.

By then, I had become aware of publications such as Barron's study guide for GRE. I devoted several months to studying and practicing multiple-choice tests using that book. I took the exam and placed in the 72nd percentile, which was much more acceptable. I felt vindicated. Columbia University accepted me, but I chose to attend New York University. I still did not know how I was going to finance my education except by borrowing as much money as possible in New York State Higher Education Loans and National Defense Loans.

One afternoon, my nephew Saleh called. He sounded down. He asked if I had time for him to come for a visit. With teary eyes, he informed me that my father had died of a massive heart attack.

I was very sad. However, I had prepared myself for such an eventuality ever since the doctor had informed me that my father had only three to five years to live. I had never divulged that secret to any member of my family in Iran. As there was no treatment at the time, there seemed no reason to alarm them. I consoled Saleh for the loss of his grandfather and did my best to calm him down.

It was no surprise that my father had donated one third of his assets to the poor. It was totally in keeping with his character. As it turned out, my share of the rest of the inheritance was large enough to ease the financial burden for the required first year of full-time study as well as the subsequent part-time years.

Asking for a sabbatical leave was out of the question because I had not been at RCS for the required five years. I had taught only four. I asked for a leave of absence without pay. I could have quit my job, but I realized that it is never a good idea to burn your bridges. I was well aware that you never know what the future holds. The board of education approved my request.

The Department of Near Eastern Languages and Literatures at NYU was well suited for me. I did not need to take any classes in Arabic or Persian for I was fluent in both. My courses centered mostly on history of the Middle East, Islamic history, and the history of sciences, as well as Persian literature. I abandoned my plan to translate the manuscript chosen by Dr. Levey to use for my doctoral thesis in the never-materialized history of science department at State University of New York at Albany because I was unable to find a suitable advisor in that area. Instead, I decided to write my thesis on the role of the emigrant Iranian press in the development of journalism in Iran. The faculty at NYU was more than helpful to me but was unable to provide me with a fellowship to continue my studies full time. In order to continue full time after one year, I had to rely on something more concrete than just spending my own money.

After completing my year of required residency and failing to obtain a fellowship for the remaining years of study, I returned to RCS to continue teaching mathematics while studying part-time for my doctorate by taking independent courses at NYU and working on my doctoral thesis.

My advisor was extremely generous and supportive. I was permitted to call collect from Albany to the Near Eastern Studies Department in New York City to consult with him regarding my progress in my research. When necessary, I took short trips, especially on weekends, and met my advisor to discuss the materials that I was investigating for my thesis. Also, I took many trips to the Princeton University library to research other periodicals necessary for my topic. I completed my PhD in Near Eastern Languages and Literatures in October 1979.

The contract between the board of education and the teachers at RCS had stipulated an increase of salary for each three-credit course above the required master's degree and approximately six hundred dollars for a doctoral degree. The superintendent offered me only two hundred dollars for additional credits. I found his refusal to recognize my doctoral degree insulting and did not accept.

Some teachers whispered behind my back that I had received my degree in Persian language. They falsely claimed that I had taken a sabbatical leave (not a leave of absence with no pay). They posted a fairly big sign in the faculty room that read: "Only physicians are entitled to be called doctors." My attempt to file a grievance was crushed by the local union leadership as well as the New York State Union of Teachers (NYSUT) representative assigned to represent the teachers of our local union.

Several years later, Jean, the science department chairwoman at RCS, received her doctoral degree in education. The superintendent refused to raise her salary. She fought back and that time the union backed her. She came to me one day, agitated, nervous, and extremely upset saying, "Mohammad, now I understand what you went through. These people are devoid of decency and intellect."

I appreciated her remarks but added, "Thank you for your sentiments and forthrightness. However, you'll never know what I went through because you have never experienced racism and bigotry."

She agreed.

Some time later, the situation improved. The local teachers' union changed leadership, and there was a new superintendent. Negotiations between the board of education and the teacher's union were underway, and one of the items on the agenda was "Jean's doctoral salary step." I forced them to include my name as well by threatening to sue the school, the local union, as well as NYSUT. After the step was approved, we both received a couple thousand dollars retroactively, as well as a large annual step for our doctoral degrees.

Why did I not apply for a full-time position teaching Middle East history in college after completing my degree? It was largely because of timing.

During the years I had been in the United States, the U.S. government had had a very good relationship with the Iranian government under the Shah. American and British oil companies had a large number of workers in Iran. The U.S. bolstered the Iranian government as a foothold against the Soviets who were also interested in the country. American manufacturers sold large numbers of armaments and planes to Iran, and the U.S. military trained Iranians in their use.

Large numbers of Iranian students came to the U.S. for education, and the Shah donated a lot of money to fund university programs expanding cultural awareness of the Middle East. Many of the Middle East languages and history programs in major American universities were funded by grants given by the Shah.

In 1979, Ayatollah Khomeini finally ousted the Shah. The 1979 hostage crisis[36] followed soon after, and Iranian/American relations were completely reversed. Money for the Middle East programs dried up. Departments were reduced or closed. While well-established professors scrambled for the remaining jobs, new graduates were largely left out in the cold.

I received my degree in October 1979. While there were a few opportunities, those jobs were fairly tenuous in terms of long-term employment. I had a job, and my family needed security. I decided to remain at RCS and direct my interests in a variety of other directions.

---

36 On November 4, 1979, Iranian students took over the American Embassy in Tehran, and held American diplomats hostage for 444 days. They were released on January 20, 1981.

CHAPTER 41

The Iranian Revolution as Seen from America

URING THOSE TURBULENT and difficult years of my life, many other events were developing. In 1977, one of my cousins, Jalal, came to America with capital to start a restaurant in this country. He was headed for Las Vegas, where his older brother had connections. I wondered why he was intent on abandoning lucrative businesses in Tehran, preferring to come to America to start a restaurant. But I soon found out.

The political situation was becoming uncertain in Iran. The Shah had exiled Ayatollah Khomeini from Iran to Turkey in 1964. From there Khomeini went to Iraq and years later to France, where he continued his stinging attacks on the Shah, agitating for his ouster. Some Iranians with vision and means realized that a revolution was coming and knew the outcome would not be beneficial to their well-being. Within two years the revolution came.

Washington was the scene of anti-Shah protests on November 15, 1977, and tear gas had to be used to disperse the rowdy crowd. It was comical to see the Shah wiping his watering eyes while President Carter was in the midst of formally welcoming him at the White House. On his visit to Iran in December 1977, President Carter delivered a warm speech in which he praised the Shah's leadership and called Iran "an island of stability." America had missed the point, again.

The streets of Tehran exposed the error of Carter's description. The economy was in shambles. The country's system of agriculture had declined steadily following the Shah's land reforms. Food shortages had caused rising prices.

The nightly news covered the increasing dissent in Iran. In addition, we were beginning to receive cassette tapes from Iranian students who had become friendly with us and occasionally came to visit. These cassettes were recordings of Ayatollah Khomeini's fiery speeches delivered on various occasions. The speeches offered more information on Khomeini's line of attack on the Shah's rule. Khomeini opposed the Shah because of his many deficiencies: his subservience to the West in politics, his encouragement of emulation of Western values and mannerisms, his opulent style of living, his political blunders, and his use of a brutal and insidious secret police (the SAVAK). To top it off, the Shah had given another excuse to Khomeini when he celebrated what was called "The 2500th Year of Foundation of Imperial State of Iran," on which he spent some $200 million in October 1971. This was a lavish and expensive ceremony where the most well-known designers and planners were hired from France, and even the food was imported from there. Khomeini called it the "Festival of the Devil." Even some of the Western media criticized the huge amount of money that the Shah spent while the country suffered from poverty and a widening economic and social gap.

The concept of *Vilayat-e Faqih* (Rule of the Religious Jurisprudent) had originally been a subject of discussion among the scholars of Karbala, Najaf, and, possibly, Qum, but it was Ayatollah Khomeini who popularized it throughout the world. This idea, arrived at through the use of *ijtihad* (intellection or investigative reasoning) was that, in the absence of the Twelfth Imam, the rightful representative or ruler should be the foremost-recognized religious jurisprudent. In pushing for the Shah's ouster, day after day, Khomeini persisted in his condemnation of the Shah's policies and his subservience to the United States. Khomeini's determination and tenacity never diminished, for he had made it his personal responsibility to rid Iran of a ruler whom he considered illegitimate.

He was not alone in his efforts to dethrone the Shah. There were dozens of writers, both secular and religious, who opposed the Shah's policies. Millions of Iranians devoured their writings, paving the way for an intellectual mass revolution rather than a military-style takeover of the country.

The enthusiasm Khomeini generated was astonishing to me. Some young Iranians who studied in the United States gave up their educational pursuits and left America to join what they considered to be the dawn of a better life in Iran. There was great anticipation among many Iranians but also great foreboding among a smaller group who saw the Shah's push for modernization to be the hope of the future.

From his home in exile in France, Khomeini announced a revolutionary council to replace the Shah's regime. In Iran, there were daily demonstrations against the Shah, and some of them were violent. The Shah had no choice but to leave the country. On January 16, 1979, the Shah left Iran for Aswan in Egypt. Shapour Bakhtiar, the last prime minister appointed by the Shah, was unable to control the situation in Iran. Events were moving fast, and many Iranians, in the country as well as abroad, wondered and worried about the kind of government that would replace the monarchy. Khomeini returned from exile on February 1, 1979, to be welcomed by cheering throngs of Iranians. The Islamic Republic of Iran was proclaimed soon after.

While I had been leery of the establishment of a religious government all along, I became more so when I heard that rules had been issued regarding women's attire. Iranian women had been instrumental in bringing the Shah down. Some women who were not in the habit of wearing a head covering, proudly wore the scarf as a symbol of resistance to the monarch's despotic rule. During the revolution, the scarf and the chador had come to represent women's militancy, not subservience. Yet, after the fall of the Shah, rules were instituted to eliminate the right to choose what to wear. The most important role for women described in the new constitution of Iran was one of being good housewives and raising children. That did not sit right with me. When my own niece decided to leave the U.S. and return to Iran with only one year left to finish her bachelor's degree, she insisted that she could finish the rest of her study at Tehran University. Alas, she was rejected because her *marja'-e taqlid* (the Ayatollah she followed for religious guidance) was Ayatollah Mohammad Shirazi and not Khomeini. Though the idea of replacing the Shah had been my ardent desire, I began to feel a sense of regret regarding the change of events. I believed that a secular government would be more suitable for Iran.

After the revolution, I became interested in reading the works of some of the many Iranian thinkers who had called for a change in the government, writers such as Ali Shari'ati, whom Ayatollah Khomeini called a martyr of the Iranian Revolution. I began to realize that the revolution would not have occurred had it not been for the metamorphosis in the nation's consciousness shaped by those writers.

I was very enthusiastic about presenting my personal observations to the American public about the writers who had influenced the Iranian Revolution. I spoke to many groups who were interested in that subject. I also wrote a book entitled *Ideological Revolution in the Muslim World* that was accepted for publication by American Trust Publishers (ATP), a publishing company under the aegis of the Islamic Society of North America (ISNA), which was primarily a Sunni organization.

My book was published in 1983, but American Trust Publishers' name was absent from it. The printer's name (IGPS) was indicated instead of the actual publisher. I was beside myself but kept quiet while simmering inside. I accepted several invitations by ISNA to deliver speeches at University of Wisconsin Madison, and the University of Illinois at Urbana-Champaign. It was in these two places that I realized that ISNA was interested in me particularly because I had been critical of some of the superstitious beliefs of Shi'ites. They thought that they could use me to their advantage.

My day of awakening came when I was delivering a speech about the controversial concept of *ijtihad,* one of the bases of law in Islam. *Ijtihad* allows for change if and when a community is faced with new circumstances. Around the thirteenth century, most Sunni Scholars came to agree that they had created a pure system of law that should not be corrupted. Therefore there was no need to add new amendments. Thus, they "closed the door of *ijtihad.*" Since that time, any suggestion of "innovation" in the law has been regarded as unthinkable to most Sunnis. However, some modern Sunni thinkers have advocated the use of *ijtihad* in order to solve issues that confront the Muslim community. Muhammad Iqbal (d. 1938) was one such Sunni scholar. On the other hand, the Twelver branch of Shi'ite School of Law ardently and stubbornly clung to *ijtihad* as a tool to address newly arisen circumstances.

The ruckus that my speech created made me realize that most of the audience were not as open minded as I had been led to believe. The audience became gradually restive as the members commented to their nearby neighbors. Several had their hands up as I was speaking. They looked hostile. While Muhammad Iqbal, a well known Sunni scholar, had sufficient credentials and standing in the Muslim community to suggest reinstating the use of *ijtihad* to produce progress and change in Muslim society, I did not. Some of the audience gleaned from my talk that I personally was a proponent of *ijtihad* (which was true).

During the question and answer period, the mood of the audience took a turn for the worse. Accusations of *bid'ah* (innovation) were hurled at me. This accusation is extremely serious. One member of the audience indignantly asked, "Do you think you know more than the great scholars of the past who closed the door to *ijtihad*?"

I took a placating stance. "First of all, I never claimed to be wiser than other scholars. Secondly, I am only presenting the views of Muhammad Iqbal, who was a Sunni scholar and much revered by all of you." When they insisted that they were not talking about Iqbal but were interested in my personal opinion, I responded, "I am a man who thinks. I believe anyone who is capable of thinking is entitled to his or her own views." The audience was enraged, and for a couple of minutes the noise was deafening. Derisive shouts of *bid'ah* (innovation) filled the air. I stood there silently watching them. After the moderator quieted them, I had the opportunity to put in another sentence. I gazed directly at the audience and uttered defiantly, "If you're the best and the brightest of the Muslim World, God help us!" No one said a word. I left the podium.

Later, a friend consoled me, saying, "What bothered that mostly Arab audience is that they are madly jealous that Ayatollah Khomeini, a Persian and a Shi'ite, 'stole' their Islamic revolution."

It was time for me to break my relations with this group. I contacted my lawyer and asked him to formally demand the return of my publishing rights. An agreement was reached that ATP could sell the remaining 2,700 copies that had already been printed, but that no new books were to be published and all rights would be returned to me.

My association with American Trust Publishers and Islamic Society of North America was over, and I was able to concentrate my energies elsewhere. I did my best to do a good job of teaching my classes both in high school and college. Of course, the education of my daughters took priority over everything else. Furthermore, I was invited to join the NAACP (National Association for the Advancement of Colored People) Board of Directors in Albany and also the local board of the Arab American Anti-Discrimination Committee and to serve four years on each.

In those capacities, I associated with two open-minded and progressive men with whom I formed life-long friendships: Michael Dollard and Irv Landa. Both men were social activists in Albany. I enjoyed their company, working with them on the NAACP board of directors as well as socializing with them personally. At times when the world seemed to have gone mad, conversation with these two freethinkers reassured me that there were still some people possessing universal human values who were ready to speak out against injustice.

CHAPTER 42

Misperceptions

*A*FTER I RECEIVED MY DOCTORAL DEGREE in October 1979, my hopes of finding a full-time position in a reputable university had been dashed by the reduction in Middle East programs following the Iranian Revolution. However, I did look for an opportunity to teach part-time at a local college.

When the university students took over the American Embassy in Tehran on November 4, 1979, and held the diplomats and staff hostage, Americans became fixated on this crisis. There suddenly was a lot of interest in the Middle East. As it happened, I had already agreed to deliver a speech about the Iranian Revolution at the annual meeting of the New York State Social Studies Teachers Association in November 1979. Several hundred teachers attended that session, and its enthusiastic reception encouraged me to pursue other opportunities. From 1980 until 1995 I taught courses in Islamic history and culture at Union College in Schenectady, New York, and I taught similar courses at the University at Albany from 1995 until 2007. This turned out to be one of the most enjoyable periods of my teaching career. I found the students to be interested in the topics and fascinated by my comparisons of societal habits in the Middle East to similar habits among people in the United States. My classes were usually full.

In the spring of 1999, I was teaching History 388, Islam in the Middle East: Religion and Culture II, at the University at Albany. The lecture for that night was entitled "Veiling and Seclusion of Women." I had promised my students, mostly junior and senior history and political science majors, that I would cover the topic as thoroughly as possible in the time allotted.

As I entered the classroom, in my peripheral vision, I saw what seemed to be a black garbage bag placed on the chair behind the first desk on my left. I turned quickly to take a closer look. I realized that the middle-aged woman occupying that chair was wearing *abaya,* including a black face covering. Since my classes were offered in the evenings, some of the students were adults. I did not recognize her at first. But, by virtue of being in that particular seat, which matched my seating chart, I knew that she was one of the older students. I'll call her Mrs. Forty-Five (her approximate age). She had taken a couple of my other courses previously and was industrious and genuinely interested in history. I heard her explain sheepishly, "I am wearing an *abaya.*' I hope you like it."

"No, I don't like it," was my quick response. She said nothing, and I began my lecture:

> It is true that Muslim women today are often restricted and, in many places, are secluded and compelled to wear a veil. In discussing this issue, we must address an important question. Is Islam, the religion, the cause of this practice? Does Islam dictate seclusion and denial of women's rights? The answer to this question is definitely "No." Islam supports women's rights to own property, to be educated, to vote, to inherit, to divorce, to travel, to work, to own and operate a business, and to fight for their rights in courts.

I was interrupted by a young female voice shouting, "We want to talk about genital mutilation of Muslim women!" I looked toward the corner wall where I noted the presence of a woman who had escaped my attention when I had been taking attendance. She was not on my list and therefore not enrolled in my class. Obviously, upon hearing from a friend about my forthcoming lecture, she had snuck in. Almost all the students turned to see who she was.

"It appears that you are in the wrong classroom, Miss," I retorted. "I am not going to ask your name, nor will I ask you to leave. However, I will comment that genital mutilation is a custom prevalent among many African tribes of a variety of religious backgrounds, including animists, Muslims, Christians, and Jews. Recently, there have been some articles in the papers that have erroneously blamed this barbaric habit on Islam and Muslims. The author was obviously ignorant or tendentious. Tonight's lecture is not dealing with that subject. While the topic is interesting from an anthropological angle, it has nothing to do with Islam and is not relevant to this course. You may leave if you wish." She gathered her backpack and walked out.

After she left, I continued my lecture:

> The rights that I just enumerated were afforded women in the seventh century, in the time of the Prophet, and many centuries afterwards. Even now, to a certain degree, women enjoy these rights in some Muslim countries. Today, the Western media tends to display Muslim women in veil and imply that they are oppressed and stripped of all rights. In addition, a perception is created that veiling and suppression of women has been imposed by the religion.
>
> It behooves us to study what Arabian women wore before Islam and what, if any, changes were introduced during Muhammad's time and after. Historical evidence indicates that prior to, and in those early days of Islam, it was not uncommon for men to accost women in the streets, propositioning them and even groping them. Surah 33, verse 59, alludes to this problem and suggests modesty in dress. "O Prophet, tell thy wives and thy daughters, as well as all [other] believing women, that they should draw over themselves some of their outer garments [when in public]: this will be more conducive to their being recognized [as decent women] and not annoyed. But [withal,] God indeed is much forgiving, a dispenser of Grace!"[37]

---

37 Muhammad Asad, *The Message of the Qur'an*, Dar al-Andalus, Gibraltar, 1980, 33:59.

Reading the verse carefully, it is clear that it is not an injunction but a recommendation. This verse, as well as many other verses that discourage an action, ends with a note of forgiveness and mercy. The last sentence of the verse cited above makes it clear that if women choose not to cover themselves with some of their outer garments, God is indeed "much-forgiving, a dispenser of grace."

What the verse was addressing was modesty. My memory takes me back to the late 1940s in Karbala, Iraq, when Bedouin women, whose lifestyle had changed little since the time of the Prophet, came to town to sell their products of woven baskets, live foul, and more. To my total surprise, some of these women did not even wear underclothing beneath their tunics and long skirts or dresses. It was quite possible for an observer to see their breasts and sometimes their genitals as they moved about stretching their legs while sitting on the ground. As for their breasts, the long and wide opening in front of the tunic left nothing to the imagination. Walking in the streets of Karbala, occasionally I witnessed Arab men wearing *dishdashah* (a long white robe) while climbing date palms to prune their fronds or to pollinate the trees. Not only did I see dates hanging down but also the man's "chastity," which was quite visible. If I witnessed some Bedouins wearing such outfits in the late 1940s, then Prophet Muhammad's concern about modesty in the seventh century was probably well-founded.

Laughter filled the classroom. I laughed as well but continued:

If, in the 1940s, some Bedouins did not cover their "chastity," I am sure you can imagine how many people walked around half naked in Muhammad's time. Indeed it was the habit of many Arabian women to circumambulate the Ka'bah semi-nude during the hajj.

I waited for the laughter to subside and the chuckles to abate. "I am sure you know I would never make up these stories." I continued my lecture.

> Surah 24:31 cautions a woman against drawing attention to herself in public by displaying her jewelry or "natural charms." Islam proposed modesty in public for men and women alike. It was a custom of Arab women to open their tunics, bare their bosoms, and dance, thus encouraging their men to fight courageously in wars and return home safely to be rewarded generously. Islam discouraged such customs.
>
> Covering one's face or hair was not a custom until the tenth century during the Abbasid Dynasty (750-1258), as a result of the influence of the Byzantines and others upon Muslims. When Arab Muslims pushed out of Arabia in the seventh century, they encountered diverse groups of people with a variety of religious beliefs and cultural differences. They encountered Jews and Christians who secluded and imposed veiling upon their women. The Bible mentions many instances of such a behavior. Muslims slowly began to imitate those Judeo-Christian customs. However, as time elapsed, Muslim scholarship waned, and the cult of masculine honor grew. The custom of veiling, originally adopted from Christians and Jews, became incorporated into Muslim tradition.

It was time for our fifteen-minute break. Some students stayed to ask questions. Most left to smoke, eat a snack, and rest. I saw Mrs. Forty-Five take her *abaya* off. Her face was flushed and sweaty. I looked at her and said, "I hope you're feeling okay." She approached me while struggling to get herself loose from the *abaya* that had two sleeves clinging to her sweaty arms. I began to chuckle to break the ice.

"I am really sorry, Professor. I thought you'd like to see me wearing the *abaya*."

I told her not to worry.

She continued, "Your lecture really opened my eyes. I had no idea that wearing veil is just a custom and not a religious injunction. Foolishly, I thought that you would like to see women in veil."

"Where did you get it?" I asked. She had traveled in the Middle East and had purchased it in Baghdad. Her assumption that I would like to see women wearing an *abaya* reminded me of another episode that had taken place two years earlier.

In the fall of 1997, I was teaching History 387 (Islam in the Middle East: Religion and Culture I). My college students were scheduled to take their midterm exam. As it happened, I had to attend another meeting on the same evening. Instead of cancelling class, I notified my students that my wife would proctor their midterm. On the appointed date, my wife and I entered the classroom early setting up for the exam. She sat at the desk while I chatted with the incoming students. I had about an hour before my meeting began, so I stayed until all the students had arrived.

One of the incoming students asked me if my wife was there.

I said, "Yes, she is here."

He looked around and was puzzled. "But I don't see her, Professor. Where is she?" he inquired again.

I replied, "Do you see the blonde woman sitting at my desk? She is my wife."

He looked surprised but a sudden realization of something that ran contrary to his perception appeared on his face.

At first, I did not fully grasp his astonishment. I was too busy to give it a thought, but his reaction nagged my brain. I rushed to my car to go to my meeting. Sitting in the driver's seat, revving up the engine, my mind suddenly clicked, solving the enigma. He was expecting to see a veiled woman. Since my name is Mohammad, that should imply not only that I am a Muslim, but also that my wife must wear a veil. Images imprinted, intended or not, leave permanent impressions on people's perceptions.

One by one, students returned from their break back to our classroom in 1999. I continued my lecture on Veiling and Seclusion of Women. I talked about the fact that while the Quran encourages modesty for both men and women, there is nothing in the Quran that specifies that women must wear a veil or that the custom started because Arab Muslims were influenced by the customs prevalent in conquered lands beyond Arabia. Seclusion of women and veiling started to become common among Muslims in the tenth century, at a time when rowdy and immoral behavior had also become widespread and the more "pious" people sought to "protect" their families. By the sixteenth century, the habit was well entrenched in many regions of the Mediterranean world. Religious leaders reinterpreted certain Quranic verses to make them more stringently required and applicable to all women rather than just the Prophet's wives. The habit of veiling of women, which was actually a social custom, was thus retroactively justified to appear as part of the original teachings of Islam and thus spread farther east into Iran, Pakistan, and beyond.

Furthermore, I discussed how modest dress has been common in the United States until recently (early 1900s), and how some forms of veiling exist even today among the Amish, Mennonites, Nuns, and Jewish Orthodox.

Many people in the West find this practice of shielding women from the view of strangers to be quaint and humorous. I have encountered it among many other people outside the Muslim world, even in the United States. In the early 1990's I visited a small town in New York State where a man was making jelly by using fructose rather than sucrose and selling it from his home. We called and arranged to meet him there. We found him alone in his house. He appeared to be Amish, but in the course of conversation he told us that he was Mennonite. His sixteen-year old son was mowing the lawn outside and his wife, we were told, was asleep. It was a family operation and he took us for a tour. We were very impressed by his ingenuity. He had converted the entire basement of his house into a small "factory." It wasn't a simple jelly-making apparatus that any household might have. He was making enough jelly to market in some of the area's farm stores and even supermarkets. That's how we had found his business' name and address.

The gentleman took us from room to room in his house and proudly pointed out how he ran his business. Meanwhile I detected a ghost-like figure of a woman wearing a long dress moving furtively from one room to another as we wound our way from one hallway to another entering the rooms. This "apparition" appeared about three times. Having been born in a religiously conservative family, I immediately discerned that she must be a conservative Mennonite. They similarly emphasize modesty for both sexes. In some conservative circles, a Mennonite woman should not be seen with her hair uncovered. Women have to wear bonnets, tied under their chin, to cover their hair in front of strangers and I, a male person, was *namahram* (any man not permitted to see a woman without conservative covering)!

My students listened to my tale with rapt attention. We still had some time left before we proceeded with discussion and comments, and since I was in the habit of telling "stories" when relevant to the point, I related a tale of my childhood experience when I first began to question the habit of wearing a *chador*. As I spoke, my feeling that people across the world are not much unlike one another was reinforced. We are what we observe, learn, and experience in our momentary journey on earth. The degree that separates us from one another is the way we come to regard our perceptions as facts.

CPSIA information can be obtained
at www.ICGtesting.com
Printed in the USA
BVHW030047120720
583518BV00002B/364

9 781887 043670